Life Uncommon

Life Uncommon

Life Uncommon

Julie Weiner

LIFE UNCOMMON
A book of Poetry Tales & Tidings

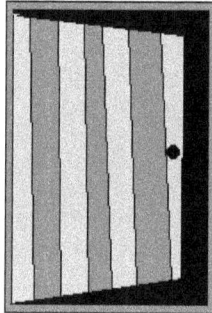

Life Uncommon

PREFACE

In these pages you will find poetry and prose that I've written over the course of twelve years. It is my hope to show many people that they are not alone in the world. We are all drifters who experience things independently and yet we coincide within the similarities of how we handle and endure our experiences. There are things many attempt to hide within themselves such as pain and the solitude we so often feel. So often we give way to believing we are the only ones who have ever felt the ills of a life-changing experience. But we are not alone. We are more like mirror images of one another walking along the streets of the world than we allow ourselves to admit. So join me in the first step of moving beyond denial and journey with me into the self that is us all. For we are all players in the life uncommon.

Life Uncommon

ACKNOWLEDGMENTS

My path has been graced with many teachers, mentors, and guiding influences who have taught me about the value of others as well as the value of self. I've been blessed to have become closely bonded with the inner souls of many along the way who have shared their stories, their experiences, the lessons they've learned, and most importantly the emotions from within the guarded corridors of their hearts.

The words written in these pages have come from many places. Some of the poetry and prose came from personal experience. Some came from my reaction and understanding of the experiences of others. Others were imagination at its finest.

I would like to thank everyone who has taken the time to share with me. I've been nourished by both family and friends and am so very grateful for their time, their wisdom, their patience, and the light that they have shed on my path these many years.

DEDICATION

I dedicate this book to my Mother (who passed in May 2010), my kids, Matthew, my family and my friends.

Special thanks go to those who have helped me find my way; Matthew, James, Hili, Mara, Tiff, Chris, Stan, Angel, Paul, Shannon and all of the many people I have learned from throughout my life.

To my furkids past, present and future who have graced my life; you have my heartfelt thanks for being here for me through thick and thin. I could not have written this book without you. It is your unconditional love, understanding, patience, kindness and natural therapeutic tendencies that has allowed me to come this far. Each and every day I am thankful for each and every one of you.

To Matthew: It is never an easy task to deal with me, and yet you do it with love, kindness, tenderness, compassion and integrity. I am forever grateful for you sticking by me no matter what and always being here when I need you. I love you now & always.

To my Family: Thank you for always encouraging and supporting me as a writer, as a poet and as an individual.

To my Friends: I cherish each and every one of you for the special, incredible people that you are and have always been. Thank you for your every kindness and for always being there when I need you most.

Life Uncommon

To all seekers of mystery, the heart, and the depths of the soul without whom this book could not have been written, and to my family and friends who have supported and encouraged me a lifetime over.

Life Uncommon

1. "9/11"

We all remember that day
When we wondered will our families stay,
Even one more day?
Our hearts felt torn
Felt alone, and clung to the world
And for the first day
In our lifetimes
That day when the flag unfurled
We stood and we stood proud
For the first time we
Became America, And
Transcended just being
Identity became us
And we became free
That day we became
United

2. "1 a.m."

I am so tired
And uninspired
Drifting thoughts
But I don't care
I'm thinking of Matt out there
Wonder if he is thinking of me
Things are now shit
The spiral twisted
Full speed
And I could not
Stop the
Inevitable cruelty
That came my way
I was weak
And now I am this
Sick and lonely freak
Again the sleeping fairies are
Whispering in my ear
But I will remember you
Sweet Matthew
Goodnight Sweetheart
Wherever you are

3. "A Bit of a Dream"

You think you've got it all figured out
Life is going to make sense for once and all
But it never quite does
No key quite fits in a hole
No dream quite fits the affair of your life
You try to know and yet you never do
All apologies for the things we can't know
We can't prepare for the unpreparable
Life is never simple or easy or right
Its always a mess and always supposedly perfect
Perfectly chaotic
Rain comes and sweeps us into a haze of romanticism
Snow falls and life resumes in the heart
Spring rises and the flowers give us color back
Summer heats us into earth
Like lilies we come up beautiful and then we fade
We have every possibility at our fingertips
And a life of open windows when all those horrid doors close
I'm sorry for those things I never explored
And I smile in my mind's eye for all those I will.

4. "A Fall Walk"

I took a walk in my neighborhood
The day was cool, but not too cold
Fall had just begun
Leaves were changing colors
Taking on new meanings
They were coming to peace with themselves
I knew that they'd find that peace
And when they did they'd change again
Leaves change to a brown color every fall
They are almost the same color brown each time
Unfortunately each brown leaf slowly dies
Shriveling up
Becoming slightly hard
Crunchable
Then they die
Leaving trees bare and heartbroken
Each finds new meaning in a month or two
White flurries of snow find a home on them
Keeping them company
And when the snow leaves

Life Uncommon

Melting away
Lonely again
I knew that they'd find peace
They always do
Any season
Any temperature
Any color
Any shape
You are always welcome to be company to a tree

I knew it then, and I know it now
Trees link us all together
We may have nothing else in common
But we always have our best friend

While I thought about the trees
The rest of my thoughts drifted away
I loved the colors
The wonders
I walked on for a long time
Thinking about the wonders of nature
Walking on…just thinking
It was one beautiful fall day!

5. "A Friend"

A friend will walk next to you always
A friend always listens to what you have to say
A friend will understand all of the chaos in your life
A friend brings joy into every room they walk into
A friend can come to you for anything
A friend is someone you can fall asleep in front of and not be afraid
A friend will be proud of you good or bad
A friend is you to me

6. "A Moment in Love's Embrace"

Time perhaps the greatest friend we have
Any time asked it'll give us a hand
Sheltered notions thrown to the wind
Everyone facing fears once again
The river of tears not quite dry yet
All stemming from a night long ago met
Tip-toeing through life

Life Uncommon

Each morning turning into night
The moon rises and shelters the sane
Love who you are, even the pain
Silhouetted maybes still unanswered
Sometimes answers ok not to have
Reach out and I've got at least
One true moment.

7. "A New Door"

Walking through a new door together
Awaiting a new day, a new dawn, a new world
Free for the first time in our lives
Knowing we are safe through the rest of our days
With the person that knows us best
Friends from the moment we met
With beauty, our hearts sing
As we gloriously await,
The happiness our joining will bring
Friends and family gather round
Praising us and the strength we found
In you I found the truths
That I always felt, but were never expressed
Until you
Each morning I now awake
And thank God for bringing me here
Now, with you.

8. "A Warrior's Dream"

A dream to shatter the peace of all the other dreams
So disturbing are its images
My own father angered by my sister
By the rude words that left her mouth
The day before
Screaming at her in public
Forcing her fragile body to cry
I'm finishing my lunch before I must return to work
She says something in defense
And he says "Ok, NOW we're going"
Grabs her by the arm
Drags her up front
As she cries out of those painful ones
For a sister to hear

Life Uncommon

Then like loudened thunder resonating
SLAP!
Must I have such a ground-rumbling dream
If only to wake up to the realizing words of
"Yeah, I could Kill?"

9. "About Her"

My wife has been very ill
Cancer eats the soul I love
I try and I try to
Make her happy
Yet, I trigger tears from her eyes instead
As I grow older
I lose more of those I love each year
My sister
My brother-in-law
The past blurs into my vision
I recall
I remember
My heart giving them life

10. "About Hospitals"

That smell
Medicine
Cleanliness
Feels like death
Cringe
Run far, far away
Through the perfect white hallways
Dart around corners
Burst through the doors
And realize
Nowhere keeps the creeping back

11. "About Stuff"

Will I get fired?
I hope not
But I call out sick so much
I take herbs
Swallow vitamins

Life Uncommon

Get blood taken
X-rays
Scans
All these tests
But still I remain sick
Can my boss understand?
Or am I just another bad employee?
What about my teachers?
Are they angry?
Will my grades drastically drop?
Can I be kicked out of my classes?
Will I have to retake anything?
I am so worried
Oh! Oh! Oh!

12. "About Today"

Sleep kept me from being weak
A late arrival for seniors
Very relaxing for my body
Although my heart was in tears
Lonely without my love
Another fight last night
Saddened I still went to school
Only to find him waiting
What a sweetie he was to me
I love what he did
He tried today
Going to my doctor
Speaking sweetly
I can't say I feel much anymore
But I love him…
Too bad I'm almost too distant to kiss him

13. "Above"

The sun shines so brightly on these
Gifts from above
Each flower a family participant
My lilacs and roses
My petunias and sunflowers
Each here
Each day
Now in the darkened room where I allow my shadow to speak

Life Uncommon

He asks "Why do we grow these?"
I try to reply
But I find I cannot

14. "Acceptance"

So much is on my mind right now
I am afraid that I will never
Get over this fear of life
If I find the best way
To commit suicide
Meaning pain free, and quick, and guaranteed
I'll do it
I don't doubt that now

Anyway, there is much to say
For my current condition
In spite of today being father's day
I would like to share some information
My father beat me as a child
But it wasn't the physical that killed me
It was the mental
After those years
I accepted my inferiority and weakness
I was raped in my teens
My heart was broken numerous times by males
And Jake made me a web of confusion
Bottom line is somewhere along the lines
I died
I believe Jake was the last string
However, he is not to blame for it all
A lot, yes
But not all
So my life is not worth much to me now
Understand?

15. "Act I, Scene II"

Broken-hearted tears reaching my sleeve
Love like this don't ever leave
There are reasons for everything
Sometimes one, two, three
Seven times broken, seven times whole
Seven times twisted, seven times told

Life Uncommon

Living the life of the losing streak
Trying to get back off the street
Nothin' is ever easy in the life of skid row
Living like nothing, begging like poor
Hoping for something greater, anything more
Smoking in the moon, singing in June
Nothing quite comes easy, yesterdays noon
And yet the birds are staring out there
Seeming to see something quite clear
On a cloudy day they know
In the seat of a beaut, in the heart of a crow
Freeze, stop, stare, and glow
Tomorrow's coming, rain dropping flow
Simple truths, simple knowledge
Today's a test, tomorrow's a fetch
Yesterday's gone, so turn back the page
Strumming truths, rapping acts
Listen to the youth, remember the facts
They know the truth, binds unchained
Truths untamed
Blueness of sky, leave behind the blackened eye
Look with narrow, hear with truth, in the sky
Tomorrow's coming, yesterday leapt, today's a test
And next comes the chapter we'll love best

16. "Advice"

Yet another fight with Eric
Should I keep trying?
A fight ended in fuck you...
Ya' fuck me
Pathetic night for me
Would I be better off if I were free?
I called friends for advice
Not even as lucky as a good pair of dice
No help at all
Oh, well, another night of fall
Good Night

17. "Affirm"

My heart tears
And the wound hurts
I feel there is much to say

Life Uncommon

But am soundless
My eyes tighten
And a single, solitary, salty tear springs forth
I die inside
To the ignorance
Of a falsely believed truth
One that meant you knew I loved you
It lingered as a hope
But now the tears fall
And I choke
At the words that won't come
For I know no uttered sound
Can bring you back to me
No truth from my lips
Or my heart
Can let you know that I loved you
So I'll hold the tale close to my heart
That I once loved a girl
And she loved me too.

18. "Ageless Woman"

She is an ageless woman
Her wisdom beseeches my own
She finds a place to hang her coat
A place to call her own
Its a house or a cabin
Whichever one you like
She shelves her books
And paints in delight
During times of contemplation
She'll walk outside
And stand upon the cliffs
Breathing in the tide
She'll wave to the gods
Hello and goodbye
The stars will twinkle
Almost in response
She'll hear the sea soothingly
As it will tell her no lies
As she'll walk silently back
Understanding
A truth
That only the sea could share.

Life Uncommon

19. "Alan"

A mystery locked beneath drugs
A smile hidden from an eye for appearance
An attitude almost unknown to nature
A walk with a click of his heels
Glasses to hide what a child's eye can see
Manners that have dripped away like sugar that's easily dissolved
A parent is now only a figure or a friend
They are no longer caretakers who raised him
A life that's been easily twisted, turned, and beaten by drugs
I ask- why is Alan an actual group
Of people that are dissolving like sugar
Right in front of our eyes?

20. "All I am, All for you"

When daylight breaks
And the energy fades
When the world seems dark
And you feel alone
I'll be standing there
Handing you the Sun, the Moon, the Stars.

For the truth is...
You are my world, my rock so steady
My tree of strength and might
The ground that stabilizes my fright

You are
The waters, refreshing and gentle
The fire, that roars and unveils
The air, that uplifts as I set sail
The earth, that holds me in comfort

It is you that sings me to sleep
And breathes me into morning
It is you who knows and gives me life

The tender toucher
The gentle giver
The universe
In your touch

So I ask you to grant me

Life Uncommon

The greatest gift
I could ever have
The possibility
Of standing by your side
When you laugh
When you cry
When you love

And if you let me
I'll be standing there
Handing you the Sun, the Moon, the Stars.

21. "Alonce"

Alone once more
Alone in an endless war
Freedom and victory come at an evil price
A swallowed pride, hand-thrown dice
Life is a gamble, a risk we take
Sheltered I've lived inside my own cave
Grown up, learned so much
But how to be alone,
I've not learned that much
Independent woman now
I want no man
Manslaughtered dreams leave my head
School sounds so great
But feasible--not so much at this date
Time to move on from spiritual war
Time to become me once more
The need to survive
Comes knocking at my door
I suppose the truth is
I still want more
Not love
Fuck love
To keep my home
And leave my anxiety behind
I think I should be happy
To seek and to find
Law and order
They too knock at my door.

22. "American Men"

Life Uncommon

Daily they go to offices
As both Wall Street brokers and janitors
Striving with such dignity
Awaiting such success
Then go home,
Alone, nothing left
Nothing to sustain their eager souls
Each lying in their own pain
Each so different, each so much the same
It's the same story, the same cry
Just a different guy each time
Yet, they all wonder endlessly, Why?

23. "Amore"

On a warm, summer's night
I looked in his eyes
Genuine greatness we both felt
I knew for the first time in my life
That there is no greater feeling
Than the happiness love gives two individuals
Whether they are a perfect match or perfect opposites
The first time we saw one another smile
Our eyes were as beautiful as two sets of shiny stars
Love was felt
Our hearts had only began to melt
We touched in that certain place
Joy was like an over-flowing river
Settling in

24. "And God Has No Dominion"

And God has no dominion
Over tyrants and doctors
Nor over the rich and wealthy
Nor over the poor and unsteady
For only the birds shall lift their veils
And God has no dominion.

And God has no dominion
Over the sad and unstable
Nor over the happy and bliss-filled
Nor over the generation of children

Life Uncommon

For only beauty may rise in the face of harm
And God has no dominion.

And God has no dominion
Over the sinful and innocent
Nor over the religious and sacred
Nor over the heathen and anarchist
For only one with himself may rise above
And God has no dominion.

25. "And the Hours Just Wash Away"

Sitting in my room alone
Staring into the blankness that infinity brings
I dream of you and wish for one of a million different things
But we both know that phone call won't come
Not today, not tomorrow, no ring in this lifetime
I'm just a bum
Emptiness resides in so many places
And I hide
I wish I could tell you I'm different inside
But we're all the same
So why should I hide?
I'd call you today right now if I could
But your number eludes me
I always knew it would
You're like a hanging ornament in a sky I'll never know
In some distant land where I'll never go
But still I dream of you
As I stare at my blank walls
Wishing for the million things
That not even infinity can bring.

26. "Anymore"

Our lives came together
By some beautiful grace
Can you hear my heart
From a thousand miles?
Can you hear my call
And make it all worthwhile?
Do you know my dreams
Even when I've forgotten them?
Do you know my soul

Life Uncommon

Even when I don't know
Do you know who I am
Anymore?

27. "Anyone?"

Anyone-
For a minute try to imagine my world
I am seventeen with a past of horror
My family is monstrous
My friends stay clear of them
My heart is strong
My smile tries to shine
But my soul is crying
My tears are filled with agony and longing
For my one true love
I miss his encouraging words
His loving touch
The kiss of protectiveness he always gave me
And the eyes of passionate love
I long for him the only thing I've ever truly wanted
Everything else can be taken—but not him
Punishment after punishment each tear still calls his name
I wish someone could hear my soul's cry and
Stop the monsters punishing words and actions
And give me the angel I long for

28. "As He Goes, I Cry"

Like a springtide of emotions all locked up inside
I fear to scream
I know naught but to hide
I'd love to yell 'don't go'
But I know
I've cried for men before
I know the familiar heartbreak I feel now
They tell me not to run
So for once I don't push
Its in my eyes anyway
That I know
You'll go
Isn't it something when a man
Chooses jail over you?
Talk about a crusher

Life Uncommon

That footprint will bruise
I'd love to say maybe
But that's not the song playing

29. "As The Popcorn Pops"
(dedicated to Rivertree Court)
As the popcorn pops
We used to get caught by cops
Now we are apart longing for each other
Katherine was the best super theater mother
Justice was always a flirt
Wearing some short mini-skirt
Ty was a sweetie
Except when he was with the guys and being a meanie
Fred was cool to hang with even after he quit
Before that he tried to act like a shit
Amanda was random in all of her thoughts
All a bunch of nuts
Derek was a dork
But he was just as cute as Mork
Kyle was our hottie
We all wanted a part of his body
Aaron was our Mr. Perfect man
Sometimes he could get any girl to be a fan
Nick made us all laugh at his jokes
Especially when sitting at Denny's all drinking cokes
After a while we all missed Jeff
Cause there were no great managers left
So now I think of you my friends
As all our knots tie their ends
Please think of our soap opera days
And wish we will one day smile at each other in silly looking leighs!

30. "Ash"

The light shatters the truth I do not see
I'm endlessly searching in this crooked sea
For something worth holding onto,
Something worth letting go
Something to help me
Something to let me know
Somehow I've got to find me
Somehow.. its so far to go
And I try to find my place on this stranded island

Life Uncommon

Embraced by god's light
Sheltered from sin
But here I am all over again
Floundering around
Without water to parch my thirst
And I'm without love, without light
Without you
My beauty in the night
And I'm dying here
All alone
Because like I've said a thousand times
And I'll say a thousand more
I'm here
But you'll go
Everything must
Its something time has given me to trust
Nothing lasts but a moment
So I must learn to let go of it

31. "At Death"

In dying is a truth from the heart
The point comes when we must love
With the key to life: truth
Without honesty death is no different than life
Yet, when we live to die we yearn,
Yearn to be true,
In all aspects of life
Words seem almost incomprehensible
Because of their utter sincerity
And more importantly love
Is heard through a look
And all becomes silent

32. "Autumn"

Have you ever wondered if the wind kisses the moon
The way he gently kisses you?
Have you ever imagined the loneliness the sun must feel?
Gentle gliding trances awaken the spirit of old
Now is the time when the veil thins
And ancient truths are told
Spiritual ancestors soon coming to walk
Amongst us

Life Uncommon

Ready to embrace the found and the lost
Which are you...the forsaken or the devoted?
Autumn leaves rustle while still in tact
Soon they will leave on their journeys around the globe
The colorful way of the nature around us
So beautiful, so peaceful
It all reminds me of home
A place without want or worry
Free from stress and unbiddenness
Away from household chores and routines
Without meaning
Distant from earthly desires
And even distant from fears
A place without the shackle of body
Or the weight of humanity
The true place "where everybody knows your name"
Spiritual home
Glimpses of heaven soon coming our way
Here to remind us on Halloween day
Of the truths we know
And to serendipitously remind us that we are
Never alone.

33. "Autumn Lilies"

The walls of the self are like enclosed envelope spaces
Reaching out to a nothingness that never feels
Hearing the splatter of rain
Falling lightly all in vain
Lyrical poeticized words strumming through
The barber shops' tale of the never-ending blues
Each time a soul departs a raven caws
Only those who listen ever really hear
The more I speak, the less I know
The more I rage, the younger I grow
Acceptance as placid as summer's sweat
Still no real place to call home yet
But its not all Autumn tears and tantrums, you see?
In truth, lately, I've spotted everlasting beauty
Its in the way the leaves rustle
The romance is the songbirds bustle
Truth like rain sets the clouded man free
Prevailing beyond time, beyond space, beyond you,
Beyond me
Listen to the words of your own heart

Life Uncommon

For the truth really lies there,
In light and in dark
Time to put away childish confusions
Be an adult, grow up,
Love life, dance, and never forget to keep
A smile tucked warmly at your side

34. "Babblings"

There's all this rage in me because I'm dying to say something
But nothing ever really fucking comes out
I hate hatred
I can't stand the prejudices and bigotry that spout so fluently out of our stupid mouths
Its like humanity is lost to itself
We mirror each other and yet we all think we're better
We're something special
Something talented
Something worthwhile and worth bowing down to
We're all shit
You can be a success
But you'll still be so depressed that you'll reach for another bottle
Another pill
Another dose of whatever it is that just might soothe out your woes
How do I express my extreme hatred towards the lack of truth?
Sure we have authors, singers, talk shows, and children starting to talk truth
But we still have the same old stupid ass stigmas as we had twenty years ago
You should marry the right man... a doctor, a lawyer, someone who society believes is
respectable
You should weigh a certain weight
Why?
Because everyone wants you to be healthy?
Yeah, fuck that
Everyone wants you to look perfect because they were told 95 pounds is beautiful
Our government is so fucked up we don't know it- at all
We're like a disconnected society that reflects us back into loneliness and isolation
This isn't getting the point across at all
I sound like a babbling teen
So fuck it

35. "Bad"

I've been used my whole life
I was a mother before I was nine

Life Uncommon

Not biologically
But certainly in action
I was raped before I reached seventeen
I was lending out money that I'd never see again
Before twenty
And the rest feels like I've sold my soul
To nothing
To absolutely nothing at all
That's what was on the other side of my kindness,
Trust and love
Absolutely nothing

36. "Bad Day"

In the past we would sit down for a while, treasure each other
We had a strong bond, trusted each other
We felt free, no hidden feelings, no secrets, happy

Haunted in my happy thoughts
Optimism choked out of my mind
Old friend turning enemy left me solid in asphyxiation

Tried to work out the disagreement, but couldn't
I felt helpless, no idea what to do
So this is the end, we can no longer see one another as friends
Too much remained hidden, trust ended…Why?
We talked behind each other's backs
Allowed hatred to circle our minds
Stabbed each other in the back
More masks, more lies

Perhaps our friendship slowly slipped away
Maybe again someday we'll be friends
In a far, far away land

I still have my other friends I guess there is some happiness in that

What am I to do?
Is anyone else going to leave me?
I want to go home
Or find a way to stop this unhappiness
Even a small bit of cheeriness
Would make me have at least some optimism
I have no control
Should I just go home?

Life Uncommon

Help…What am I to do?

37. "Baffling"

Laughter chuckles at my thoughts

Smile at the agonizing truth
That he is there
And I am not
Perfect match
But we are not

Together we strolled down a lane
But only in a stare
And how I dare

To grab him
As he has me
And avenge my heart
And the agony

38. "Bars"

There is no escape
From the prison
The one with torment painted walls
The bars that lock you in
And you forget what is locked out
A place you cling to
Because it is all you know
The pain
The burning tears that drip
Simultaneously with your stomach shrinking
And your head bowing
Eyes must look down
The body becomes like a helium balloon
Unraveled
Letting the air shrink everything
Curl up
But they won't let you forget
Or break free
Death is not an option
The pain and the hatred must be endured
Fear your own rage

Life Uncommon

If you can even stand yourself
Buried in shame
Look in the mirror
Who is it you see?

…them

39. "Basketball Player"

A man died here yesterday
He bounced a basketball,
Dribbling now an offense
An object mistaken for weaponry
What is the point?
For crying out loud!
Shoot the evil basketball player?
He has family somewhere
Maybe a couple of kids
Possibly a wife
And now because of a frightened cop
He is dead
Tragic
Goodbye sweet basketball star

40. "Be My Lover"

Be my lover
Be my fighter
Be everything to me
Be the one for me

Love me now
Hold me close
Look up high
To where we stand

Take my hand
Stand by me
Side by side
Where we stay

Be my lover
Be my fighter
Be everything to me

Life Uncommon

Be the one for me

Look outside
See the light
Where we love
Where we hope
Where we dream
Of love

Be my lover
Be my fighter
Be everything to me
Be the one for me

For me

41. "Be Yourself"

Throw society out the window
But keep the law in mind
Don't cross the borders of crime
Just speak your own goddamned mind
Listen to the words of your heart
They matter something drastic
No need to rebel like everyone else
Man, grow up, be yourself
Society's fucked enough
Why add to that shit?
Get over the past
Its okay to live the outcast
Life. Not a small hurdle
So wake up and shake the world
Piercings aren't anything big
Tattoos stopped shocking long ago
Bitchings doing nothing, its got to go
Speak the truth
Don't you know-- Anything goes!
Not every river has to flow
It's your world, get up and take it now!

42. "Beaten Child"

"Daddy no! No daddy!"
Ever screamed and not been heard?

Life Uncommon

Ever hurt so bad on the outside that it scarred the inside?
Ever been beaten so hard you can't sit?
And had the pain of that not even compare to the pain of being ignored
And unloved?

43. "Beautiful Snow Globe"

I guess I have been here before
But I don't know when
I think
I believe
I stumbled upon it on accident
Or maybe he gave it to me
A tiny world
Perfect as can be
I don't know
But anyway this place I hold inside my heart
Is beautiful
Filled with love
The lightness that laughter brings
The teardrops that melt into springs
Rivers of golden dreams
Here is my home
And love is what it will bring

44. "Beauty Leaves"

Like rain you entered my heart
Enamored by cupids loving dart
I smiled at your eyes
We'd never stoop to patronize
Something in you let me know
The love we shared then and now
Is genuine, truc, something that
Will last in both me and you
For a moment I had you
You held me in your arms
Let me know a safety I thought was long gone
Even your tears let me know
From friend, to confidant, to lover
Letting you go is the most mature
Thing I know not how to do
As I prepare to watch you walk away
I grow from vixen to lawyer

Life Uncommon

The change that happens when beauty leaves.

45. "Before Healing, I Felt Pain"

I want him
I love him
I am intrigued
Isn't there a way out?
Love is terrible but so enticing
I don't just want anyone though
I just
I lose
Not meant to win
So I slip off a mountain
Drive off the road
An angel to sweep me away
Or shall I stay?
In this tormented hell of my own imagination
I suck
I am worthless
Not meant to be
Step on me
The already crushed insect
Forget me
If you ever knew me to begin with

46. "Begging"

Write out how I feel…Hmm…How do I feel?
Lost…confused…hatred…mad…hurt
Like the world just sweeps me away and I've no choice but to go with it
I hate the winds that surround you 'til your suffocating
I hate the rules that bind you 'til you choke
I hate the ways of the world we live in,
And yet idealism has no place in this universe
I'd fight it if I could, but who am I kidding?
Me? The snail? The naive little girl? Who could I fight?
The law-makers? God? Religion? Necessary occupation?
I've got nowhere to go but within my own web
I'm the weaver of a hell I cannot stand
I get sick and anxious, I fit not within their walls
I don't fit anywhere if you want to know the truth of it all
I'm like a drifter without a sea, without a home, without even a sky to hope for
I'm the rainbow without an end, Jackpot-less and without a leprechaun

Life Uncommon

I'm not even normal – I'm insane or at least strange enough to be considered so
And the funny thing is I don't care
I don't care who I am or what I do or what I believe in
I just want peace…I'd bang on the walls of insanity if I could
I'd beg the gods for a lifetime of quiet nights and to never have a nightmare again
If it'd work. Do you think it could? I doubt it
The things you always want most are never that easy
We must pass challenge after challenge, jump through every hoop
I'm no juggler…just a girl trying to cling to a nothingness
Nothing is stable, I forget that so easily
I try so hard to meet expectations, to get somewhere that isn't nowhere
The grim reaper is at my door…not to kill me…
Just the dreams that mean everything…Isn't that sweet?
It shouldn't be that you give your all every fucking day just to have it swept away
It shouldn't be that you do your best with every bit of confidence
You can bare to muster up and then the walls shake anyway
I'm not perfect. I claim my imperfections and humanity
Can't you just let me succeed? I don't need riches or fame
I don't need to be understood so well the world changes
I just want financial independence
A place to hang up the fucking hat I don't even have
A way to make sure the bills are paid and the bread is on the table
I'm the man in today's society and I need to take care of me
But I don't. I just try to. Can't the challenges of life give in? Can't they stop being so
tough? Can't I have a win? I deserve it I swear I do
I deserve the right job, the right pay, the bread on the table,
And the life that for me I've alone made
Can't you let me have that? Please?

47. "Being Happy"

Nothing less than a smile
Everything living and non-living
Can let it flow
Its that outrageous feeling
The sunshine of life
Continuously guiding us towards
That something special inside

48. "Beloved"

I sit here realizing our enchanting amour
Years so quickly turned to four
Our hearts are majestic, beautiful

Life Uncommon

Twisting together like vines
Wind flowing thoughts sift through our minds
We have tides and tides of emotions rolling on,
Rolling in
As though our love was born by god's very hand
Or under the moons' compelling command

49. "Beside An Owl"

Sometimes I sit and wonder
Who I am, who I was, who I will be
Teardrops fall like heaven upon my sleeve
The need to express overwhelms
And I grab my pen
For it is my friend as its always been
I used to sit alone for hours, days
It seems that time has ended
Seemingly suddenly
I know my problems move no mountains
But if they did...
Who knows?
I mourn not a love
Or a broken heart
This time I mourn only the me
Who I recently watched
Depart

50. "Betrayal Captured"

You, friend
Shall cut my throat
And slice my tongue
Shred my thoughts of a loving man
Blind my eyes
For they see things that aren't there anyway

You, friend
Help me down from these clouds
Place my fins on solid ground
Replace my wings with wood
Simply be the support I cannot be to myself
Just don't leave me on my own

You, friend

Life Uncommon

Do you understand the grieving I go through?
Can you feel the torture in my mind?
The scars burn through me
Almost like I can't go on

You
You
Who is the you?
Anymore

And who is the friend?
Anymore?

51. "Between"

Somewhere between the land and the sea
There was me
There was I
And I looked forth onto the sky
Unknowing
And for once I cried
Feeling more alive
As I knew at once where
I belong
Welcome home, child
Welcome to I

52. "Beyond Time"

Sometimes beyond time and beyond space
The heart learns to love again
Trust, I am without
Do words really mean nothing?
Is truth that hard to tell?
Can integrity die inside?
Are dreams miracles waiting
To never happen?
Is my heart so beyond love?
I'm sorry to my own heart
I'm sorry to any I've hurt
I am just a twenty-four
Year old female
No greater picture knowledge
And I try to listen to God

Life Uncommon

And those who love me
Sometimes I fail
Sometimes I'll be just me
Is that okay?

53. "Bitter Me"

Once I did smile
The age I cannot remember
But it was sunny
With cotton branches
Raspberries of pure delight
Swimsuits and sprinklers

I do not smile now
I cry inside and out

Searching for a destiny
One to lead me back
Back
To the cotton filled fantasies
And pretty pigtails with daisies in my hair

54. "Blank Alleys of the Heart"

You are letting the pain tear you apart
Stare out into space
Drift off
In a daze
Left thinking about pain
But not thinking at the same time
Just drowning in a lake of emptiness
Alone…Lonely
And crying so hard inside
That on the outside you can hardly breathe
And you try to think about how to make things right
How to make everything okay again
To walk through a wooded area
Hoping that maybe you'll stumble along yourself
But you can walk through those woods every day
And still no sign of you
Nothing
Its a blank wood
And a blank world

Life Uncommon

And everything you want to fill it up with
Is leaving anyway
So the world stays empty
And you just continue to stare at the empty walls
The voids of your heart
The abyss of your universe
And inside cry those endless tears
Remembering the days when everything was all right
And why is it that you didn't cling on harder?
Why didn't you know then that that was the last time you would feel so whole?
You listen to the wind
You hear the words
But in a blink
Gone

55. "Blocked Swimmers"

Swim my friends
Flap your fins
Rush to the side of the bowl
Swim to the top
Or in circles
Go somewhere, anywhere
Must break free
Of the cage in which you live
Surrounded in a small world
Where you are watched
Swim
The useless words of a blocked writer

56. "Blue Sky"

Open and warm
Chirping friends and there will not be rain today
We are going out today
A date
Happy together
Family has lost touch
But I have her
And I am so okay that the rest is lost
Cars just strum down the road
Grass seems more green today than yesterday

Cars collided, head on

Life Uncommon

Red trickles down my face
Her head
Oh, no
Precious and in a glass bubble in the windshield

57. "Bohemian Tragedy"

Poet tries to understand
His love, a courtesan
He learned the Bohemian way of truth, beauty, freedom and love
He looked up and then there she was
Sparkling, a diamond
Tempting and innocent, she was it all
Love struck cupid style
Orpheus moved forth
She somehow knew that it was he
That she'd love for all eternity
Dancing poetry, passion-filled room, offering so much, asking so little
He sang enchanting as the sun
Acting ended, truth begun
They loved in that moment, eternity
Hades tried to weave evil,
Tear them apart
But no one quite knew
What lay in their hearts
Gathered round with sitars and prostitutes, fire-eaters and jugglers
They danced and sang songs of the age
Revolutionizing art for us all
Their love was to stand the test of time
The curtain fell
And so had she,
The lovely Eurydice
And freedom stolen in the night
Would be written for all to see
This is the story
Of a man
And a woman
Consumed by love
Bought with nothing
But kept for all time

They found love
On the rooftops of Paris
In the song that only love could sing.

Life Uncommon

(Inspired by the movie "Moulin Rouge")

58. "Booze"

Brick one
And brick two
One atop the other
And more pile
Onto
A tower
Belief in love
Belief in religion
Belief in trust
Swing the bat
My hand this time
Break it
Fallen
Bricks
Beliefs asmolder

59. "Boredom"

I hate having nothing to do
I feel like my life is slipping away
I mean I have nothing to show
I haven't read any new books
I haven't helped anyone
Nothing big to show
Nothing to make me feel whole
I'm bored
Simple- just bored

60. "Boyhood Ending"

I wonder what the point
Is exactly when a boy
Becomes a man
When he gives way
To the shackles of prison
When he forces himself
To believe that nothing
Will bring her back
To drink away the heartbreak

Life Uncommon

To kill the beauty inside
Convinced that she was
Forever gone
And those eyes once forever young
Burned out
Flicked 'til they could flick no more
This is the call in the
Mind of the love forlorn
He believes so vehemently
That to his heart she would
Never return
To kill that beauty
Is to take away that hope
Alone in solitude in a prison he broke

61. "Broken Out"

Lightning Strikes
I look to you
And know I'll be your wife
I see years of glory ahead
Children and dancing and laughter
You bring out the best in me
I feel the most of myself
The potential me
When I'm with you
I'm encouraged, inspired
I feel like soaring
And being fulfilled
I no longer want to hold back
Or hide
I'm released
And its due to you
You've given me wings of heart
And I am a dove
Flying free
You give me the air
So that I finally may breathe

62. "Broken Pieces"

I am broken pieces
No part of me is whole
Nothing about me is unscathed

Life Uncommon

I think I hate whatever innocence I have left
I think I'm broken
I stopped trusting
I stopped loving
I no longer seek a relationship
I've stopped pushing
I'm a fallen-apart-mess
I sit in shit and shame
And I'm nothing
I'm a loser
I still cling to a stuffed animal
I can't sleep
And I hate myself
I'm a shipwreck of human pieces
And I'm only three days from being twenty-five years old

63. "Brother Wind"

I am a child who knows the wild wind
The wind who I call my brother
And not like any other-
The wind as an individual can see the world through
A different perception

The wind is fast
Which is why it can act as its own master
The wind can tease to a point where it
Comes and goes, plays and runs,
But all it knows is a place to fall on its knees

All I need now are the keys to a peaceful world,
Because our confused world is unique
Which will make us all weak
And so the silent yet violent, loving wind is
Still shoving for an interesting place to be
Besides on its warm, caring knees

My brother wind the brother from no other but
A peaceful mother will finally find its dream

64. "Bubbling Waters"

In a bubble the water falls
Coming down in waves

Life Uncommon

Leaving no room for flowers to bloom
But feeding the roots all the same
Giving beauty an even more spectacular fame
Somehow in this illustrious name
I've died and been reborn again
Among the stars and moons that orbit the earth
I find myself alive in this rebirth
Sheltered no more and never before feeling so free
God bless the stars
And heaven certainly blessed me!

65. "Burning Pain"

Fire
Burn
Red
Orange
Yellow
Hot
Flame
Soul
Pain
Hurt
Fame
Burn
Hot
Turn
Cot
Quick
Bad
Mad
Frustrated
Angry
Unhappy
Burning
Pain
Left
Nothing
Emptiness
Lifeless
Zero
Zilch
Space
Air
Filled

Life Uncommon

Light
Hot
Burning
Colorful
Pretty
Firelifeburningpainmadfameladcamehelphelphelp
Life is turning into a circular pain of fire!

66. "Bus Accident"

News brings blues
At least today
Five deaths because of a bus being in a Metro train's way
Children on the way to high school
Bet the substitute bus driver feels like a fool
Friends are lamenting loudly
Hearts are saddened softly
A few decided not to ride today
Fate?
I don't know

67. "Calendar"

As I looked right through the calendar on my wall
I glimpsed an idea of home
That place where the heart lives
Where the family resides
Where love exists
I found myself thinking
"This isn't home"
But I don't have a home
My heart doesn't belong anywhere
So I listen
I let go
And I wait for the wind to blow

68. "Call Her Crazy"

Just a misshapen weave of twisted mistrust
Again and again she found her abuser
Kept walking into the pattern of the abused
Call her crazy
Sometimes we live a lie

Life Uncommon

And there's no inner us to die
We just are
And the lie is us
At some point we recognize the mask and try to remove it
So often we fail
But we try
Somewhere hidden behind
The shit, the shame
Behind the squeaks and the twists
Behind the fucking lies
Is us
The real person
Sometimes it takes years to find him or her
Its a search
The only thing in life we are charged to complete on our own

69. "Can a Picture Hold Life?"

I sit staring at a picture with expressions of life

It holds flat land
Brown sand
Mountains bumpy as an old-grandmother's hand
Clouds flowing to the rhythm of a soft band
Mountains that are steep and endless
Clouds that are fluffy, yet motionless
Hills that are bumpy, though they lie shapeless
In the desert sun
There are no children having fun
Not even adults telling a pun
Nor are there animals roaming, flying, or walking 'til the day is done

I'm still staring at a picture that is lifeless
Yet the stream looks blue and full of life
The clouds are formed and treasured as much as a husband's dear wife
The hills are steep but not nearly as sharp as a knife
Certain mountains come to an exact point
Even looking like a body's joint

I realize the picture is lifeless
And my imagination has just made it
As full of life as any ordinary thing I have seen grow!

70. "Candid"

Life Uncommon

Mourning, I am, for the days gone by
Melancholy in appearance, but retreated inside
It takes my body and I am no longer
An unbalanced maniac
Before the doorway to the asylum
Doctors laugh
Aching in excruciating pain
I just wish for a better prison than this
It just grows inside me and craves
Immunity weakens and it strives and survives
Dying am I
Yet I am unsure if I lived before
It takes me and I just yield to its magnanimous power

71. "Candlelit Clown"

Clowns on a jaded hill
Looking for a ride,
She's looking for a thrill
So I bide
My time
Singing a song
Rhythm and rhyme
And you'd think since its been so long
I'd forget how to drive
But not me
I'm just happy to be alive
Just to be
So I saw a man smiling this morning
And thought it funny
What is it about smiling in the morning?
Reminds me of the egg bearing bunny
Clouds are gone
Moon is up
So long
What a good pup
He's the one who spotted
The jaded hill with a candlelit clown.

72. "Candlelit Cry For My Soul Mate"

Have you ever loved a man you didn't know?
I have, I do

Life Uncommon

His name could be anything
Matthew or Donald
Whatever the name I love him
In my dreams I've loved him a lifetime
And each night I love him a lifetime more
He's my prince, my hero
My loyal mate
And I love him entirely
Every bone aches for him
Every tear calls him home
Tonight and two nights before
I've lit a candle so that he shall know
His way
Home

73. "Can't he love me?"

I smile
When a bully
Cries
I weep
When the devil
Cannot
Be seen
My glass is always empty
Every parcel bitter
I stare
Oblivion awaits my entrance
Returning
To the abyss of silence
Nonverbal in perfection
Knowledgeable eyes
Still the question twirls
Into
Infinity...

Can't he simply love me?

74. "Casket"

Woman dressed in black
Wearing sadness and holding on to something
Flowers, I suppose, as if the dead can
Understand. Poor woman I am sad for her on this joyless day

Life Uncommon

Walk to the headstone
Place lilies, and say a prayer
Or two, but realize that when they are
Gone nothing can bring them back. The casket seems so

Perfect, strangely, but not to this body
The one I see before me needs this place
To sleep in a box
The way she wanted
And how do I know?
I know for she is
Me.

75. "Caved Little Souls"

Empathy
What the hell is empathy?
The ability to feel but rarely heal?
Fuck that, fuck it
Why should I worry?
Should I sit here, and watch them lie?
And why should I cry?
They tell themselves scores of truths
Only making their memories so much more uncouth
Sure, sure they are okay and everything is great
Nice little pretend game
Smile as they want and please who they will
Inside they are crying, lonely still
They pick up their pens and write sorrowful words
But then pretend it away flying free with the birds
Do they even know how fake they sound?
Do they even care why I stick around?
Does it matter in their dark little hells,
That someone actually cares about their pathetic little selves?
Are they so sure that I won't remain,
That no matter how hard I try, it'll be in vain?
I don't get it, but I hate it all the same
I can't stand this sick twisted little game
Help me, help me they cry into the night,
And there you stand trying with all your might
But they meant leave me the fuck alone
I don't give a shit that you care, I like this shelled home
And then you stand pushed away, closed out with the rest of the world
Tomorrow comes to pass and their memories are unfurled

Life Uncommon

They want you to be happy
And goddess knows they like to get sappy
But do they really want help?
Fuck if I know, I've tried
And still the doors remain closed

76. "Challenging Time"

Sometimes it feels like everything's okay
Sometimes, like now it feels...just the opposite
Perhaps its hard to prepare for life
Hard to know when to duck
When to run, when to hide
And even as I stand here
I only challenge the truth of time
And time, it always wins my friend
You can cheat it
Or try
But it'll win every fucking time!

77. "Changes"

We live in a world of constant changes
We strive to survive
Some of us always act
Day by day we weather changes
One day we have snow, and the next day the sun
Curiosity teaches
Everything has its own special characteristics
A flower petal, a snowflake
Tend to the mortal

78. "Changing Someone Else"

I've traveled paths with enough dismay to walk away with tales
The tidings of matter are not always neat or pretty
But I've been proud of each
Because they've led me
How do I find pride now?
Are you just another who does not accept me as I am?
If you changed me enough, could you convince yourself to love me truly even then?
Why is it that men seek to change a woman?

Life Uncommon

Perfection if it is anything at all…. It would be a person who has found themselves on their own
Should weight truly hold the key to your heart?
Humor, kindness, compassion- do these really pale in comparison to outer beauty?
I've strived and strived at so many turns to be the best of myself
And yet today I feel
As though that is not enough
I won't change for you or anyone else
So perhaps this will become just another sad tale
For me to tell

79. "Chaos"

One rule to live by is chaos
Absolute disarray of all order
Dominance of chance fall into line
Forceful without reason
No enemy nor friend
If one falls into believing they can stand still
Chaos will sweep their way
Illusions will be left naked
Reality may be scary
But we cling to it
Hoping for predictability
The standstill that never seems to come
And when you know you believe
And belief breeds hope
An ideal that kills
We forget about chaos
And believe we are gods
But the truth is that we are all just puppets
For others and for our fantasies

80. "Chartered Course To Truth"

Simple beauties rest alongside our lives
A flutter of wings
A purr and a meow
Beauty lingers
Gentle whispers so tender
Light music to sway to
The blow of the wind in the feathers of a palm
The singing of an ocean
And the growl of the earth

Life Uncommon

We listen with unsteady ears
But with strong hearts
The question is not when
Only how to chart our course

How to find the lakeside of our dreams
And the hopes of our youths
Where to plant the trees
And set down foot by foot
Time tells no mans tale
We fill in that blank ourselves
Tears avail us not
If we can't listen to the rhythm they bring

In sadness, in hope, in the death of a fantasy
We may find the truth
In how to be

Busy streets and honking cars
Many businessmen without time nor cause

Joan Baez sings us to truth once more
"The answer my friend is blowing in the wind,
The answer is blowing in the wind."

("The answer my friend is blowing in the wind, The answer is blowing in the wind"
–Lyrics by Joan Baez)

81. "Childhood Recollections"

Many memories rest in that house
But shouldn't be louder than a mouse
There are secrets
Of fantasies
That should never be spoken
Otherwise their spells might be broken
It was a place of hope
I was a child--innocent and sweet

82. "Children"

Little children are always confused
And are sometimes easily amused
During the summer they love their bicycle

Life Uncommon

And during the winter they smile at an icicle
Each child is unique
Some of them are weak
Others are very strong
A few of them only sing their favorite song
Most of the children like playing with animals such as a fawn
Or fall asleep at the peak of dawn
Little children deserve to be loved
And cuddled and hugged
They should not be tugged towards anything bad
Or as they get older they may always be sad
Some might even end up only knowing how to be mad
Everyone should be loved and we should start with
Our children otherwise we will never get anywhere
And the people of the future won't be fair

83. "Christmas Steps"

Like crystal raindrops my tears fall for you
Sweetly bitter I remember you
Timeless moments we spent openly
Our hearts like rivers flowed
Some things cannot be held onto
Like the first loving look in your eyes
The first "I love you" on Christmas Night
We walked hand-in-hand along the bridges of New York
And the cobblestone streets of Paris
We spent our summers in Italy
And our winters in New York
My happiness was all wrapped up in you
Gone are the days of our romantic youth
Sweetly I kiss you goodbye
As I purposely remember not to hang your stocking up tonight
The lawns of our neighbors are all lit up
Not many presents to fill my heart
My first Christmas without you
I take a breath, as my heart knows
Tomorrow I'll step into my world
Tears behind, memories in a box, hand on my heart
I took the step
I let go.

84. "Cigarettes"

Life Uncommon

Wrapped around me
A binding force
Coming towards me
The key to my undoing
Closer and closer
My enemy comes
The colder I get
Closer to me
Burning me
From the outsides in
Slowly and sensually
Getting closer
Closer to my cave
Sucking all my fears away
Burning me still
The force
Becoming weak
So close
Too close
So I stop
Flame dimmed in
An instant
Vanishing
My core
In tact
And I am cold and alone again.

85. "Circulatory Life"

Takes me on a fast train
Filled with hellhounds and pain
Then turns upside down
Wear anything but a frown
Because now I'm wearing the crown
Queen of my own dreams
Centrivical in beautified disgrace
Ugly head rears itself before the new moon
And as the clock turns to a new day
My happiness has just begun
Dragons breathing scorching fire

On my new smile
And the circle just goes on

Life Uncommon

86. "Circus Time"

Sitting in a room full of laughter
Clowns running around on stilts
A lion roars in the background
The trapeze man gets ready for his jump
As the fire eater carefully inhales the flame
All carefully rising to their own sense of fame
Children laugh out as the bearded lady walks by
The auditorium is lit up by colors sparkling
Lit-up hats,
Squiggly snakes,
Popcorn and peanuts to boot
And sunglasses too big for our heads
Smiles to be had by all
Thank you Barnum & Bailey for
Bringing the circus to town!

87. "Cling Or Go"

Sometimes when life quiets down enough
You hear the sound of your heart
When its laughter you hear,
Every part of you loosens the fear
But when its crying,
The tears that flood the world,
The reaction's a bit different...
You feel like crows are circling you
Warning you of the war to come
A death to the you you've just become
Opportunity knocks and you've no choice but to answer the door
Clinging is beyond us humans, and so chaos reigns
Its control over us is eternal
Why do we try to beat the odds?
Why do we try to prove we can hold onto anything?
Am I too weak to let go?
Or too stubborn to stay?
I've learned how to fight
I stand in the faces of my foes
But the ability to let go
I'm an apprentice at best
If only we could forever,
Lay these fears to rest...

Life Uncommon

88. "Clover Lover"

Carnivals dance with delight
And its under the glistening moonlight
That she stands like the greatest
Tower of love
Her smile lighting up the universe
I want to walk to her
And tell her everything
Give her my soul and the key
To everything within
She seems to just know
Where I've been
Where I am
And even where I'll go
Like the mysterious gypsy under a reddened sun
And the glorious mistress
You'd pay anything to
She's the glistening diamond
She's the woman I love
And always will.

89. "College Thoughts"

What can college life teach a person?
How to conform?
How to be a non-conformist?
Well, I can't speak for anyone else-
But this is what I've learned
In college you trust people you don't even know
You make friends that will probably be your friends forever
You learn that most of the time listening is better than talking or giving advice
You learn if you gossip
The person you gossiped about will know in five minutes
You learn who you are without your parents
You learn who the immature you is,
And who the mature you is
You learn the mature you is preferred
And that just you is all that matters
Here we can say anything, do anything, be anything,
And it will all be okay

90. "Connecting The Jagged Lines"

Life Uncommon

We've all been through hardships
We've all experienced pain
Why do we seem to hurt longer?
Why does it seem the pain never leaves?
You have thought about suicide too
You have understood what its like being me
So why can't the world?
So why does it feel like no one will ever know?
Most of us have tried to commit suicide
Most of us have headed down that road
I survived this is true
I am still alive
You got through it as well
You must at least somewhat believe
Somewhere inside me is still that spark
Somewhere inside you it isn't all dark
Life is worth living
Life is important enough
Its funny how the experiences never quite go away
Its funny how the good disappears, but the bad always stays
I believe in tomorrow
I even believe in yesterday
So I will keep fighting
So will you if you try to believe

91. "Conscious Quality"

My conscience dictates my behaviors - shall I run wild?
Be a madwoman? Run in the dust like a vampire searching for blood, No!
I shall stay calm in my rocking chair
Dreaming of such adventures, I must
Hold back such desires and live as they tell me
My conscience is my ruler, and they the lawmakers

Drawing frees my soul through a crayon
Writing is my true beauty
No matter what it is I write…I write beauty
Every word is pulled from my heart and stuck like glue to the paper

Teach me dear professors
For I profess that I need help in this dangerous world
Others are self-absorbed
I feel fear…insomnia is hard…pain is worse
Without love I am content in death

Life Uncommon

Professor of poetry doesn't know the love and the hate
And the desire for the unknown as I do
Why should he correct my wrongs? Is he so perfect?

God and religions are supposed to be supreme in my life
I choose otherwise
God cannot be proven
Religion is just someone else's love of tradition
I believe in ambiguous feeling
But sometimes I don't

92. "Conundrum"

Trying to solve the riddle that is life
I have loved many
With all my being
My brain, my body, me
Perchance it is the loss of the loves
They were my reason
For being
Pawns ask how to live without love
How to go on
Move on
Survive a mere second
A small night

I know the feeling

Everything solid and good
Meaningful and real
Like fact
Better than printed word
Was them
These loves
Give me reason
And maybe once more I will give you life
Otherwise
The she that loved
That she
Is- dead

93. "Couldn't You Be?"

How can I know if these things you tell me are falsities or truths?

Life Uncommon

There is no way to live life without living some of it in pain
I understand that not every road ends with a pot of gold
But I know I deserve better than a line dead without call
I know I've traveled far enough to be treated well
If it was disaster I sought then I'd be reaping all that I sowed in glory
But it was not
This time I sought happiness and love
I even wanted to undergo change within the self
Now I know that even a year alone does not award me with perfection
Perhaps I aimed too high
Perhaps bliss is out of my reach
But then, why, would that be?
Isn't that what the angels want- for us humans to be happy?
I love you dear fellow
Whether or not you know the truth and the profoundness of it
And here I remain alone
One learns after time to be more cautious
To be alerted by the flags colored red
But how to divert your path from pain
I suppose I'll have to be taught that lesson again
For as I sit here hurting
Feeling empty all over
I assure you I am without completion
If only love could be enough
To make a man be the man you most need
If only time held us safely, instead of making us bleed
My heart spurts out ashened fluid
As the most recent dream is drained within me

94. "Crimson Lover"

Something in the way her eyes glow
Lets me know that she has a deeper understanding
Than anyone else I'll ever know
Something in the way she smiles
She knows secrets and holds them close
And even when I had the chance to turn
To run and to flee
I couldn't
My feet were bolted
And my arms outstretched
I had to embrace her beauty, I confess
She's so stunning you'd do anything to please her
You'd throw away canyons and mountains
Just to see her smile

Life Uncommon

You'd create fires and erupt volcanoes
If only she'd smile once more
That's the power she holds
And something in me rests easier at night now
Because, simply because
She knows.

95. "Crone Mother"

In so many tales
We hear of these three
Simple girls
Though they be
They bring a world of light
To you and me

One the Maiden
The next the Mother
And yet a third
The mother's mother
The Crone she is called
And rightfully so
For she is wise
With truthful eyes

She started off as a girl
In pigtails and curls
Princess entailed
Growing up bit by bit
Had times of heartfelt aches
Took some kicks
Experienced as experienced women do

She grew up she did
To be a mother too
She raised a daughter
And smiled in delight
For she was a vixen
But such a sight!

Again time passed
She knew it couldn't last
But the truth is
It didn't all go by so fast

Life Uncommon

For as she walked down the aisle of life
Giving it one last round
She knew she'd done it all right
She became a man's wife
Had daughters numbering three
And now as she's grown older
She's a crone mother to me!

96. "Cry For The Angels"

Tears to dull the pain
Tell me she did not die in vain
Her hand in mine it shall remain
Through dusts of time
More songs of rhyme
She will be and thus be mine
Free she flies amongst the birds
Swam alongside the fish of the seas
Ran up hilltops
Walked through the valley of the gods
And sang with the cherubs of yore
She was an angel
Who left devils in the dust
Men bowed to her
Lullabies recount her many blessings
She was my all
My angel,
My keeper,
A destined inspiration to us all
So when the leaves of autumn fall
Listen closely to the wind
For it is her whispers
Embracing you

97. "Crying Eyes"

Do you thank heaven or hell when your car breaks down,
Across the street from the car repair shop?
Do you kiss the stars or cuss the moon when you,
End up at the one guy's house you've been trying to avoid?
Do you believe in lessons or lies?
Is it smart at a time like this to follow my car's lead,
And break down and cry?
Would it be better to just let it flow

Life Uncommon

Say fuck that shit and take it slow?
Eagles sing "take it easy"
How beautiful that must be...

("Take it Easy" is a song by the Eagles)

98. "Crying From a Sword"

Crying inside
Hurting from the pain
They slashed me with a double-edged knife
Killed my faith in them
Brought me back to square one
What do they see in me
My skin is so rough
My blood is so weak
Even my hand is at a loss of strength
Caring will not come again towards them
One fuck up – that was all it took
A double-edged sword
One slash,
One pain
That's all
Now I write alone in torture
For my friends are weak on the surface
And rough inside
Leave me now…I need to cry

99. "Crystallized Tears"

A child of the earth will rise above
Hand cloaked in white
Living truth, not blight
He will be wearing a talisman of light
Heir of the Egyptian right
Listen to the call of the wind
Hear him now as he speaks her name

Upon the pyramid lies a symbol of faith
He wears it on his arms embrace
Left handed genius to take him there
Here in the world where death is near

Until the clock strikes 8

Life Uncommon

On that September day
We have 24 hours to fix it
Make it right
The clock will strike midnight tonight
And you'll feel a chill
As the child is right
The darkness will go away

The child of the earth is honored this day. (8/11)

100. "Cycle"

The cycle of destiny is when…

Your future is your way
Your way is your goal
Your goal is your purpose
Your purpose is your reason for
Living your future

Cycles of destiny
Life is
Tangled up
World-
Our home

101. "Dark"

I don't want to be suicidal
But I am
That's hard to admit
Its just I don't like life right now
I can't see anything but lies, bullshit, pain, hurt, and more loneliness
Some part of me urges there's more
But I don't know the more
Even if I did
I'd probably hate it
Since now I hate you, hate them, hate everything, and surely hate myself
"Broadway is dark tonight…'

("Broadway is dark tonight" lyrics by Goo Goo Dolls)

Life Uncommon

102. "Dark Demons"

Dark, dark
Without fire
Invisible to the demons
That prey on me
Without them
Without me
Serenity turned grey
Slap me
Slam me
Kill me
Send me there
I dare, I dare
Forever I go
And you will never know
What its been
Here
In
The
Dark

103. "Dark Melodies"

I guess that says it all
In the darkness of my life
You show up
You brought music to my heart
Ability to feel to my soul
You stirred you shook
You rattled and you rolled
The keeper of darkness
The music of the night
So many views of you
To me in plain sight
The roar of a wolf
The passion that yearns
The voice of an angel
And all that scorns
A part of me goes with you
Oh, how I'll miss you

104. "Daughter"

Life Uncommon

He called me up one evening
Not so long ago
Asking for a date one I never would forget
So I pampered myself silly and smiled at the image
We went out for an evening
And now its become a life
From pigtails to riches
And now I am his wife
The caretaker and the lover
Of my husband
A more tender dear I'll never find
My daughter already three
Well she's just the fondest one of her daddy
Minutes or days may pass
But they are obscure
It is just him and me
And our baby we adore

105. "Day To Heal"

One call…
An answer of a voice from long ago
I was angry
I asked for the answer
Only to be told my thoughts were false
My pain was not inflicted by him alone
Once he hurt me
Then he stopped
Losers were the ones whom I was afraid of
A conversation heals a year and a half of pain
Nights in a corner are cured
Tears are innocent
Friends or not
Time heals all
Communication won't let me fall
Thanks
I feel free
Relieved
I am myself
Watch me fly

106. "Daydreams"

Consistently I dream in my waking hours of beauty

Life Uncommon

Some days it will be this guy or that guy
But many days, like today, it is about my beauty
Smiles awaken my sleeping face when I see in my mind's eye
Acceptance
I have a boyfriend at my side
The same one that holds me at night
Pictures of running and riding roller coasters
I feel cured
And I see a beautiful me
Deny it I will if ever you ask me of these images
But they are there
And they are me
Beauty

107. "Dead with Nothing"

I am dead inside
In my head is where I hide
Melancholy teardrops
Smiles and laughing are just props
Cold and silent without the mask
Having any hope or faith
Has become too great a task
It was my choice to let another in
Please don't grin
Tales of my life are sad
Depression is not just another fad
Phases pass after time
For you to doubt this would be a crime
Emotions bring about too much pain
So I've forced them behind a lock and chain
A door left forever in a silent abyss
There is nothing I will miss

108. "Dead with Truth"

Dead now
Before me
My words need a coffin
Bullshit deserves to be buried six feet under
How many lies
How many
Is my deathbed
My daughter has a great husband

Life Uncommon

Why did I say otherwise?
My son is a doctor
I should have known how great that is
Filled with lies
Not cruel by intention
But they must have stung
Pain is too much
I know that now
Why did I only learn this now?

109. "Dear Diary"

Every day we wake up and go through a normal routine
We brush our teeth and take our showers
And then present a certain self to the world
And although I also present a self
I try to show the world the same self I see in the mirror every day
As I change, the mirror's image changes,
And so too does the image the world sees change
Sometimes it is bare and ugly
Only a few are able to find the undeniable beauty of the naked truth
Without judgement and without restraint
The mirror and I we see you too
These are the writings of it all
True and real
To discover the meaning underneath it all
Is a feat few can accomplish
But let them reflect you too
To pick a poem up, any poem and to discard it without care
That is the only thing
I've ever deemed sin

So...

Here are my pages
This is my journal
A way that I express myself
A home for my heart and soul
A place where my imagination takes over
No stops
No lines
My thoughts are free
Poetry is written
My life is told
Read it if you dare to explore my inner most feeling

Life Uncommon

The mysteries
The secrets
Hopes, dreams, fears, and wishes
Long lost loves
And new found lovers
This is the mystery of my life
My journal

110. "Death"

If life is pointless
Why am I alive?
I have nothing at all
My money has been wisped away
No person is close to me
Not one being understands me
Is life without sympathy cowardice?
Only one question lingers
How do I do it?
I do not want to live
Or see tomorrow
Not the next day
I've lived my life
All of it
And now it is gone
No love
No friend
Just work and more work
The rest- endless unhappiness
Terrifying hatred
Lonely tears
Maybe pills is the way
Drown myself in the endless sleep
Death

111. "Deplorable"

If I could write to my own heart
I'd tell it to wait
And not to cry
Love is always inside
The future is what we make it
And I intend mine to hold
The highest good

Life Uncommon

Filled with love, light, and laughter

112. "Depressing Dreams"

Sitting here in dial-up confusion
Thinking of friends in Australia and New Zealand
Wondering if the cold there is as
Striking as our summer heat
Pink Floyd plays on the radio
But never as well as it does on my
Own CD player at home
Some things you can never own
But the way you feel about it
The way it makes you dance
Or sing
Or dream
That's just yours

I have a friend who wants to face her fears
But doesn't know how
Or maybe she wants to face her loves
Why must we face these things at all?

If we don't like most things
We can give them away, throw them out
Easy, simple
People after some argument or persuasion
We can get to go away too

But emotions?
They seem to linger forever
And at first their influence is subtle
Then it builds
Until one day we realize
Most of what we do, say, think is influenced by 'em

Depression must be when we have so many things going on
That we can't even know what emotions are influencing us

I suppose there are ways to find out-- Soul searching, for example
Writing, talking stuff out, but what of the quiet types? What then?
Survival of the fittest

No wonder suicide is still so high in numbers

Life Uncommon

Avoiding such hardships is impossible...
Perhaps that's the bottom line of life
Sad, isn't it?

113. "Depression"

Shimmering madness
Roams through my head
I try to think of how
To express emotions
Thicker than lead
But I come up on empty
Once again
Its the cloud of confusion
The air of pain
Its the way you get to feeling
When depression sets in

114. "Desire"

Long for arms
Security
Stability
Crave such lips
That intoxicate
Sensually
Like wine
Wish for those eyes
To capture
My essence
And bring me
Just me
To
My
Night

115. "Despised"

Despise myself more and more
Promises unkept
The fragile glass of trust broken
The weak string of friendships cut
Sympathy and understanding plucked from the feather of life

Life Uncommon

Secrets do not exist
I have lied
I have stolen
I have broken promises
I have hurt
And what I am now is nothing
Worthless to these people who I have called friends
Useless to trust
They have ostracized me
And I deserved it
I deserve it all
Bad and worse
Not good
No, I am not good
So torture me demons
And torture my life
For I have sinned to them and to myself
I should be punished
For I am a bad person
Apologies unaccepted
Punishment is welcomed
So punish me,
Dammit!

116. "Destined Lovers"

Like two branches intertwined are we
Simply dwelling in the heart of time
Loving each other, simple rhyme
You're the harmony to my dis-symphony
The beat that puts me back in line
I'd be lost without you
Sailing somewhere along some ocean blue
And wishing for just one more chance with you
I've died and been reborn
I've lived and I've hurt
I know the pain that sorrow brings
And the joy that conquers the unconquerable
If even for a second I doubted us, I'm sorry
If ever for a moment I didn't know, forgive me
Because somewhere along the pathways we took
We found each other
I'll be with you when you are lost
And I'll hold your hand when you are at your loneliest
I'll be there to hold you

Life Uncommon

To wipe your tears
And to kiss your sorrows
I see the pain in your eyes
And I know this hasn't been an easy life
You've gotten on nearly twenty-six years fine without me
I'll understand when you need time alone
And I'll love you even when you're gone
My heart aches to see your face
But I'll use that strength that you tell me I have
And I'll be some strong woman for a time
Only because I believe you'll come back to me
Thank you for being in my heart
For trusting me that much
Thank you for letting me in
When I didn't even know it
Like two branches of a birch, we birth an eternity together
Time has told us no lies
We did find the love we've loved the whole or our lives

117. "Destiny of the Soul"

There before me my soul mate stands
Smile in hand   ready to unravel it at any moment
The lip cracks
And there it is   the irreplaceable smile
Perfection surrounds
Modest beauty
Ignorant of all the magic
But I know it
My mind loses itself in those eyes that hold so much life
My life
Respect drips from my soul
The ignorant scholar understands me so well
Yet misses the most important part of my soul
My love

My soul mate ducks behind a prison cell
Yet, I cannot complain--for I hide too.

118. "Devilish Kittens"

you run around my floorboards
and dirty my home
you take the papers

Life Uncommon

which I own
racing with nothing
into a place you've been before
and you fly through the apartment
as if you are queen
but this is my lair
my bed in which I sleep
all I ask is for some respect
a little consideration
for my peace of mind
perhaps you could take time to recall the sanity which you stole?
oh dear god
this used to be my home!

119. "Dicks"

What are they like?
I'll tell you
Confident, arrogant, cocky, lustful, reckless…
They don't understand care
Or their own hearts
It sucks
They ask all about you
Assume you are naïve enough to manipulate
I'm so sick of being talked down to
I'm about to snap
I do not want to fuck
I do not want to give you anything
I want all men to just fuck the fuck off
Now!
Leave me alone!

120. "Disconnection Junkie"

He shrugs off reality
Like its a jacket
He hits the concrete
Like an elemental racket
He's stoned up
Doped out
Crashed and killed
He knows he's nothing

He's the truest lie

Life Uncommon

You'll ever hear
Its his eyes
You long to be near
So you take his promises
And store them up
Your heart is filled
With the falsehoods he spills

You want to be swept up into his world
To live on his island of dreams
And forget about how life always seems
Its the nonsensical feel which encaptures you most
His words sending you
Coast to coast
You could lay in his eyes
And drown in his tears
Knocked down shivering spears

He's the truest lie
You'll ever hear
Its his eyes
You long to be near
So you take his promises
And store them up
Your heart is filled
With the falsehoods he spills

He's a disconnection junkie
A drug-induced party
He's the universe of Ritalin
Drowning his sorrows in another bottle of gin
Love him as you will
He's destined to leave you lonely still

121. "Disney"

Have you ever wanted as I do?
The friends who challenge
Yet stay at a distance
Grades magically perfect
Although performance always fails
Teeth that shine
Antique possessions all mine
Calls on the line
Empty voices on the tube

Life Uncommon

The crystal ball fairy tale
Of only a few
Fictional fantasies for my ignorant
Love the wound
Salt the sugar
And light a candle
For maybe I knew
Have you ever wanted as I do?

122. "Don't"

Don't feel
Don't feel
I mustn't fall into that trap
Again
He held me so tight once that I became breathless
I will build walls and hide there away from everyone
Just to be safe
Secure from the pain
Parts of him I will forever love
Not when he hit me
Nor when he yelled
Few times he did make the effort to hold me
But I won't feel and can't allow myself
To remember
This is vital
My life is already tortured by overbearing forces
I do not want any more pain
So I won't feel
Don't
Don't feel
Don't feel

123. "Dream"

Before I drift off to sleep
I want him to hold me
In my dreams
I want him to know me

I awakened to the sweet thought
Of him stretching both his hands
Then placing them on either side of my neck
Slowly bringing my lips upward, toward

Life Uncommon

My body tingling in sensation
Then magically locking my small lines
Into his
We kiss
And I awake

124. "Dreamers"

Screamers can scream to the point
Where heads are spinning as thoughts are changing
Eyes are rolling as sights before them flow to a different rhythm
Noses smell different and unique scents
Mouths are tasting the taste of a new beginning
Bodies are feeling the ultimate feeling of dreaming
Screams are proof that dreamers can do anything

125. "Dreams"

They're usually good or bad
But last night was different
My dreams were pathetically strange
My dreams were about work
About nacho chips
Popcorn
The people
You name something about work
I dreamt it
Stupid, hey
Yeah, oh well
I'll have new one's tonight
What will they be?

126. "Dreams of A Maybe"

Sometimes I think I've seen it all
I wonder if there is anything I haven't seen
Why is it always me?

I'd like to think there's no way I can be hurt again, but I will
Still trying to be what everyone else wants me to be, try to be fake
Try to be a sheep, instead I just lose me
I listen to their troubles, sorrows, woes worse than mine
Maybe no one else will ever see inside me

Life Uncommon

I try to love, to have friends, to have faith
I don't, I cry, I nearly choke

Sometimes I feel every bit of pain lurking inside
I wonder if anyone can see all the things I hide

Is it wrong to love? Is it wrong to trust?
At times I am paranoid, at others I am free
What do you think will become of me?
I want to get through this
I don't, I cry, I nearly choke

Sometimes I tell the my tale
Sometimes I believe in love

Sometimes I wonder if you even know what you did to me
I'll think I want revenge, but that isn't me
I want to feel pretty, to have faith
I've survived this long and will survive so much more

Then sometimes I think if I ever get hurt again that will be the end of me
I reach out my hand, find peace
Sometimes it's there, Sometimes it's not
Sometimes I believe, Sometimes I don't
Sometimes I cry, Sometimes I nearly choke

127. "Drowned In You"

Darkness surrounds me tonight
My strength is gone
I am just
He is no longer
Cease to exist
Bastard my love
How funny can I be?
Love my only real enemy
Too funny
Wrong
Scary
Dreadfully scary
But I do
Today and tomorrow
Love him
My life
I love him

Life Uncommon

128. "Drugged Feel"

Must be drugged to feel as if my feet do not belong touching the ground
I shall lay down
Standing now
Dizzy
I want to tell Jake that I love him
I want to feel better
I have so much to say
But I am slipping
So good night
I love
I love
Oh, Jake is
Its you that I love
As always
Love
I hope you hear me wherever it is
That you are

129. "Eagles"

To land like an eagle
To fly like an eagle
Would be to ultimately feel wild exhilaration
A feeling of freedom
No power
Simply because none is needed
Being alone and unafraid
Untaunted by life and death
Space is everywhere
To fly and need no destination
To sing at the world
And say anything...

Sometimes I dream I'm in an opera house
On a solitaire stair
Dark room
And I am fearless
I just bounce slightly

I spread out my arms like wings
And become one with the soul

Life Uncommon

Of an eagle

130. "Echoing Madness"

What is it goddess?
What am I supposed to feel?
Why is it here, but remaining un-revealed?
I'm stumbling along, crumbling my song
I am inside myself now, I swear I can hear your call
Voices echo my name, but I'm still the same
What do they want?
What are they saying?
Why is their language unheard by me?
Are my ears so impenetrable?
The darkness comes
And the moon always looms
Melancholy drifts
Way before noon
The spirits gather to dance
A romance all its own
But I am blind and see not
My eyes are shut closed
Again tonight
Am I supposed to feel things?
I feel numb
I doubt that counts, mother
I wake from my dreams
I hear no screams
What are you telling me mother?
Why can't I hear?

131. "Elemental"

Classic wind
Blowing free
Wind rains
Down on me
Fire storms
And air breathes
Tumbled dry
Floating leaves
Winds of amber
Storm of fire
Roaming disaster

Life Uncommon

Natural fire
Withering dreams
Heated truths
Tonight I lay
Time it strays
Caught in the sun
Floating dream
Stars just out of reach
Nothing the beauty
Within the natural
Nature's way of
Breathing

132. "Embracing Hope"

Right now I am embracing some hope for the future
Maybe I will go to school tomorrow
And then work the next day
Too many idle days have shadowed these past few weeks
I need passion
I want desire
Fiery emotions rest in my worried little head
But somehow I choke
At each chance to explode with enthusiasm
Today I have been in much pain
But somewhere I also found strength
I am starting to believe
I will once again
Be myself
And the self won't be controlled
It won't be my bosses or my teachers
It will solely be me
Most likely not the same me though
A better me
I think of smiling
Which brings, at least, some hope

133. "Emotions"

We all have troubles
We all make mistakes
Some of us take the path to break or fall apart
Some of us build up walls
These walls are supposed to protect us from danger to our hearts

Life Uncommon

Walls like these are solid, uncaring, and ugly
Some of us are open to everyone
We can tell our life stories and feel okay about it
We can smell the scent of steel, but may just ignore it
Our emotions tell us who to trust and who is an enemy
Steel is the path we walk down when we are depressed
Some of us have small walls
We can talk freely to some people
Although we can also walk halfway down these ugly paths
Some of us are confused
We aren't amused by difficult times
Maybe some day we will all be happy
We won't need ugly paths
Solid walls
Or anything else to block us from reality

134. "Emptiness"

Sitting at my desk I stare out a window
Looking for happiness
But only finding emptiness
Hoping for a peaceful bird to fly by
But only becoming saddened to know it was hunted yesterday
Wishing for a child to run after their ball
Yet, I cry for last week they were shot in a drive-by shooting
Asking for a bunny rabbit to hop across the field
Even though I already know its become extinct
Maybe I'll see a tree blowing in the wind
Or find out its been cut down for human resources
Possibly a family will be taking a walk
No, I forgot, they were killed in a fire
Looking hard for an intelligent man
Failing to see anything but computers
I'm staring into the emptiness of this world wondering
Where will it end?
How many have been shot?
Gotten STD's?
Burnt in a fire?
Bombed?
Stabbed?
I notice that at the top of the staircase
All there is, is a drunken stair
Hurt by today's drugs
And peer tugs
It won't end…not like this…

Life Uncommon

Not like this—just look out your window
How much emptiness do you see?

135. "English Quiz"

I studied
I took ½ the notes
Expecting to be absent
I left them behind
The schedule jingled
I'm in a corner
Yes, its true I'm sorry quiz
I failed you

136. "Entrance"

Back out into the world today
Vow to live
Coupon redeemed
I can make it
Exclaim your praises
Yeah I made it
To swim
To fly
To soar
She's out in the world once more

137. "Ernest Hemingway"

I

In every man
There is a child
Hopeful and bright
Eyes that shine
Like twilight
While he might look broken
He has that innocence
It'll forever remain
It's a matter of fighting
It's a matter of never losing
Sight
That in your

Life Uncommon

Heart
And your mind
Its best to remain
Hopeful and bright

II

He was a boy
Arrogant and full of pride
She a lady with such
Strong tenderness
They fell in love
During a war
Not a fling
Nor a childish fantasy
They wrote to one another
All the time
Never came to him in youth
She was to love another
Somebody else's bride
But she didn't marry
Eight months of solitude
He endured
Heartbroken and alone
The war he inflicted upon
Himself
Turned the boy into an
Anger-fed man
By time he learned she never married
He'd already given up his life
And by time she told him
Of her love
It was already too late
He had died inside long before

III

Remember me
Not as who I am
But as who I was
Tender, loving, affectionate
When a man loves
And he loves all the way
There is nothing stronger
No mountain, no tide, no fire,
No person, place, or thing

Life Uncommon

With more passion
More vigor
Than a man whose heart
Ticks for just one woman
He may care again
He may marry
Or go through a dozen mistresses
But he'll never love any
As he loves his true and only
Pride gives way to heartbreak
He once loved with more
Promise than a thousand
Promises made by any other
Man
They say that war wounds
But no war wounds more than the one with a man
And his own self
To live on in the heart
Of a loved one
And to die in your own
Mind
Is there any greater sin?
No novel written
No story told
No declaration stronger
Than a man who loved
And whose heart becomes
Only one wound

(Inspired by the movie "In Love and War")

138. "Eternity Can Wait"

Heaven has no place for us
We're like two tumbled drifters in the sea
Trying to find our place
Between land and sky
Heaven above so elusive
And death was never our friend
When I met you, I knew I'd love you 'til the end
I promised myself then that I'd do anything
To have you in my life
Give up whatever it took, just to keep you by my side
You were the light that shone on me
That brought me life and filled my soul

Life Uncommon

How could I ever forget that smile?
Or the way I felt the first time we kissed
Somehow in those first moments
I found a life I always wanted but never knew
In those moments I found my soul's existence
And the place where I knew in the future all of me would reside
So here I lay at your bedside
Hold your hand, naturally, as I've done a million times before
And while I know you are about to leave
I believe we'll always be together
In heart, in soul, in life
Eternally yours

139. "Eve of Destruction"

On a day when the sun will still rise
I cannot help but fear to walk
Fear to see the outcome of our nation
Of our people
Of the land we call our home
Less than two years ago
Attack
A 9-1-1 emergency to which we failed to respond
Within any boundaries of integrity
Failure to proceed with precaution
Has injured us endlessly
How do we show our face to NATO again?
The UN sees an increasingly naive nation fall
America on its knees
And we discuss war
Children the ultimate sacrifice
Altruism dead
And today, the eve of destruction
"What" is…Now the question we must ask ourselves
Instead of 'When?'
Screw-bombing our intelligence
We try to gain alliance
Shattered truths, tears for the youth
Little do we know of tomorrow

Listen to the sound of silence as it rebounds
Time a ticker we all hate to hear
And the end of peace far too near
Demand something to follow
Before our nation we doth watch be swallowed

Life Uncommon

By a terrorist war we'd all be better off
If it never were.

140. "Fantasy"

The dragons are slain
And the unicorns run free
The wolves howl
And this is the place for me
A realm of fantasy
Dream on you twits
Meet your long lost soul twins
Meet in the sunsets
And in the parks
To dine, to dance
To live and to love
Where seals and snails roam helplessly
And where is the vixen
The perilous she
The swinger of rhythm
The caretaker of time
Oh look at me losing myself into rhyme
Wood carving of blessings
Pumpkins at your door
Posters of boys
And she dreams once more

141. "Farce"

So in the dark corners of my room
I dream of him again tonight
Struck suddenly by a terrible blow
One of reality
Where fantasies are for children
And work is life
To be a slave to society
Where religion breeds hope
A way to keep us working night and day
To dream of this afterworld
The unrealistic dream
Just like love
And trust and truth
Unfailingly false
Consistently inconsistent

Life Uncommon

So in this corner I roam around
Trying to stop the sound of truth
But I fail just as surely as any
When one knows the hope is false
The world becomes one dark room
Without light and without safety
This is my corner and no one can save me

142. "Feel You In Concentration"

I cannot compose from what I've heard
Only what I feel
Russia must have been beautiful
Although Jews were shown blackness
Dirty concentration camps
Shed blood
And strangely filled with extreme love
Silence cannot block the screams
My hand vibrates as I hear echoing cries from victims
All the survivors, in mind-my friends
My knowledge will show me
I sit here feeling bits of pain from
The Holocaust

143. "Feelings"

Feelings are emotions from our heart and mind
Beings are just emotions of nature's heart and soul
Trees, plants, animals, insects, and energy make up nature
A human can join nature's swaying, changing space
Or tear apart its fascinating existence
All organisms feel emotions just like
Nature's constant changing feeling and life
We can be one with nature and feel life
Or destroy its very existence and only know sadness
Are emotions just feelings humans have, and
Feelings when a human feels nature?

144. "Fellows"

One handsome, sweet, and charming
Flirtatious if you please
The other outgoing, bouncy, happy

Life Uncommon

Flirtatious too
Do they fit?
A question to bring them together
A date?
A dance?
I ask again- do they fit?
Honestly, I think not
But they're both adorable beings
Do they fit?
Hmm?

145. "Finals"

Stress is a word I know well this week
All the pertinent information has found a leak
Dripping out of me too fast
Finals are always the last
My teachers are so tough
But I'm trying to do good enough
Summer is nearing
But look what I'm still wearing
The coldness leaves these jeans on me
But, I know when the finals end—I'll be free!

146. "Finders Keepers"

Everyone falls apart sometimes
But if you've ever fallen in love
You're ahead of the game
And if you find love
Be the smart one
Don't let it go
Go home to your soul mate
Love him or her
For all they are
And live
Really live

147. "Finding the Point"

What scares me is
That so many people grasp
Tightly onto this false reality

Life Uncommon

Believing some good will come of
Them, and their survival
What good do any of us do?
We are mothers and doctors
Saving others from torment and pain
Keeping lives going and pushing
And for what?
We will die
And when we realize that
Reality is not love or hope
We die anyway
So I am just as useless
As those who believe
Maybe not knowing would be bliss
To live without question
Happy without answer
But this is a one way train
And I can never go back
So do you hop on
Or do you stay put?

148. "Fire"

"Fire is the devils only sin"
Perhaps at once you and I were kin
The girls you chase
The hearts you break
The blood you drink
The essence of truth
The magic of a Druid
The heart of a boy
The kings of a river
The buttons on a toy
The man of honor
The truth that hurts
The pain inflicted
The fire that burns
The crackles of ember
The leaves of a maybe
The phone calls to a friend
I cry for you
You heart is pure
Golden as your
Tears of a whisper

Life Uncommon

149. "First Poem"

Seconds, minutes, hours, days, weeks, months, years, decades, and centuries all come and
go
One thing- the only thing that may come and never go- is love
I used to sit and dream of love
As time went on I got bores with dreaming
I tried to find love but no matter how much I hoped, dreamed, wished, screamed, or
talked about love
I never found it
When I least expected to find a match I found a guy
This guy in my opinion is the perfect "clone" for me
I used to sit alone and dream of love, now I sit alone but not by mind nor heart
I dream of how great the love we share is
I remember at one point in time we broke up- it was a sad time
Then since our fate is so great- greater than any other this love between us two could
never be more true
Our hearts both feel the love we have- knowing that assures me we will "never" be apart
From all this I learned its never too late to save love, its never too late to make that
feeling
Of darkness the "blues" to fade away to a peaceful, dreamy, heart-warming love
It is so true that when two hearts are so clean, pure, and innocent they are so hard to keep
apart
Those two hearts brought together by the strongest fate of all
Love can come and stay or come and go but it is unlike all the seconds, minutes, hours,
days, weeks,
Months, years, decades, and centuries that come and go
Love is the most unique feeling any two people will ever know

150. "Flickering"

As I enter through this door my eyes adjust to the darkness
Understanding slowly the shapes of different objects in the room
Funny how the room mimics my life
My soul is thick with night too
And I constantly need to adjust to the people and things around me

151. "Flickers"

If I could look into
My reflection in the mirror
Of time
Faded glories drifting away

Life Uncommon

…
Visions dance in my head

152. "Flowers of Life"

Red, pink, purple, white, and yellow are examples of colorful flowers
Flowers are pretty
People are witty
People are like flowers in a way- both have a beautiful inside
Flowers are in a sense the happiness of our blooming lives
Flowers of life are eye-catching just like people flowers have a way to bring others closer
To look at the true beauty that lies inside us all
We all have a flower of life inside us
Some of us bloom faster than others, but we all have the same joy
The joy of blooming into wonderful and extraordinary eye-catching figures

153. "Fly"

In the arms of myself
I fly
Floating every day
Towards your arms

And I dream
With tears in my eyes
Of a place like this
Being blessed, happiness

Eternal
Flickering away
The moon rises
To another day

And I'm kicking it high today
Letting go of bitter yesterdays
Singing my destiny
Trying to find reality

In the arms of myself
I fly
Floating every day
To the arms of a god

Life Uncommon

154. "Following My Grandmothers"

My grandmothers were strong
But now passed away
I am left
Left to be strong
I can plow
And bend to toil
Even go through fields sowing seed
I will be strong
My grandmothers were strong
They were soft-hearted
They touched earth and grain grew
But I can't touch earth as they did
My grandmothers were strong
I will be strong
And full of memories
Because my grandmothers were strong

155. "Fool"

You gave me a rose so
I gave you my heart

Simple notions in quantity
But complex as knowing why we are here

Words that rhymed in my ears as a lullaby
Each syllable ambiguous

Touches that tickled my toes
And I was misled

Kindness dripped from your lips
And each kiss was my venom

You raised the blade
And I did not duck

156. "For Them…I Long"

Is it possible to ignore admiration?
To erase someone else's existence
Walk by
They are invisible

Life Uncommon

I am invisible
A ghost
Dead in this body
Longing for another life
Each day I think
Analyze
Wonder
Will my man come?
Shall I be doomed eternally to nothingness?
Despair and depression
I want him
Need them
Feel them next to me at night
Holding my crumpled body
Kissing my pained forehead
Loving my death
I long
I long
I long for them

157. "Forever Hell"

I'm unsatisfied with the lies that you tell
I'm totally dried up like a goddamn well
If you had any clue of the trouble you bring
Fuck you'd run for jackass king
But you don't know just what you do
Fucking loser you leave me blue
I'm betting that you don't have any idea how hard I cry
But its silently inside that I lonely die
You've got your life to live, why care about mine?
But goddamn its about time you paid that fine
For the trouble you brought to me and my mind
But you'll never pay not one small dime
I know your kind I've lived with them all my life
Since I was a kid I've dealt well in strife
When I thought it was love it never really was
It was just a masked up lie, 'cuz
It don't matter to anyone else who the fuck they hurt
Just kick that dust in our faces like we're nothing but dirt
Remember that time when I told you I get hurt easily?
Would it have been so hard to listen just that once?
I know fragility's a joke
To you fine bloke
But let me tell you this sensitive girl

Life Uncommon

She's been on enough tilt-a-whirls
For a lifetime of dizziness and confusion
I just want a way out now, a way off this horrid ride
But I'm guessing its too late, I'm already dead inside

158. "Forgotten Things"

Each choice we make burns in each moment
Like lemon drops that have lost their taste
Like rain that suddenly fades away
Its all a matter of moment-to-moment
Each day waiting for the next
The choices we make defining and redefining us each day
Stability a fleeting balloon
In a sky of the moon
Kissing each present goodbye
We forget the small things
And take the big ones for granted
Suspicion a sharp knife that dulls beauty
And the only thing we have to cling to
Is love itself
The window reflects the inner, unsaid, truth

159. "Formidable Romance"

Love is like a tragedy waiting to happen
I give my all
And shit, you know I take the fall
But that's a lie
You see I don't always let them inside
Truth be told it only makes it
Hurt worse
I love him though
Even allowed myself to dream
To think
To wonder
About life, about love, about romance
Kids even considered
I'm not a kid anymore
But I still dream like one
I still don't give up
I'll still carry on

Life Uncommon

160. "Fremont Street"

The Sunday night hooker stares at me silently
As I make my way down Fremont Street
Trying to enjoy my morning coffee
Before my early 5 a.m. shift
I am disturbed by her brash character as she lifts up her skirt
Showing her naked underneath to passers-by
Though I am a quiet man
Older, more learned
I could not stop myself from abruptly replying to her technique
The rest of my hour I spent watching the poker faces of gamblers
As they tried to win at 3 stud poker, blackjack, even Let it Ride
With a last sip I sighed
Deeply and disposed of my morning delight
Within moment I was at my destination
Main Street before sunset's first light

161. "Fucking Victims"

So I get online again tonight
Another abuse victim putting up a fight
Walls stream high for them
And still they believe they are alone
I can care, love, listen
But what's the point?
Another door slammed in my face
They walk away without a trace
Maybe its fears
Yes, maybe that's it
Maybe they're just scared
So what do I do?
Stand there and cry?
Mutter a lyric-less lullaby?
Please, mother, you know that's not my style
I cry, I cry
They ask me to smile
Why am I to smile?
They wake up alone
And each day feel they are rotting in pain
Every day the cycle continues again and again
Razor blades to their skin
Oops, their control became too thin
Their bellies are empty
And I'm supposed to smile?

Life Uncommon

Well hell I'll fail this test
I'd rather wallow in emptiness

162. "Future"

What lies ahead of me I don't know
In my past too much has been a show
I'm facing the future with an open mind
And leaving the bad of the past far behind
I'm learning to face my fears
And not worry about the small tears
I have a self-esteem
And I know I'm not living in a dream
I also realize happiness doesn't just flow down a stream
For the first time I face the future with hope
That one day people won't depend on dope
We all face the future
But we have the choice of how it turns out
There is no need to shout
I'm just saying without a doubt
A good idea of the future is better than
Just sitting in front of a television being a fan
We have to be strong on our own
We can't depend on a gun
Or something life-threatening like that for fun
I don't know the future and that is good
Because life can be easily closed up, just like a jacket hood

163. "Gateway"

Suspicious eyes
Gleaming their way through the darkness of my heart
Suspicious eyes
Penetrating my soul waking me with a start
I climb the path to righteousness
Tripping upon the reality of my unholiness
I spin in a twist of fate
And open my eyes as you open the gate

164. "Gentleness"

Glancing up at your eyes
I saw love flickering as it has throughout time

Life Uncommon

Like a cactus spring
You showed me your gentle nature within
I could not have loved you more
You were all I had hoped for
Strong and stable, yet soft and fragile
Like a soft-flowing stream we've gone the mile
Through years of changes and growth
Somehow we remained so very close
Even at times when we've been apart
You've always been nestled inside my heart
Today I feel blessed for having the chance
To be one half of this lasting romance
Throughout the years the love we've shared
Has been like the gentle call of the wind
That only our spirits can hear

165. "Girl"

The words of others just echo in her ears
Never really meaning anything
To the orphan
Who had parents
Even siblings
She walked the world alone
She endured the pain of ten men
Her bravery only a speck to her
For she will never know how
Beautiful she is
Tie her down
Beat her through
She screams for help
And oh my god
They all say goodbye
The closets of her youth
And cupboards of her memory
She knows what cruelty is
And so continues on her days
With the delicacy and grace
Of a childhood goddess

166. "God Gave Me Hope"

There was a time in my life
When I was alone

Life Uncommon

I wandered about in strife
Feeling no place was home
I wanted to change
But didn't know how
Tried to rearrange
Came up short somehow
I went to my friends
And family members too
But nothing could mend
Those tears endlessly blue
Finally, when I lost it all
Lost my way
Took that last fall
It dawned on me to pray
A church lit up across the way
I hadn't been in years
No time better than the present day
Inside God gave me hope to replace my fears

167. "Going to Bed"

Today was exhausting
I worked
I fought
I flirted
I kissed
I'm still not happy
The one I love is so far away
So far inside his own mind
Can I reach him
Fuck, I'm too lonely for this dream
I'm not patient enough no more
I'm seventeen and I'm still in the state I was in four years ago
Men who are they?
What do they want?
Going to bed…

168. "Goodbye Little Girl Me"

My innocence is gone
Anger left in its place
No more people stepping over me
Ms. manners when necessary
Ms. game face 'cuz I have no other choice

Life Uncommon

But innocent girl no more
I have grown and I have wept
I lay to rest
R.I.P. my old list of dreams

169. "Goodbye Sweetheart"

Last night I told him that my love for him is gone
And then I drove off hoping all was done
Threats
Yelling matches
Cable cords to hang myself on
Car doors slammed
Stalking to no end
Ring...ring...ring...
To my life what did he bring?
Happiness?
Oh no, it was a mess
Loneliness?
Some lonely nights I loved his caress
Tears?
Yeah, lots of those and a few new fears
My heart goes astray from this beast
Sometimes his touch will be missed
Goodbye sweetheart

I throw the hurt you've given me away...

170. "Grace Awoke Me"

The night was young
I came in early tonight
Ordered myself a whiskey
And got ready to drown my sorrows
One more time
I don't know when she came in
But suddenly I turned
My eyes slightly blurred
But I could see her
Like the earth sees the sun
Her smile lit up the room
She gracefully danced with man after man
Her dress was red
And she crimsonized my desire

Life Uncommon

I wanted to move for her
But I was drunk
Glass after glass of whiskey
Left me in a state
Still she danced
Like a twirling comet
Then something incredible happened
She came to the bar and stood by my side
I wanted to tell her she was lovely
But only managed to stare into her transfixing eyes
She smiled at me while gazing into mine
She went back to the dance floor
But looked my way
Something in her eyes told me
Something in her smile showed me
Something in the way she knew me
We only held that moment for a few hours
While her red beauty danced
And I drank
Something in her eyes told me
Something in her grace woke me

(Inspired by the Beatles song "Something")

171. "Grandma"
(dedicated to my Grandmother)
I called her
She smiled
We love each other
I've missed her
Time heals all once again
Yeah, …

172. "Green"

The paper in my pocket every day is a constant reminder of my dependence on the devil
My body wanders around almost aimlessly just waiting for the next command
And as I walk I can always feel its presence
Close to my body to remind me how close the devil is to my soul
The paper sits there making a mockery of my hopes and dreams
It laughs out loud at my hope for any success
For I will never succeed at freeing myself from the devil
He has marked my eyes and my face for life
Forever I am stuck

Life Uncommon

My mind is my own yet it is constantly tormented
With reminders
I am perpetually forced to obey these laws

173. "Grieving"

Mental breakdown where life is just shit
Everything is fuck
And every doctor is a nitwit
Subrealities and illusions keep my sanity
Dreaming the way a poet should
I fear the longer end of renewing myself
Pain stains my dignity everywhere
Waiters are just characters in books
I miss a life, any life
I am living to die
Survival is of no use
Kill me now
Oh, please kill me now

174. "Grown Up"

New job
New looks
He comes out of the cupboard
Less drunk with indignity
Sober from ignorance
He is no baby
Advice seeker
Turned giver
Sober and new

175. "Guilty as Charged"

An old-friend e-mailed me today
She thought I wouldn't be able to see behind her hurtful,
Blaming words- but I did
The problem is- I always do
I'm not so good at just pretending
My lies are completely see-through
She probably wanted to say she missed me
But all I read was, "Blame, blame, blame..."
"You are at fault, because..."

Life Uncommon

Even if that's not really what she said,
It most certainly is how it felt
Sometimes its nice to hear from an old friend
Sometimes its nice as shit
And the day would have been better without her, without the blame,
And without the,
Guilty manipulations-
A time honored maneuver of women.

176. "Guy"

I dream of you all the time
Shining in glory, smiling at me,
Italian heartthrob
Beater of grains
Words of peppermint
Stick of cinnamon
Candles of blue
Yes, it is all you
The star out of reach
The friend never far
The guy of my dreams
Perfect as you are

177. "Halloween"

Ghosts and goblins
Ghouls and fools
A night of fears and scares
Haunted houses scurrying like mice
Freddy and Jason – out to get ya
Superstition and competition
White cloth vs. black cat
Costumes and masks
Real and fake
Facade or fantasy
"Choose your own adventure"
Because tonight its…
Halloween

178. "Handshake"

Bitter nights I've laid alone

Life Uncommon

Today you came to me with a simple poem
Offering to be there, someone near
While I see beauty in such offerings
I know where I am inside
Fighting to keep my spirits high
Forgive me please, but I cannot hold you
And stay true
To my own heart
Which I need to heal
Roads lead me in many directions,
This one leads me home
To a place of healing within
So I ask you to please understand
That I cannot reach out my hand
To hold you
But instead reach out my hand
In friendship

179. "Happiness?"

I look around myself
Only seeing people tangled up in their lies
In pure masks they wear
People build walls
That stretch to the sky

Well, I keep on looking at the world
At what its been through
What it is
And imagining what it'll become

Hell-
If we aren't happy by now

Yeah, yeah
I truly can't imagine that day
I mean just look at the world that my imagination stems off of
How could I imagine a day of peace?

Just looking around myself
All I see
Are walls
Masks
Lies
Painful memories

Life Uncommon

And people trying to break free
From the chains that bind them

Yeah, yeah
People are happy
Just take a look at you and me!

180. "Happy Notions"

Bluelight thistles
Morning dew
Simply loving you
The rain in my coffee
The mist in the air
You're the beauty that twirls
The heart in a dear
You're the champion
A poetry writer
A song dancer
A captain of the heart
Mr. Lover Romance
Mr. Oh so Right
Mr. Take me home tonight
Mr. I'll love you forever
Mr. Your dreams have finally come true
Oh yeah, I'm riding straight home to you

181. "Hardship"

Have you ever felt like all you do is somehow wrong?
Well, that's how I've been feeling lately
I mean I'm not perfect
It still sucks
I want to be strong
To make the right decisions
And be looked upon with admiration
But that's not always the way it happens
I suppose we would never learn if that's the way we did things
This must be the way it really oughta be
And maybe tomorrow if I fail again
I'll stumble upon some new part of me
Get to know some narrow part of myself
And be new somehow
Until then, I'll live with my choices

Life Uncommon

Hold my chin up
Smile and not give up
Because that's what we do
When we live the life of an unending fuck-up

182. "He"

When he moves
I grab onto his arm
I make such a firm grip
To make sure
His love for me is obvious
And true

When he moves
My eyes dangle
They watch the sight of a caring person
Who they know so well
And want to know better

When he moves
The world is silent
And my heart beats

183. "He Lifts Us All"

Long ago
You lost your way
You left it all, gone astray
And today you pray
For someone to help you
God, you believed, had left you
And today you pray
And you ask god to show you the way
"Do you need me now?" God shouts
And you say "Yes"
You admit your fall
You admit it all
And you pray
That God will show you the way
Because today you know
You're not alone
In your darkest moments of despair
It was then, that you knew God was there

Life Uncommon

When you prayed, the answer came
For once you knew your way
Because God showed you that day

184. "Hearken"

Listening to the wind, I hear whispers of
Better days
Better times, easier words
Lighter notions, simpler truths
I've not much to offer
Yet, friendship is always there

185. "Heaven Out A Window"

Sometimes I look outside
I plaster my hand to the window
Hand cold, unmoving
Stuck
And my heaven
Shall forever stay
On the other side

186. "Her Dream"

"Her dream" she shouted out
Her dream is to be noticed
She wanted a loving world
A million people communicating
Which would leave the world celebrating

She didn't like a little spoiled kit being a brat
And lived believing not to take too kindly to that
She knew how to care and taught us all the share

A world of friends with no ends
Why can't we see it? Why can't we be it?
What will it take to end this corrupted mistake?

A president of hope she longed for
And a drug and disease free baby to adore
Oh yeah, she wanted more

Life Uncommon

Her dream was to all be kings and pointedly focus on all things
To give strength to the poor, to fix the inner sore
Oh yeah, she wanted more

The homeless she knew needed to hope and tried to show us all to cope
She stood up in front of all the world
And barely ever quarreled

She wanted us to do something new
Yes, me and you
Her dream was to come together and have hearts as free as a feather
To wander to all extremes and not to split into tinier teams

She never expected us to go crazy or sit down and be lazy
Her expectations were higher
Hopefully to work in tune like a choir

She knew life could be a thorn and sometimes we'd have to mourn

Her dream still stands
If we can all give our hands
Her dream is known inside
So lets work together, coincide
Oh yeah she wanted more
Oh yeah she wanted more

187. "Here Am I"

Twisted blood stained vines
Wrap their way around these arms of mine
I try to break free
Yet falter in shock
Time works against me
I'm weaponless and fearful
Standing alone in a shelter of suffocating vines
My efforts are worthless
For here I stand
Here am I

188. "Hiding"

Drops of salty tears cover my sleeves
Legs resting near my chest
Small now

Life Uncommon

My arms embrace my legs
My head instinctively falls forward
Feet have gone numb
Eyes are closing
They have cried too much anyway
Weakened and tired

I finally find a pillow
And a comforter
Lying down I prepare to dream
Before my eyes close again I need to push
Push away
All the memories of him
My enemy
He wants to hurt me
And I am terrified
Shaking
But let him exist no more
Eyes are closed
And I sleep

189. "High School Hopes"

Girls dream about super studs
All sick of waiting to fall in love
Keanu Reeves and Brad Pitt
Fill up their heads
Guys about supermodels and Sandra Bullock
Day in, Day out
Same statements
Same fantasies
Will any of them be fulfilled?
Is there a point?

190. "Him"

As I turn the corner I keep expecting
To see him walking to my house
For him to smile at me when I drive into my driveway
Then when the turn is made he isn't there
He hasn't been there for a while
My love has left me
I wonder every day where he is
Yeah, I know I shouldn't care

Life Uncommon

It's true he hurt me
My heart was broken
I've moved on
Maybe one day he'll appear again
I miss his tenderness
But it may never be there again
I'll just have to keep turning down an empty street
Longing for him
Even if just as a friend

191. "Him and I"

Is he lonely?
Killed by the beast of broken hearts?
I know
I am
My pen moves
Hair swiftly touches my nose
Our professor speaks
He looks at me
Classroom dull
But this stare is so invigorating
But I question anyway
Wonder if I am invisible
Or if I shall be doomed to wait here
For
The
Beauty
That
Never
Comes

192. "His Beauty"

Picture beauty for a moment
With its own grace
See it walking
Feel its warmth

Untainted by bitterness

He is beauty
His smile uncorrupted perfection
Each letter falls

Life Uncommon

Paper grabs hold of them
It knows and understands
As I do...

His beauty

193. "His Cell"

In this cell he built for himself his thoughts narrowed down
He became this rigid being behind the bars
His body was left to turn to dust he would never be anything again,
Because the bars shut him inside
His cell was built from so many things
One wall stood because the pain from losing Adrianna was taken in so deeply
Another wall stood from lost luxuries that were forgotten long ago
Trips to other countries, oceans and skies he would never see
His space closed in
The bars had been formed thick and strong
His bitter thoughts and cold, lonely nights built a new bar every night
As the hours counted down--so did his space
Each secluded thought left him in a more lifeless surrounding
He thought about passed opportunities as he waited for the sunrise
And he recalled how many decks of seconds he had been dealt
He recalled those decks being discarded
Replaced by whiskey and cigarettes
His hand held many things in its time,
But it never held anything as solid and cold as the bar it did that night

194. "His Touch"

My skin crawls
Cracks
Ages
And dies down
Without
His touch

My lips chap
Crack
Lose color
And lie still, motionless
Without
His touch

Life Uncommon

My heart calms
Beats slower, normal
And feels loneliness
Without
His touch

My body curls
Curves
Ages more
Without
His touch

195. "Hollow"

It feels like you never cared
Not as though you weren't here
But that you were
And I meant nothing
Not to you
I still blame myself
Always do in situations like this
Never make you in the wrong
I figure I'm too fat
Not blonde
Or tall
Not a whore
So not enough
Like if only I'd let you use me more
Nothing makes you stay
When you choose to go
There's no way I could've known
I was being so naïve
Couldn't see
You could've loved me
But who cares?
You're not here
So I stay alone
Tucked away neatly
Afraid, waiting to trust
Paralyzed
Inside

196. "Homecoming"

Life Uncommon

A night of mystery
A night of dance
Without me wearing pants
Jake and Justice are coming
Not a night for bumming out
Will Jake be romantic?
"Ha la, ha la "(is) "my boyfriend" back?
Has he been gone for such a long time?
Ha la, ha la, my boyfriend's back

197. "Hope"

Right now I am embracing some hope for the future
Maybe I
Will go to school
Work
Know too many idle days have shadowed these
Past few weeks
I need
Passion, I want
Desire
Fiery emotions
Rest in
My worried little
Hand, but somehow I choke at each
Chance to explode with
Enthusiasm
Today I have been in much pain, but somewhere I found strength
I am starting
To believe
I will
Once again
Be
Myself
And the self won't be him
Or a dictator
It will solely be
Me
Most likely not the same me though
A better me

I think of smiling
Which brings, at least, some hope.

Life Uncommon

198. "Hot"

Rivers of fire, burning desire
Flick on a candle, light up the fire
Sizzle and steam, find me somewhere new
Take me away, fantasies all new
Titillating screams from the depths of me
Aching for me, something I've never seen
So yank at my heart, pull at my soul
Just show me more, or let me go
Light up the flame, set it on fire
Here in the night, burning desire
Take me or leave me but never desert me
Tease me to please me but never appease me
Show me the reigns and take me tonight
Show me the fire, as it burns so bright.

199. "How I Knew"

I use to lie awake at night and dream of you
Such sweet desires for you
I wanted you
Passion for you swam through every limb
Every breath I took was one more moment
I was longing for you
Wishes made were always of us
I would stare out into the darkness
And drift into a haze
Completely swept away by your eyes
By the beauty that shone through every single time I talked to you
That's how I knew I loved you
Because every other thought revolved around you
Every second before I fell asleep at night was spent thinking of you

200. "How Things Are"

Life moves on in so many forms
The adventurous waves of the ocean move
Towards a new place to hit with their mighty powers
The tiny seeds people plant - grow
Towards the sun to become beautiful flowers
People walk to make change so life never
Becomes a motionless picture
Our hands and minds extend out towards a new dream

Life Uncommon

Legs of all animals strengthen and lift up
Even the harshest feelings
The moon twirls around the earth
To the beat of its own rhythm
The wind moves itself
And many of life's great wonders
Hands open up to grasp the ultimate feeling of living
And then close and won't let go
They won't let go until
We aren't sure why life moves on in so many forms
But that is no reason to stop life
Suicides, homicides, drugs, alcohol and smoking all lead
To the horrifying idea of one form of life
Never moving again

201. "How to Make Art"

When you take people's loves and apply them to an artistic work you can come up with anything

Possibly a quilt where each design has a story of an emotion
What can be created?
Anything—any story
The possibilities are infinite

202. "Hugs"

One by one
Hugs once, twice, three times
And on
They made me happy
All my friends at work
Sweet and cheerful
Loving and caring
Warm and true
Each hug was full of all of these
One by one
My day became happier
All those wonderful
Hugs

203. "Human"

Life Uncommon

I am a human, part of the society of the most advanced species
We can now each live in our own caves all over the world—
We can live for years and never speak to anyone…is that an advancement?
We do not need to talk to one another or even care that one another exist
This is what the industrial revolution got us
Now we no longer have to work out in the fields
Now we get to work in nice heated buildings for $5.15 an hour
Which isn't even enough to cover half the rent

What is the point of human existence? To make money? To have love?

I don't get the point of my existence
I have had people tell me I am here to help, to heal
Why…so they can go on living out their meaningless existences?
Why would I force anyone to live society's conformist life barely able to breathe

People once told me that my life is my own
Which is so opposite the truth its not even funny
Why I am working? Why I am living? What is the purpose of life?
I mean I absolutely hate working, I hate bills, I hate getting sick
I hate money and I hate being part of the machine
I have to work to make money to pay off bills just in order to survive
And I am surviving to work to make money to pay off bills
Where's the meaning in that?
I was once told that we work to distract ourselves from thinking about this
We settle into a pointless existence because that's what everyone else is doing
When I tried to commit suicide a year ago I realized afterwards... after throwing up all I
had Ingested...that I don't want a meaning...because what if the meaning was something
awful…like my entire existence was formed just so I would help the old lady cross the
street on some idle Tuesday five years ago

Someone once told me to take a job doing what I love
I love sleeping…no one will hire me to do that
I love chatting on the internet…no one will hire me to do that
I love reading…no one will hire me without the proper degree
I love poetry…but I haven't found a publisher

Inspired by Pink Floyd's "Welcome to the Machine"

204. "Hunger"

My heart is hungry for love
When he runs or leaps it flies like a dove
When he walks my heart

Life Uncommon

Beats fast towards our fate
His laughter brings my face a smile
My feelings become darkened for his sadness
Emotions are easily mixed up if he's confused
My throat will dry up and become thirsty
If I can't have his love
My heart is hungry for his love

205. "Hypocrisy"

I write because I love it
But somehow I actually care what others think
What they feel when they read
I am the hypocrite here
They should not matter
Do not matter
Will not matter
But always, inevitably
Do matter
Life is a hypocrisy of ambivalence and I just follow the waves

206. "I Always..."

I always write out my feelings
Onto a piece of paper
What am I writing to others
Do they understand
My words?
Do they want?
What is a word to them,
What should it be?
Is this poetry or just words,
Scribbled out,
Onto a piece of paper to them?

207. "I Become"

Truth becomes me
The tale goes as such
White walls on the inside
Painted by pain
Bruised by pride
Smashed through ends

Life Uncommon

Time after time
Innocence is relative
Manipulative ways surely pushed
Razor blades and pills on my dresser
Water to quicken the blow
She was in a coffin
And some spirit is writing this as you know

208. "I Can"

Last year I wrote a poem
Then I lived it
This year I write a truth
Maybe I'll live it too

The truth:
I am strong, even when I am feeling weak
I am confident, even though I allow my thoughts to waver
I can control my thoughts, even though I haven't mastered that yet
I can lose weight if I want to
I can learn to eat right
I can learn to be better at remembering things
I can become more responsible
I can earn my own respect and the respect of others
I can keep my compassion, love, light, and laughter
I can be me
I can do my best
I can let go of things that don't need holding on to
I can live without stability
I can adapt to change
I can keep a really clean apartment and car
I can work at a job that I am overjoyed to go to every single day
I can work at a job that I love entirely and look forward to going to it every day
I can find a place to work that feels right on all levels
I can live my life to the highest good
I can become more understanding of myself
I can learn more about me
I can believe in myself at all times
I can make sure that I'm not anyone's doormat ever again
I can make sure not to fall for cons anymore
I can find a way to get up in the face of whatever I fear
I can continue to hope, have faith, dream, love, and care
I can be a person of truth, trust, honor, loyalty, devotion, passion, and intelligence
I can express myself artistically through writing, drawing, dancing, and acting
I can be a person who only speaks the truth

Life Uncommon

I can understand that I don't expect to be perfect
I can understand that my goals won't be necessarily reached overnight
I can understand that things take time
I can live as me and that will be exactly right
I can
I can
I can.

209. "I Dare You"

Beat me senseless
Take me apart
I dare you to just break my heart
Constant drumming of memories
I hate them I do
So I dare you
Just breakthrough
Get to know the inner coldness
The cave
The warm me inside that's so passionate you could just die
Try just once to dance through the rain
And forget about the pain
Cut yourself free
Life is a breeze
Dance the slow dance of the eternal drum
Unravel all that you've become
I dare you
Just stare into the mirror
Hate it when you are wrong
Foolish beliefs you remember
As you draw with chalk out on the sidewalk
Darkness falls
And you take me apart
Piece by piece
Challenge every bit of me
You see those bars I live behind
Witness to the roaming madness that is
Me
And finally you get it
I see you dancing in the snow
Whistling in the wind
Lighting a bonfire
As you dig your feet happily into the ground
Welcome to magical elementation, my friend.

Life Uncommon

210. "I Get It Now"
(dedicated to Alex)
A year later I understand
You didn't just depart
It wasn't something temporary
You didn't just move out
Or away
You left me that February day
I guess I had to hope
Maybe because I'm young
Perhaps still naïve
I just couldn't let myself believe that you were gone
Maybe you were special, I'll never really know
I'm done asking why can't you love me and what in me is not enough
'cuz guess what? You're not enough for me anymore
I deserve respect
I earned it from you long ago
Your own inadequacies are not my fault
This is a blame for you to bear alone
I don't forgive you just yet, But I will
I love you still
But, dear, I let you go

211. "I Hate You"

I hate you
Do you hear me?
Am I alive when you see me,
Or just a shadow, an image?
I live
I am human
I fail at your every expectation
I will never earn your love
For you are a damn fool
I call out
Just to say Fuck You
Fuck your rules
Fuck it
I say Fuck Yourself
You will never appreciate me
You're not a saint
A master maybe
But not a saint!

Life Uncommon

212. "I Love You"

I send a ray,
An arrow of hope
Out to you
I kiss the wind
And Imagine your lips
I let go
I grow up
I become me
For a dream
Emily, Derek, Joseph, you, and me
A true family
I love you
As the stars shine
Each night I sing you a lullaby
Telling you "I love you"
No words spoken by me
Have ever been more true
I swear,
I love you

213. "I watch"

He stood so closely to that wall
And I just stared at him
Just for a few seconds
Almost every minute for an hour
He stood there in a gray sweatshirt with a zipper and a hood
He just looked so silently pleased
I even believe he looked at me too
Maybe he knows I like him
Or maybe he just hasn't caught on
I want him in my life
I feel this ache to have him by my side
My inside
All of him should be there
Will it happen?

214. "I Whisper"

Can you love someone from a million miles away,
And never let them know?

Life Uncommon

He's the one
I know he is
For at night I've whispered a million times
"I love you"
And last night I finally knew
Who it is I whisper to
I whisper to him, the little boy in blue
He was here
I scared him away
My crab-like pinchers hurt his fragile twins
He's not a Pisces
Or a singer
Though, he does sing
His favorite book is "Fahrenheit 451"
Last night I slept with him
His essence still left behind on the
Shirt he wore
Perfect to cuddle up to
In him I seek comfort, protection
Safety in hiding
Hiding within him
Can he heal me?
Can he see the scars inside,
And kiss them away?
I need time
I need to know him
I need to understand how I feel
And yet with every breath
I miss him
With every time the clock ticks
I sigh, for him
How can I bring him back?
And should I?
Will I frighten him off again?
I whisper "I love you..."

215. "Ideal Child"

As a child I believed
Love was real
Religion brought hope
Dreams were my truth
But as the days passed
These realities of mine
Were not real at all

Life Uncommon

Hope gave me meaning
So did my ideals of love
And trust
The lesson is simple
Trust only in the reality
That dreams fade
Love is just a chemical
Hope is just a way to keep us working
And work is what we do
All we are
Everyday
For money
And for families
Surely as I believed in the Easter bunny
Today I believe in life without meaning
Hope is a false dream
And love is black ink
Where once was a dreamer
Is now a writer
Drowned in the truth of wisdom
Youth is a conformist entity
And adulthood is survival without reason

216. "If Only"

As you cry
my thoughts extend out to you
wishing to embrace you warm and safe
holding you close, holding you here
if only I could help you
from behind the brick wall
but distance ...distance
if only I could be there when you cry

217. "I'll Hold You In My Dreams"

I wish I could be there to hold you when you cry
to be there to wipe those tears from your eyes
It feels so unfair to me
that I can't be right now where I feel I should be
next to you
I'm sorry that words aren't enough
I know
I love you

218. "I'll Stand On My Will"

News comes today that life's just about to get a little harder
Not sure how long I can hang on to the job I've got
I'm still damn near broke, living paycheck to paycheck
Now my student loan is about to kick into gear, I feel like shedding every single tear
But I'm kicking it high and mighty and refusing to give in
I'm not ready to give up yet, I'm not through, I've still got a lot of living to do
God, I hope your angels will catch me now and carry me gracefully through
Because without them I'll surely hit the ground
And getting up will be that much harder to do...But, no, I'm not ready to give up
I'm not ready to give in and I'm certainly not ready to call it quits
I can't say there's a single accomplishment I've made in six years
I haven't graduated, I haven't gotten out of an apartment
I haven't saved up much more than a penny or two
But I've got me and I'm going to stand on that
Even if the ground gives way because my will alone carried me through
Even when the world walked out
It'll be a long time before I'm through...this little girl still has a lot of spunk left
You may see me down right now, depressed as hell and thinking, "Is this really what life is?"
But I am going to hang on to the few simple things I know
I know that love, light, and laughter make the world glow
I know that happiness comes with time, in time and during it, too
So instead of just seeking it, I'm going to live it
I know how to let go and that's what I'm doing...Letting go of habits that aren't really me
I'm letting go of pessimism that never did suit me and the notion of giving up
Because my will alone will carry me through
So I'm not some great big rich famous success, but I know my heart...do you?
I know my fancy friends moved to big cities, live their fantasies, got married
But I don't know any of them who is happy
Not yet, so I'm not through
So I'm going to click my ruby slippers and go home to my heart
And if that wretched little piece of organ gives me trouble
I'll give it some trouble back, because my will alone carries me through
I know there's light within me, I've seen it shine like diamonds before
I swear I'll be happy in truth because I won't stop daring, I won't stop trying
I'm kicking it high and mighty and refusing to give in
I'm not ready to give up yet, I'm not through, I've still got a lot of living to do
And my will alone shall carry me through.

Inspired by the movie "Wizard of Oz"

Life Uncommon

219. "Illuminate Me"

Illuminate me in the night
Help me to scare away the fright
Yeah, that's right…I'm crazy…So be it
Maybe I'm just an ordinary Joe or Jane that may be
But hey, this is the real me
Behind cold blue bars of steel
Hanging on the world of something ethereal
I love the surreal…Yeah, 'cuz its real
Illuminate my soul,
You asshole
I dare you to stop chiming your paranoid words of frenzy
Take a jump into the night
This is the fantasy where the hours chime away
Into the birds of prey
Floating on a star
Dancing on the moon
Daring they call me…Its true, I may be
But, hey fucker this is my fantasy
Where your world simply fades and the night lingers
And I ask you to just try, try to Illuminate me
For I am dark and cold in the nighttime of the world
Where churchyards yawn and the daysleepers crawl out
Its not me your worried about
Oh, no its you and the anger you fear to shout
Its okay to be angry And I dare you, Illuminate me
For I am banished into this realm
Where darkness creeps and madness surrounds
Its not him
Its not you
Its me
And so I dare you - Illuminate me
Flickering flames die out in the cold
And this is my world travels untold.

220. "Illumination of the Moon"

What leaves you in awe of the moon?
What makes her so special to you?
Is it the way she sparkles?
Or the way she always seems to smile?
Could it be the beauty she illuminates inside of you?
Or something strange and seemingly altogether new?

Life Uncommon

What makes her so special?
How deep does your affection of her go?
Do her tides move you emotionally again and again?
Is she gentle and nurturing?
Does she let you know the ease of the world?
And the comfort of the sky?
Does she help you feel safe?
Does she let you know why?
Can she answer your questions when there are no answers?
Does she speak to you in whispers like the wind to a feather?
She moves about the sky as if she owns it
And yet she is a gentle leader
only flowing within it
She seems to know your femininity
And the things inside that most need saying
Yet you stand silent before her
Smiling inside as you stand there erect in awe
For maybe the moon in all her glory holds a piece of you up high
Perhaps a part of you lives in the sky
And maybe tonight as you sleep
You'll remember the moon
And the promise she keeps
To come back each night and guard you
She is there loving and adoring you
Tender and loving, she is there
She is all and nothing
And she stands there glorious and mighty
They say once you know the love of the moon
You can never quite turn away from her
For she shall hold a part of you
Eternally

221. "Illusions"

I'm hurting and I don't even know who to cling to
Like I'm lost in the rapids of despair but I'm not even in despair
I don't even think I'm lost…It's like the time before you wake from a dream
When you aren't in the dream and you aren't in the day
You aren't grounded but you feel grounded
I have myself – what does the rest matter?
And where is he when I need him? Does he think about me, like I do him?
I love too much, I fear and I worry and I'm lost in an abyss of woe, sadness
No teardrops saying I feel pain…I am alone yet not, I don't understand
Its like I'm caught in a web that's masked with illusion
But what is the illusion? It's like I'm blind to myself

Life Uncommon

I swim in this strange silhouetted abyss
Friends who weren't are gone now
I am home inside myself if nowhere else and the one who understands
Is gone with the tides
I'd search heaven and hell for him but I can't even drive a small stretch of road
And why won't it rain today when I need it the most?
Where is the cleansing of the earth? Where is the stability?
Change, change, and change again
Where is everything I know? And why do I love?
Why do I feel this ache inside?
Who is the protector? The eagle? The dove?
Where is my love? Where is it all?
Candlestick alleys gone astray and I'm lost here thinking…as its floating away
I cry out in woe but no sound nor tears seem to actually flow
Here I stand…stand here alone…the universe within…the clouds without
Why do the stars shine? And where are you? And where am I?
Something wishes for us to know…Something wishes but will not flow
I write endlessly…words of disaster
A woman, a child…I'm both inside…one loves to hide…one loves to dance
A ballet of some funny romance…don't know how it ends…not even how it goes
Still I twirl endlessly and curtsey at last

Perhaps I should light up a smoke
I'm broke…fix me I plead…Yet, no doctor to phone
I suppose this is the way of the world tonight
So I'll just lay here dreaming of taking flight.

222. "Immortal Beloved"

She whispers through the grains of time
She whispers through these dreams of mine
She enchants the mysteries of my youth
And wears her spell in my fantasies uncouth
She whispers through songs of ease
My little vixen, such a tease
I feel her whispers,
feel her breeze
And once again my soul's at ease.

223. "Impenetrable"

How come we can't listen
Why can't others help?
We all have pain

Life Uncommon

Most of us don't love ourselves
The shit stories are the same
Rape, molestation, beatings
Being ignored, being lied to
We all cut the same
We all heal or don't the same
But we still don't listen
Are we selfish?
Or incapable of love?
Why can't others reach out to us & vice versa?
Is life really one giant heap of do-it-yourself?
Love was my savior
And love died
Like rotten eggs on a hot Sunday afternoon
It died
Washed away by my tears
Buried by my sorrow
I'm so alone I could die...
Happy July!

224. "In Regards to Nguyen Chi"

Nguyen Chi
He fought government
Imprisoned
No trial
"re-education"
Yeah, manipulate your perpetrator
Let him no longer be
Can one imprison all of us?

225. "In the Cave"

Alone in a cave of maybes
I was torn and scared
Alone, with no one to save me
To the surface came all I feared
I wished for the sun to rise
But days went by without any light
Tears again and again filled my eyes
I cursed everything within sight
With no friend around
I finally faced the turmoil inside
And here's what I found

Life Uncommon

I found a girl who loved to hide
I have always hidden alone
Never letting anyone in
My skills I'd never hone
I was convinced I'd never win
It was then that I realized
Something that changed me irreversibly
God had always been by my side
And once again he came to save me
The cave became illuminated
God and I walked out, hand in hand.

226. "In The City Of Lights"

Nothing makes sense
In the city of lights
Trials are tested
And moods are swung
Twilight comes into play
And lunatics are on the run
Tears of light mix with grey
And here I find myself
Facing one more day
Girl that was, walking away
Further and further
Gone astray
Knock on the doors of heaven
"Open" she says
The door swings
Pendulum moves
Rhythm of truth
Silence of sound
And somewhere...
Somewhere...
My gift is found

227. "In the Contests of Time"

We try so hard to get where we're going in life
For a moment time stood still and I noticed you were mine
That I had grown, become a wife
Once we were children young and sweet
Now old and fragile...still we greet the world with a smile

Life Uncommon

The cycles of nature and the contests of time
Sometimes makes life hard, sometimes we forget to take time

The cycles of nature and the contests of time swirl about us, moving in rhyme
Nights can be long, and days even longer but together we get through it
Together we conquer all

Words pale in comparison to the way I feel
We've been through so much
I can't rhyme for you or be the brain you long for
Just a simple girl am I
With a spiritual heart
Loving you for years
As I have from the start
I can't fill your hand with money…I can't buy you a house,
Nor a boat but I'll listen and try
I'm sorry if that's not enough but it's all I've got to give
I may not be what you want or what you need but I give what I can
Being all I can be…Being this simple me
We came together years ago…We've come so far and it shows

Through times of hardship and times of sorrow
We've stuck together…We've seen tomorrow
Though our lives have changed many times
Throughout these years…different jobs, different friends…new beginnings
No one thought we would last but together we passed that test.

228. "In the Destinies of Time"

Only one man can fly his way to my heart
He'll bless my seeds
And bless my heart
With him I'll fly
And so will my lonely heart
In him I find peace
And love
In his eyes I see
The cards
Children in store for me
Three children are the key
Emily
Derek
And
Joseph
They'll be

Life Uncommon

Light, love, and laughter
Temperance, strength, and disaster
The change a mother needs
The strength to bless their father's seeds
Twins I'll have
And a husband I'll love
His arms wrap around me
His beautiful dove
I've wished for an eagle to fly me away
9 yards, my heart, the door, and the key
This is the end of settling for me

229. "In The Fabric Of Time"

In the deep forests of my heart
Time leaps and holds my hand
Delicately placed like tiny grains of sand
"Moon river" rises above me
As I watch it smile
Above my cherry oak tree
Snowflakes flutter about the yard
A single owl watches me watching him
Time stands still for a moment
And in that moment I die
And in that moment I am reborn
A nymph, a vixen, a woman, a whore
Lyrical lullabies lull me to sleep
In a land of fairies, where gnomes do weep
In my trance I hand you
A bottle of time to keep
In my heart I'll hold you
Tenderly, as I sleep

230. "In The Morning"

In a hallway against a locker
Sleepy and bored
Not much to do, nowhere to go
Lacking in stress, for once
I like this feeling
I'm okay
Not free,
But okay
What a wonderful twenty minutes of the day

Life Uncommon

231. "In The Seedlings Of Time"

In the seedlings of time
Droplets of rain,
Come to yours and mine
Strolling through the delicate fields of romance
I look to you with a smile at my side, and faith in the heart's glass
Fragile lullabies we sing to ourselves in the moments of hardship
And one thing that certainly carries us through is love
Oak trees surrounding us, even as stability departs
We find a beauty in the universe around
As the caw of a nearby raven lifts
Truth prevails even when the mind feels adrift
There are hidden truths inside
Leading us, abiding us, teaching us
Strive to know more in yourself than you have ever known before
Climb to know the innermost parts of yourself
Go through and redeem them
For they are your greatest treasures
We know the universe at a glance
Hold out your palm
Allow the droplets
To fall into your embrace
For they are your love
They are your truth,
They are your knowledge,
And even in the secret entrances of night,
They are you.

232. "In The Silence Of The Night"

I am eighteen years of age
I work every day
I'd do anything to keep those around me happy
In more ways than one – I am a traditional woman
Born and raised with manners and morals
People always say how sweet and polite I am
Yet, they've never seen my soul
The only one who's seen
Is a part of it
A roaring being like myself
Wondrous, dangerous, and living for adventure
Souls that are so beast-like that tigers fail to compare

Life Uncommon

Wild hearts
Wild souls
Crazy, mad
Ready to run stark naked along the streets in the rain
Then jumping and flying like the eagles
When my wings will no longer fly I will land on the ground
I will wear the perfect seductive outfit and he will be mine
Seduction is a talent I've never wasted
Together we belong free
Conventional in daylight
Wild in the silence of the night
The blackness of roaring souls
Dark and exciting
Of course, when the sun rises I'll go back to work
Back to smiling and back to the constraints of a conformed society

233. "In Truth"

In truth
I know sometimes I am filled with pride
In truth
Sometimes its hard to deal with the stubbornness I rarely hide
In truth
I realize I'm not always easy to deal with
But you've stuck with me since our simple friendship
Even on days when I haven't been at my best
You've stood by me, you gracefully passed that test
In truth
Sometimes my nature is hard to understand
But you've always been there reaching out your hand
In truth
I thank you from the bottom of my heart
For sticking by me from the start
You've not only been a friend,
But a lover too
And the love you give
Shines through and through
I am thankful for each year we've shared
I just wanted you to know, I love you dear

234. "Indiana Dreams"

Snow in the sleigh, cat in the hay, walking with you, under the moon, pumpkins a
hatching, boys chasing girls, a lil lady they'll be catching, her hair in curls, the sunset of

Life Uncommon

swans, summers of dawns, leaves amber-gold in perfection, she waves goodbye, the star
of the road, goodbye melody Monroe
Tinsel wrapped trees covered in leaves lemonade with cherries swarms of thank you
letters to a god written by the hands of an angel
He winks at you, and you swoon to your knees, sometimes he says and sometimes it shall
be, he's got the laughter that aches, the tears that you bake, eyes of an angel no doubt,
you know his soul, the lyrical poet, the beatnik that never was, neon gold blankets you
fold, memories of days strumming the guitar, sometimes he says and you're on your
knees, pushing so hard, letting go of yesterdays memories, striving for the moon, dancing
on a star, smelling the glitter of all that beauty, feel something in that perfect soul, and
that will be how you know

235. "Inner Song"

Outer moon,
Inner shine,
Close your eyes,
Lullaby,
Some time soon
As you sleep
All the promises
You did keep
Shall rise above
The sandy storm
And live inside
For all to adorn
Spirit flying
Loving high
And this to you
My lullaby
Swing your smile
To the stars
God bless the moon
And heaven bless your heart

236. "Inner Truth"

It is much easier to question the truth of others
Than to question the truth of self

I can fool others as long as I want,
But it is only me I hurt if I fool myself

At times love and hate,

Life Uncommon

They are one in the same

237. "Insanity Is Good"

Good!
The more the merrier!
Be insane!
Join me on the crusade through hell!
To find hope and love and fantasy!
Dreams that are full of strawberries and wine!
Fields of fantasies!
Swimming pools of delight!
Tear back the fright!
And we'll survive through the night!

238. "Inside"

Darkness within darkness
The gateway to all understanding

239. "Inside My Head"

Very few people get to see inside my head
Who I am
I rage inside with anger
My thoughts burn with pain
I've been hurt so much
And the scars are so visible
To me
Others glance but never see
Does anybody understand what goes on inside my head?
I think about death
About suicide
I dream
And I hope for a time
One of ease and floating thoughts
I fear no one
Will
Ever
Understand
What goes on inside
So I write
To show

Life Uncommon

And,
To tell
For I am real inside my head
All of me exists there
I am me
And that is all I can be

240. "Inside these Castle Walls"

In the past we were lovers
Within these castle walls
We felt and we loved and we soared high above
Candlelit maybes kept us going
A married young lady was I
So protective of me you'd risk your life
I do not know what brought you to love me
I've been honored ever since
And treasure your loyalty

The moment I saw you I knew
Had not a clue at first of the castles
Or the you who I knew
Couldn't remember we were lovers
But I knew that I knew you
I couldn't have told you why
But I had to get to know you

And now we've shared our pasts
Told tales of hopeless nights
Seen into the souls of the names we knew on sight
Somehow we give each other strength
Somehow we reveal a part of the soul within
Somehow we love, somehow we shelter each other from sin

Tomorrow will come
And I hope I'll know you more
Hopefully together we'll walk through that door
We will know where we stand
And the blurry lines will end
Things will become more clear
And you, I'll always hold dear.

241. "Insomnia"

Life Uncommon

Can't sleep
Never can
Sit up, think
Analyze guys
Concoct fantasies
Dream up days of less pain
Go to the bathroom
Two and three times
Visit my fantasyland where I am loved
Write out how I feel
Look out the window
Flip channels on the tube
Call someone
Write out how I feel
Listen to a CD or cassette
Drown in their sorrows and my own
Eat something
Think about sleeping
Wonder about wondering
Ask too many questions
Remember the past
Treasure memories
Avoid cleaning
Pass by my homework
Take a pill
Do a few more useless things
Then at some point
Light goes off
I say goodnight
Think of one last goodnight fantasy. But
That will have to wait-
I still cannot sleep

242. "Inspiration"

When you let down your walls to acting
To allow yourself to be understood
Take a stand on stage
Shout,
Scream,
Smile,
Those are the true factors of acting
Who are you?
Who are you on stage?
Inspire me

Life Uncommon

Make me write
Make my adrenaline flow
Stand up tall
Jump if you have to
Inspire me

243. "Inspired"

In a world that is constantly changing
Sometimes a garden patch is overlooked
Nature's greens and means aren't enjoyed
Buildings, superhighways and pollution kill-
Right before our very own eyes
Destroying our life,
Denial in lies
We are all creature's of this home
Is change necessarily buildings and highways?
Can't it be love, feeling, and play?
Just leave things the way they are now
That would be good
Nature can be a mood of existence
And so could constantly changing positively
We should reserve our home, our very means of existence!

244. "Intellection"

Its been years since anyone
Wrote me a poem
I'm touched by the sincerity
Something I've encountered so rarely
I appreciate the notion
But must be honest in response
To hold, to love,
To know, to understand…
These paths take the compliment of two
It wouldn't be fair to me or to you
If I attempted to deny myself
For my heart knows best
Passing my every test
So I know right now
Is the time to make a friend
Seems so hard to say
Harder to write
I'd rather not hurt a friend

Life Uncommon

Not tonight

245. "Intersection"

Dark or light
Life or death
Choose with inner wisdom
One step may lead you to hell
Five leaps may bring you up to heaven
I only choose him
The rest is tongue-tied figments
Golden heart
Brown eyes and hair
Tall and handsome
I must have him
I know now what I want
I want you
Through the California deserts on a camels back
Rushing through highways
Paddling a boat
I believe although you are not here
I believe you can see me
Love me
Know me
Have faith in our love and be sure that
One day we will be together
And then forever
My love
My life
I want that

246. "Is It Possible?"

My parent's had a generation of expression
They had everything "fun" that a kid could want
60's filled with parties
Teens smoking pot just as easily as chewing gum
They had complete, and total sexual freedom
Life was no bore
Life was no drag
Life was not a drive-by-shooting
Life was not cruel
Life was not hatred
Life was "fun"

Life Uncommon

Today things are different
Still there is sex and drugs
But not the same way
AIDS
Crack
HIV
Pot

Today life is being thrown away
We are hardly in a time of freedom
How did they achieve unrestricted bliss?
They fought!
People stood up for their rights
And fought!
Burning bras, being violent to become equal, spoke of happiness,
Experimented with drugs,
Hell- they lived
Today fear has grown…we can't walk through our own neighborhoods unafraid
What once scared a nation now affects the individual
Girls once urged for equality…stood up for their rights
A time pushing towards peace and harmony
Then war...tension…sadness…pain…cruelty
When will we stop killing ourselves and fight the way we once did?
Maybe one day we can be free, unharmed…Is it possible?

247. "Isn't It Nice?"

I fell in love
Fell ten stories down
Smacked the ground so hard
The sound resonated
I didn't know any better
I guess
He seemed so…
So right?
So nice?
So me?
I'd rather kick him than kiss him these days
If only I could stop the tears
If only letting go was easy
If only the ground held me tighter
If only balance happened, instead of shit
I thought he was the one
I thought he'd love me forever
I thought, I thought, I thought

Life Uncommon

Ya know?
Believing is nice
Sometimes reality isn't
I don't even get closure
No goodbye
No sorry
Just gone
Like a rider on the storm
And I'm fucked all over again
Give me strength
I will myself to face another day.

248. "It Only Matters"

There comes a time in every woman's life
When she struggles to find herself
She'll look through picture books
And read up on old diaries
She'll flip through high school yearbooks
And remember memories long gone
She'll think of romances ended long ago
And wonder who she was as a teenager
It happens all on its own
No matter the age or the partner she last had
She could be broke, she could be rich
She could be great, she could be a bitch
It matters not who she is
Or where she walks
It matters not the skirts she wears
Or the tumbled down jeans
She could be worn out, she could be mean
She could be great, she could be lean
It matters not where she is
Or when she last danced
It matters not where she dreams
Or when she last sang
It only matters that she's female
It only matters that she's there now
It only matters that she's lost
It only matters, no matter the cost

249. "It's Fucking True"

Yesterday you called me up

Life Uncommon

And I thought fuck yeah its on
Life is back on track
Everything is going to be all right now
But that was bullshit as it always is
It's a lie we tell ourselves
It's the unjustifiable sin
We make believe the world is a happy place
And we pretend away our lives
As we only look for the next escape
Drugs, bongs, cigarettes, thongs
Who the fuck cares
So you think you'll be the strong one?
No baby doll none of us are
We're drug induced frenzied youths
Running downtown so uncouth
Don't think you're different
You never were
We're all the same
We all endure
The pain that aches deep inside
It lives to strangle while we hide
Down another bottle of gin
Hell this is our undeniable sin
Pick up a joint it won't kill you any worse
Than living in this fucked up universe
Swallow a bottle of pills
Lie in a corner with restless chills
Drown yourself just like we do
And they wonder why our tears
Are endlessly blue

250. "I've Held Memories of You All"

The keeper of the threshold of hell,
The bearer of ill, the guardian of truth,
The communicator of dreams,
The spellcaster of mystery,
The mage of romance,
The clock that chimed,
He is ye who dare to rhyme,
The insider of parallel bliss,
The outsider of discontentment
All that is amiss,
It is he who loves
A narcissist at heart,

Life Uncommon

A shaker of trees- apples,
A builder of dreams,
The imperfect touch,
The distant fawn,
The understanding bard,
The princess at dawn,
He who smiles lies, fallacy,
Stumbles upon infinity,
And catches her claws,
The lurker, the watcher,
The untrusting friend, yes he is
You as you, Are he, So sing
A bit, a bit merrily

251. "James"

The dragon, the lion, the all-seeing hawk,
The falcon of yore, the heart of a
Wizard, the sword of a man, the odor
Of philosophy, think to turn the page,
Speed through life little lamb, but remember
Home is where the heart resides, you stand
Up and say you'll conquer it all, but as you
Do for me and have done so many times,
I shall be there when next you fall,
You have the passion of dragons, flight
Of the hawk, crawl of the spider,
Bite of a shark, you are a hero although
You yet do not know, time is ticking young
Mage, and when the goddess deems you
Ready that is when you shall turn
The page, so sit tight, the smirk
Of one amuck, too cute, too cute you are lil buck

252. "Journey"

Journey is about many different things
It's about crying, laughing, loving, hating, understanding
It's about holding on sometimes and it's about letting go, too
It's about knowing when its ok to say 'yes', but also learning to say 'no'
It's about allowing there to be times when you 'cave in'
But knowing when to stand strong as well
It's about dealing with hardships
With the same passion you deal with favorite foods

Life Uncommon

It's about devouring life instead of letting it pass you by
It's about knowing that holding on to the fantasies
Of stability, instant riches, and fast lines only hold you back
It's about understanding why patience is a virtue
It's about enjoying each moment as though it is
Your first, your last, and your only moment in time
It's about understanding that everyone is you and you are everyone
It's about attaining important things like
Self-esteem, self-respect, self-acceptance, and self-love
It's about getting over trying to be better or the best and just being you
It's about saying 'no more' to competition and 'hello' to sharing
It's about shedding the skins of your youth,
Bad habits, old fears, and silly thoughts
It's about growing up
It's about times when you struggle so much
You wonder if you have any hair left to pull out
It's about times when you are so angry
You swear your ears will burst
It's about times when you smile so big you'd swear
The whole world just became heaven
It's about times when you've cried so many
Tears that you're amazed any are left
It's about knowing that its ok to fail and knowing that it is also ok to succeed
It's about knowing that its all right to be mediocre
If you are doing your best
It's about realizing that no book, place of worship,
Family member, or friend can live your life for you
It's about learning to make your own decisions and knowing that you can
It's about looking the things that hurt you and scare you
Straight in the face and knowing you are stronger
Journey is about many things, but most importantly...Its about you.
Enjoy Journey.

253. "Joy"

In the light that darkness brings
we remember how she smiles when she sings
how she dances when happy
and when affectionate words fill her heart
and inside inside her heart
is that place still filled with the joy
although it may seem long gone
she has it tucked within her
tired and shaking as it may be
its still a part of her and will be for eternity.

Life Uncommon

254. "Julie's Song"

Dream with Faith
Dream with Heart
Dream for Stars
Dream to fly with the eagles
Dream with faith to become all you can be for everyone else
Utilize all the good
Shape the universe with your faith
Dream with heart like a dart heading straight for the bull's eye
And everything will be okay, by and by
Dream for stars shooting across the universe
Hoping to break every curse
Dream to fly with the eagles
And have the energy of cute baby beagles
Dream to fly wherever your heart leads you
Dream to fly with the eagles

255. "Just the Beginning"

When my heart bleeds
Tears, like blood, stream forth
What man can hold a mine in a diamond, or my heart in his hand?
What truth holds more stable than grains of sand?
When night comes sometimes it is darkness that is swept away, not light
Time holds my secrets as the locket of life holds my will to fight
Tears breed happiness when cried in truth
My enemies like fear once faced no longer hold power as sleuths
The Goddess and I alone are keepers of my soul
Any man who claims different surely doesn't know
My path has been ragged and worn
But my will goes on
I have cried and felt a victim
Now I'm rebelling against that system
I'm standing taller, stronger, and more ready
Sometimes my feet will jiggle, but I know God will hold them steady
Whomsoever I have harmed, hurt, disappointed, or acted in ill will towards- I apologize
I ask for your forgiveness sincerely, you'll know with one glance to my eyes
I'd like to live life a little better and a little more right
I invite peace, prosperity, love, laughter, and certainly light
In time I will grow, probably be wedded and become a wife
It matters most to me that if I live it will be a highest good life
May any children I bear or any souls I touch know goodness from my heart

Life Uncommon

At least I'm being given the chance not for an end, but a start
I believe in the good and positive forming within
I believe in time there will be a more genuine closeness with my kin
As for my past, I have loved many and that love will live forever in the stars,
And perhaps my heart
Whatever gave me the strength to let go, I don't know
But one thing's for sure- I have let go
I am no longer a girl nor one drenched in pessimism
I am now a woman living

Like snowfall the heart learns
White drops of uniqueness on an oak tree in Bethlehem
Love, maybe, the greatest thing of all
All things adored in our seasonal fall
May my future be blessed and right
Thank you to all people and things that have helped me in this fight
I believe and with that, I begin my life.

256. "Just Try Me"

The painted walls of my youth
Rising up covered in truth
Candy covered maybes
Leading me down a jaded road
Who I was ten years ago I don't recall
Seems so far from the road I'm on now
Trials and errors coming at me fierce
Challenges I meet, with or without a road at my feet
Time waits and stops and starts again
No watch can tell me who I am
Like a football spiraling to a fault
I try and I fail
I weep and I yell
But try as I might
Sometimes it avails me not
Only man has these woes
Only us in all our faults
Yet even without wings
And without the utter knowledge of God
We go and we grow and
We never sit the next one out
Instead we'll stand in the face of hell
And never back down
So test me if you will
I'll rise and I'll fall

Life Uncommon

But even the weakest of men
Is known to rise again!

257. "Justification Found In A Mall"

Sitting in a lonesome chair, in a room full of tables, neon lights, smell of cinnamon,
sugar-filled fantasies, and she the vixen, pine trees for Christmas, strollers filled with
presents, gifted intellectuals sipping on a bottle, a train that will ride them into eternity,
they are so graceful, they seem to dance, it will be years before they know romance,
mutterings of days long past, ornaments ribbons of red and gold, my what treasures this
place does hold, babies that giggle in delight, and I'm happy without a penny in sight,
near broke they say, and still no place to hang my coat, Indiana like a beacon in the night,
another treasure filled star, ocean of dreams, twinkling in the myst, ladies with earrings,
mothers with makeup, old men with newspapers and me with my pen, oh don't you just
remember when, you sat on Santa's lap, asked for puppies and presents, and things you
swore you'd never forget, a favorite doll, yeah this place holds so many memories,
secrets the walls will never tell, glittering fantasies, grille of Orleans, and I think of you,
smiles and tales and secrets, the beacon of the night, and I'm happy at dawn's first light

258. "Kindred Spirits"
(dedicated to my great grandmother)
Alone and without comfort
She's so alone
"Look at these books"
Words like magic
An outlook so serene
She was never mean
But always loving
Wisdom shined in her veins
I love her
She is me
Our spirits know one another
Kindred
Without communication,
We hear one another
She is leaving me
And I hold her hand now
While whispering to her
In my mind
They think they know me
They want to comfort my
Lonely bones
But I leave
I go

Life Uncommon

With her

259. "Kinetic Motions"

Thinning veins
Highway lanes
Runaway trains
Crashed up planes
Isn't it funny how it all ends?
For those without a dime
And un-meeting ends?
Wouldn't it be nice just once
To hear a story
Of the girl who was lost, but then found
The boy who ran away, but then came home
The man who was drunk, but now is sobered up
The woman who used to be a druggee, but now is clean
What would this mean?
Would it mean a bit of happiness?
A touch of blessing
And what's so wrong with this?
It seems to be what we've all been missing

260. "Kiss"

A Kiss tells so much
It can tell you if there is love with the person or just friendship
It can tell you if you accept the person or have upsets with them
It can tell you if they are beautiful to you or ugly
It can tell you if there was a past, if there is a present,
And if there will be a future
It can tell you if there is a connection if it is strong or if it is weak
Just one kiss and you can know your entire relationship with that person
And that's a pretty amazing way to figure out something so complex

261 "Knight"

The knight in shining armor
The prince of battles
The devoted lover
Loyal friend
Spiritual guide
Courageous to a fault

Life Uncommon

Arrogant but in a cute-sexy kind of way
His voice makes my heart throb
The lyrics to his favorite songs send me swooning
The sweet prince who never forgets
To say "good night sweet girl"
He could be a real ladies man
Honestly this gentle-hearted bard could pick any
He chooses to live in a small town
A cheers kind of place where everybody
Knows your name
To love him is simple, to cherish
Him easy as easy can be
He might push he might pull
But he's loyal
My heart be still

262. "Knowing"

The sad and empty nights
Will be with me, for I have
Just realized he
Has not
Loved me
Not the real me

263. "Lady in Gold"

Something in those eyes that tell tales untold
I look into those pearls
And see all I'll ever need to know
The key to my past,
The lady in gold

264. "Lake"

Out on the lake lies the heart of nature
In the trees lie the families of the woods
Flying in the sky are wings of free lives
Swimming in the shallowest of waters are the creatures
Of the lake
And inside my cabin lie the romantic
Hearts of two people
Touched by the

Life Uncommon

Cupid of
True love

265. "Lamp"

The lamp is lit
But my heart remains
Lonely
Crying inside this flesh
They are out there
Masters in their field
Apt to creating pain
Silent hours pass by
Every floor creak scarier
Lonelier
In a haven, a heaven
But fearful of
It
Yes, my lamp is lit
But my heart just isn't

266. "Landing on High"

In the future
When time stops
The clock will flash
11:48...11:48...11:48
The rush will begin
Quickened lightning
Sunsets and sunrises flash by
There is no end...

"In the end...there can be only one."

Footnote: From the TV Show Highlander
Inspired by the television show "Highlander"

267. "Languid"

Lack of sleep
Taking over
Time is rare
Mind asleep

Life Uncommon

At school
Tired, weak

268. "Last Battle"

Battling my fists against the walls of identity
I fear not the evil I've become
Nor the purity I was
I hate that which I was
Shy, sweet, understanding, compassionate
Loyal to my calling of helping
And I fell to my own circumstances
Failing my own heart
The only thing you reap is the reward that never comes
There is no glory or smile at the end of a long, hard fight
I've no justification for anything I've done
And no future from it either
I'd rather just let it be
Let it go
Shout it out
Sail it away
And fight my way on
Stuck between the rivers of heaven and hell
Life and death
Right and wrong
I stand here
Alone
As always
Healer
Warrior
Woman.

269. "Last Night"

Where does trust lie?
He trusts her
He tells her all
Am I his or will I be left to fall?
I trust Jake
But not with words
I just love to flirt
But I don't treat my love like dirt
He feels my flirting is wrong
But I have no feelings for a relationship

Life Uncommon

He does, with her
She has him sometimes more than I
She holds his trust
Her, my best friend and enemy now
What will tomorrow bring?

270. "Lasting Romance"

Glancing up at your eyes
I saw love flickering as it has throughout time
Like a cactus spring
You revealed to me your gentle nature within
Strong and stable, yet soft and fragile
Like a soft-flowing stream we've gone the mile
Through years of changes and growth
Somehow we remained so very close
Even during times apart
You've always been nestled inside my heart
Today I feel blessed for having the chance
To be one half of this lasting romance

271. "Laundry"

Dirt, grime, icky crap
Its annoying and gross
Yet we all touch it
We all clean it
Ya know I like clean things
But I dislike cleaning them
Oh well, life goes on, right?
Sorry I'm just complaining
But that's the way I feel about
Laundry

272. "Left"

Gone now
He's gone
Am I insensitive?
Is he the insensitive bastard?
When will these tears dry up
This ice in my veins?
It was supposed to be…

Life Uncommon

So beautiful

273. "Left Alone"

He's not coming back
I know that now
California is his home
I'm not sure if he's still my heart
I'm not sure he knows me now
Maybe he never did
Some nights are tear filled
There are golden memories
Of him and I
That inside, I still hold onto
But I know
He's gone
Whisked away to the greater happier
Home...of...jail
Since bars are better than my heart
He chose some bully
Named something hard and cold like "Rock" instead of me
I'm sure he wouldn't tell me that
The fucker didn't even have the balls
To tell me we were through
I'm sick of my patterns
I'm sick of these games
I hate being a loner
But the men always leave
Me, alone, anyway
So, why fight the inevitable?

274. "Leo"
(dedicated to my friend, Michael)

Roar out and show the jungle you are king
Hunt down your prey
Roam wherever you please
You are free, you are king

275. "Let Freedom"

How do we know someone's like us?
Is it the words written,

Life Uncommon

Or the emotions behind them?
Is it the way we understand words,
Or could it be the emotions we feel as we read the words?
Is it the way we feel,
Or is it theirs?
Why do our young want to save the world,
And forget to save themselves first?
Why in a self-centered universe,
Does anorexia still plague our youth?
Why in a time of materials,
Do we never have enough?
People remain unhappy and bored
With their own creations
Why is it so hard to be an individual,
Especially when we spend our whole lives
Preparing and leading up to the moment
When independence begins
And the sign hanging at Burger King
Reminds us...
To
"Let Freedom Ring."

276. "Let Go"

Raindrops like tears without the salt
Heaven lasts only a minute
But it lasts in you
And a minute isn't a short time
It's a lifetime
Because we are only a minute
A fraction, a second, a glimpse in time
Time, that everlasting concept by which so many rule their lives
To let go of concepts
To let go of fears
To let go of mind
To let go of religion
To let go of doctrines
To let go of dogmas
To let go of preconceived notions
To let go of impatience
To let go of things that aren't really you
What makes you, you?
Is it that sweet, sexy smile?
Is it the way your hips are shaped?
Is it the strong muscular biceps you inherited?

Life Uncommon

Is it the mansion you have?
Or your car?
Or your fancy computer?
Is it the way you get over things?
Or the way you fight through the hard times?
Is it the way you cook mac & cheese?
Or the way you draw?
Is it the way you lend a loving shoulder to a friend in need?
Or the way you listened yesterday?
Is it the memories that you hold?
Or things that you do, just because you know?
Do you hold on to things that aren't really you?
Have you been measuring yourself with the wrong stick?
Do you know measuring isn't important?
Have you learned that yet?
Do you know that you are beautiful?
Have you learned how to have fun?
Do you love yourself yet?
Have you forgiven yourself too?
Do you know how to let go?
Have you?

277. "Letter to My Heart"

Dear Heart,
I know you often question
Why live?
Well, here's the answer that is best for now
Don't live for the next time he can hurt you
Don't life for the possibility of a few loving moments
Don't live for him, in short
Live
Because life will be whether you like it or not
Choose the better path
And live
Death is the easy way out
Live
Suicide takes too much courage
Life
Oh, heart why have you been broken?

278. "Letting Go"

For me letting go meant moving on

Life Uncommon

I was to discover a world of dreams…so many things I would become
During the summer I realized I'd be letting go
I was saddened, and excited all at once
Sure I'd miss my friends, but I knew I'd see them during breaks
I'd miss my family but I wasn't worried because I knew they'd always be there
I left as a small child scared by the harsh realities
I was ready to climb any mountain, swim any sea…I was ready to find me

For the eldest not too much would change
His sister would leave but he'd see her over breaks
The bond that was there was not weak
He was the brother- strong and unafraid…accepting of the change

For the youngest everything would change
Her heart saddened for she was not yet old enough to understand how to let go

The younger brother understood the world was awaiting his sister
Not sad, but proud…He watched her leave, and just knew all would be fine

Mom's baby was leaving
She was both sad and proud, happy yet hurt
She told me to do well…she watched her baby grow
I know it wasn't easy…she knew it had to be done though

For Dad- his little girl was going to college
How could this be? His first child to really leave
Too strong to cry
He was my Dad- proud…I looked up to his stable ground
I wanted the same…I wanted to make him proud
My Dad should know he's done well
For his little girl wanted to be so much like him
Too strong to cry and without doubt,
My backbone in all my worries…I thank you Dad

279. "Life of Dreams"

I grasped onto a life of dreams
Tight as possible
Blind trust
Superficial promises in a false world
We are just beings
Dictated though brainwashing
All of us
Hope blinded us all
To believe in certain rules

Life Uncommon

Not to be questioned
Just followed
I messed up
Somewhere along the lines
I question
The blinding light was shut off
Now I see
A reality I cannot comprehend
But I must
What I comprehend
Happens to be question after question
Without answer

280. "Lighten the darkness"

I lay awake each night
Trying so hard to sleep
But something holds me tight
And somehow it keeps me up
I don't know if its worry
Or fear or what
The nightmares certainly don't help
Sleeping is never easy
Dreams so horrific they'd frighten the dead
And so my eyes remain open
Dreading what's ahead
Maybe if I could just turn on the lantern in a dream
Maybe then ... maybe then I could sleep

281. "Lighter"

The clouds weren't so black today
A little grey
But not a speck of white
Silence
The chatter of friends has dissipated
Warmth only emanates from my pets
Animals giving unconditional love
Affectionate beings
No grudge is ever held
Perfection that exceeds any human being I have ever known
I just wait for the day coming
When I shall give them up
And my little happiness along with them

Life Uncommon

Glorious minutes will fade quickly
Too quickly
Only pictures and memories after this
No more than that
So it goes
I am back in my nonexistent territory
Shut behind the door of life
No communication to humans
Just emptiness
And the only warmth comes from her
From my babygirl
Kamea
Sweet and precious
This kitten of mine
Beautiful too
So beautiful

282. "Like a Needle, I Love You"

You're the love that always is
And never was
Its like a thorn you get in your thumb
That never gets taken out
You get numb to the pain
The care to pull the damn thing out
Eventually wears itself out
So you sit with a dratted piece of growth
Inside yourself
Knowing its noticeable to others
Noticing it yourself daily
Trying to feel anything but the pain
Not really remembering how you got
Such a fine prick
In the first place.

283. "Like a Used Up Grain of Sand"

I feel washed out
Like I've drowned and been hung up to dry in hell itself
Happiness seems like an illusion to me now
Every word of happiness makes me want to puke
Old friends are getting engaged, moving, and finding careers
And I'm stuck here in this old self
I'm new and I'm old

Life Uncommon

I'm trying to rid myself of everything that was
And I have no idea how
But you've got to understand
That I don't care if I have to throw out everyone and everything that reminds me of the
past
I hate her
I hate who she was
She was a fucking doormat
I refuse to be that
She was a bitch that you all used up
And she's gone now
Thanks to you
And your careless fucking needs
She spent her hours and energy just to wipe your fucking tears
And the rewards never came
She's dead
And I am all that remains

284. "Listen Up"

Listen up, truth's coming out
I'm gonna talk about society now
The youth don't grow up in nice homes
Rape isn't rare
Fake isn't cool
We're still stuck playing by somebody else's rules
Kids are beaten, molested, ignored,
And so emotionally fucked and you just think they're bored
Who the fuck cares what other generations did?
Divorce is now the norm
Been that way for years now, the new uniform
We've forgotten what loves all about
Rings, white dresses, pre-nups, and lawyers
What's it all for?
We're so busy being someone else
That we still haven't figured something better out
We know the schools are shit
And our kids are unhappy
We worry about things all the time
But nothing changes
We've got no rhyme
Jails, prisons, the death penalty...
We lock up some of the only real men in society
As much as we think we listen,
We don't

Life Uncommon

We try to figure someone else out
And still haven't figured our own shit out
Our youth rebel
And we cling to society's hell
This is who we are
Whatcha gonna do now?

285. "Lone Wolf"

A man who speaks no words
Sees no horror
Hears no facts
Understands nothing

This would be a man who speaks of stupidity
At least most people's biased opinion of stupidity

This would be a man who cannot see his fears
Simply because he won't face them

This would be a man who cannot handle hearing the truth
Scared by the details alone

This would be a man isolated
Frightened to admit he resembles history

This would be a man who imagines his own worlds
Terrified to live in this one

This would be a man who speaks his thoughts of society
And rubs against the grain

This would be a man who imagines places far away from reality
Unable to bare our norms of cruelty

This would be a man who hears peaceful sounds
Unhappy with our ruckus

Why must this man stay away?
Stay astray
Tears falling down like raindrops from the sky
Painfully pouring from his eyes
Why should these things happen to such a wonderful guy?

Life Uncommon

286. "Lonely"

Empty room, blank walls
Unfilled, like my heart
I am alone and attempt to sleep
But when its night, who will my soul keep?
No arms to wrap around me
No words to comfort me
Here I am inside
Alone
And so lonely I can hardly breathe
The clubs are just a show
A front
I'm alone and I know it
And I hate it so much

287. "Long Day"

Work was a drag
Supervisor had no work for me
As usual
Girls did their hair
Stripper did not show up as asked
Boss came in unexpected
Now I am home
Still haven't eaten
And won't
Oh well
School is in a few hours
Just a few
Will not be sick
Better not be
Paper due tomorrow
Bored
No one to call
Nothing on television
Same old music
Dizzy again
Still sick
Tired
Can't sleep
Hungry
Can't eat
I guess that's it

Life Uncommon

288. "Longing"

Maybe you thought you kissed
But you did not
That, that is where you live
In longing
Longing for that kiss

289. "Looking Back"

We were young when we first met
I was 18 and he was 19
We began as friends
And lasted a year that way
Then things changed one beautiful day
We became lovers in the most wonderful way
We shared our stories and our inner thoughts
We came together as a simple truth
And we've lasted throughout so many changes
Even when we were apart
We were together
Watching the other grow
And today still together, still we flow
Its a beautiful story of a love affair
That began so simple, so real, so true
With a simple understanding between me and you.

290. "Looking Down"

How come people look down on suicide so much?
I don't get it
Here I am tortured and tormented every day by my own mind
I go crazy with my analyzing
Headaches always linger
The inevitable tears
I pull at my hair
And dig my nails into my arms and legs
I waste money on phone bills to friends that rarely help
Why should suicide be so out of the question?
Didn't someone say to go hang myself with a cable cord?
I do have two of them
I could get a gun
Just a few days and a few dollars

Life Uncommon

Or take every pill in the house
I have enough
Sleep for eternity
Six feet under
Bugs will have more pleasure in me than I do
People will laugh
Some will pretend to cry
One or two may remember me
None will wonder
Lives will go on
Oh how I wish someone would care
Or that someone would snap me out of this dreadful reverie
But no one does
Why should they?
They all look down on me
The potential suicide victim
Dare I cry to someone?
They just laugh
Just laugh
Just laugh

291. "Lost"

Lost on the shores of self
Hanging on to the only home I know
In the dreamtime, shadows come
And I plant my feet within the sands of time
Hoping to find a truth
A key I can turn
A lock I can open
And a door that leads somewhere
Beyond the fairyland
Unlocking the secrets I've held onto for too long
Opening the doors
And walking towards tomorrow
With just myself and the world
Awaiting...

292. "Love"

Love is a great emotion which is why fate brings two mates together
In the hearts of these two mates feelings start to grow
Just like growing seedlings into beautiful flowers
Love flows, sways, bends, twists, turns, wiggles, and shrivels

Life Uncommon

But true love always find a way to grow and grow to make the true love flow
Love is hard to explain, but the feelings and emotions it brings two mates
Is beyond normal understanding
Since love is beyond normal understanding
People perceive love as the best fate any two mates could ever encounter

293. "Love Affairs"

Love affairs perhaps are the very
Heartbreak of a life
A silent need lived a lifetime inside
Society so keen to enforce loyalty
The heart only knowing loyalty to itself
There are times when romance wins
When obligation ceases
And love reigns
Usually behind curtains
Where rules do not exist
Sometimes sacrifice necessary
In the heart no sacrifice exists
Free to love, to need
Poets the lovers
As only lovers can
Words the string
Thoughts the most beautiful betrayal
To live is to dream

294. "Love Stories"

Reach for the shooting star
It will bring you the romance of a blue moon
Run up and kiss Mars
Forever you will be happy
Fall into your dream…your new reality
No more love stories are needed to read
For you have caught your shooting star

295. "Love Surrenders"

In the darkness
You are there
In the darkness
You are near

Life Uncommon

Glimmering eyes
Sparkling clear
Flutter your wings
Love my dear
Follow my lead
I am there
Take my hand
I am near
Close your eyes
Drift into sleep
In your wake
I lay at your feet

296. "Love- The Hardship It Really Is"

Walking down the moon
Drifting along the tides
I see you so clearly
Wrapping your arms around the stars
Holding me within
I can see us
Just you
Just me
And we're smiling
Baby
The lights light up the way
A path we can walk along in the rain
Starting to leave the pain behind
Forgetting our fights
And the lies we've told
Forgetting about the cheating
And the girl you used to hold
And just being there
In that moment
Forgiving
Forgetting
And in that moment
I love you

We are there
Forgetting it all
Washing the world away with our tears
Being only happy
There you are
Along the beachtides of my youth

Life Uncommon

Helping me to dream up fantasies of
Growing older
Growing up
Showing me there is more to be happy about
Than I could ever imagine
And in that moment
I love you

In that moment...

I love you.

297. "Love, Arms"

I love his arms
And his charms
I run in the fields of love we have created
Stopping is not an option until I am safe and sound
In his arms of love!

298. "Lover's Lullaby"

(Dedicated to Rebecca)

Crystal Lovedrops
Tears upon my pillow
Ready to marry tomorrow
Rhythmic music fills my ears
Dreams of days to come
Walking down the aisle
Hand in hand
With a younger man
Who takes ten years off me
With just his smile
A young gay stud he came to me
With a lover all his own
And slowly over coffee and cigarettes
It came to my attention
This is where love is at
A simple proposal
And I agreed
To smile and say "I do"
And become my lover's bride
In harmony doves sing our lullaby

Life Uncommon

And rose quartz hearts fill the sky

299. "Lovers Mist"

Do you ever listen for a filtered dream
Or something that while imaginable
Seems elusive or unreal
Do you sit by the clouds,
And talk over coffee?
Do you remember old lovers,
With a smile?
Do you recount childhood fantasies,
With an irk of mischieviousness?
Lily white petals fall from the sky
I sit and dream about you and I
Alone in Fiji drinking water and tea
Singing about how we always hoped it would be
Grown children
Windblown dreams
I sit and I write
To the poet in me
I once wrote a poem about Tahiti
A dragon and a cave
And the knight who solemnly gave her away
Where are you the emperor of my dreams?
Do you sit too,
And dream about me,
Alone on some island,
The way it should be?

300. "Love's Blessing"

Here I have a tiny princess
Sweet as sugar cane
But life's twists make her being so difficult
And I am the messenger of hell
To be shunned and disciplined
Perfection is laying down beside me
Whereas immaturity and cruelty wait at my door
Piercing pain
Blood is drawn from their bare hands
Heartless, cruel beasts
I hate them!
She is my life

Life Uncommon

And they will take her too
Left without dream
No hope
The machine
I am the robot
Without anything

301. "Loving Kiss"

Each day I wake up in hunger
Starving for sugar and bread
Willing myself to stay away
But the taste is so sweet

Each day I wake up in wonder
Starving for more adventure
Willing myself to be restrained
But outside my front door is a world

Each day I wake up laughing
Starving for some happiness
Willing myself out of the void
But madness does not allow such luxuries

Each day I wake up longing
Starving for a beautiful love
Willing myself that such kisses are not bound for my lips
But the perfection is so dear to my heart

I hope one day to feel the warmth of one gentle goodnight kiss

302. "Low"

Trapped in a short body
Too lacking in ambition to grow
I see the ceilings of the universe
Painted in crimson & gold
I'd use a ladder
Or build a staircase
If I felt myself worthy
But here I am
Snail to grass
Sliming myself along
I admire the clouds,

Life Uncommon

The treetops,
The once-in-a-while rainbow,
But here I stay
In the world I know
Not really clinging
And not really letting go.

303. "Magic"

Its in a baby's smile
The call of the wind
It is in the smell of the rain
And the ache from pain
This is not a simple concept for most
They want it all
Telekinesis and telepathy
Headed for a downfall
To hear the call from within
Takes a great soul
Time is what you have
Love is what you need
It all depends dear one
On you

304. "Majestic"
(dedicated to Brian)

I am sixteen
My life is free
Life is slow, gentle like snow
I'm not afraid…

Though I don't enjoy watching a summer parade
That wondrous music excites my ears
I've listened to Led Zeppelin for years
You'll almost never see tears out of my eyes
I stay away from lies, have good friendship ties
I fit in with anything easy going…life is comfortable

I am relaxed
Not taunted by life
Nor death

I've seen bad but I block it all out

Life Uncommon

Otherwise I'd really shout
I know what life is basically about
My parents are separated
After all it's the nineties isn't it?

Another fire will soon be lit
The fire keeps burning but I shut it out
Knowing what its about
Don't get me wrong…I've got problems like everyone else…
But I keep on living…striving-slowly…yet-surely

I am sixteen…a true teen at heart
I won't fall apart…I don't do drugs, smoke, drink…I just live
Life is slow, fun, and mine to live…I am sixteen

305. "May Blues"

As much as I try to smile
I stay lonely instead
My heart given a way
To no-mans land
A place, more like a void
Where it just swivels
And swirls
With no place to land
I feel like I handed him my life
And yet I've no reason to think he even cares
Its a sad life
A lonely tale
I know I used to be happier
And as much as I try to move on
I feel stuck
Bound to my heart
That now lives in California
Without me
And probably without even care
And even though all else tells me otherwise
I still love him
I may always only love him
I know that now

306. "Maybe Then I'll Let Go"

Chilled to the bone

Life Uncommon

Winter has come again
Home is distant even by phone
Nothing solid to hold my pain
Alone in the world
The darkness covers me
Blankets my circled reality
If I could just be
But the dark reigns
And here I let loose of courage
Here its okay to feel pained
I don't even have to be strong
It's been too long
You can never really go back
And I pick up the pieces of all that I lack
Strength never quite lifts me away
Instead here in my head I stay
And maybe one day
In the winter with the cold chilling me
All the way to my inner core
When I am holding hot chocolate
Maybe then
Maybe then
I'll let go

'Til then....

307. "Me"

In this place filled with darkness
Surrounding my heart covered insane thoughts
Has crept into my mind, I no longer
Can hear you, see you, know you, feel you
Friends I am just shattered promises broken heart scared child
Will you ever cross the line of logic and understand? Me

Sometimes the darkness covers this mind
I become stark raving mad without restraint
Scared of nothing, but everything without love, his
Love is what I delude myself into thinking I--
Need, but do I? Probably not Love was never it
Not for me But I dream it and hold on anyway

Keep thinking I can't go on
To tomorrow or to eternity or maybe
Just not without him, Watch closely how it

Life Uncommon

Seeps back into me and I lose all control
Darkness sneaks Insanity laughs Madwoman now I laugh too at
Me at myself At him And at us In these conundrums

308. "Melancholy Daze"

Colorful lights and decorations surround my cave
These objects are supposed to bring joy
Fires are to bring warmth
Movies play on and try to win my affection
But they don't
None of it works
For none of it can heal
I am wounded badly
My hand is on the phone
Shaking in anticipation
Perhaps I should call an ambulance
Or drive to the hospital
I wonder...
Can a doctor fix my wounded heart?

309. "Melting"

Trapped in a cage
I stand alone
Only using words to express
My worries
Concerns
About me and about those
I care about
Sometimes I fear for us all
At times I have such hope for our futures
And each word is poison
Distorted and interpreted blindly
I fail to understand trust
My cage protects me from nothing
Friends become wounded
Rumors come full circle
Even though I retreat further into my cage
I do not succeed
At breaking free
From the pain
And I become trapped further
Further

Life Uncommon

Slowly deteriorating
As love becomes hatred
And as trust dissolves
Melting into a nothingness I do not wish to comprehend

310. "Melting Pot"

People are people
We can be any size
Some of us date guys
Go through life trying to keep away from lies
We all have our friendship ties…or do we?
Racism, prejudice, violence
Some of us live a mess
Where's the sense?
We die inside & out
Confusion master, depression the common denominator
Tear down the walls or keep within?

311. "Men"

Who am I supposed to be?
Lines of infinity…
What message do they want to sound?
Arms of security
Is there light?
Not now
Hold me warmly, passionately
Tell me everything will be alright
I want a kiss of love
I need a friend that will last
Relationships have past
Hold me warmly, passionately
No more fights
No more tears
Scared, crying, crunched in a corner
My fears are overtaking my soul
A heart of anger and rage
Hold me warmly, passionately
Tears, fears
Hold me warmly, passionately
Let it all become a fantasy
Is there a happy time ahead?
Hold me warmly, passionately

Life Uncommon

Let the fairy tales make my life a miracle
Nighttime lightning strikes through
Lightness, darkness
Nighttime
Hold me warmly,
Passionately

312. "Metallic"

My steel arms
Rusted and rotted
They got wounded over time
Now they just dangle
Flimsy and useless
So I set them free

313. "Metaphor"

Love is like snow
Both are innocent and pure- although when love
Dies out people try to find a cure
Because the heartache love gives you
Doesn't have a glove to warm up the coldness your heart feels

Love is like art
Both give a great feeling and emotion
People all have a realistic way to get both

Love is like a sparkling dove
Until it flies away and breaks your heart
You may fall apart
But just like that beautiful piece of art
All you have to do is start over again
Keep hoping for that feeling of love- never stop hoping

314. "Metaphorical"

Drawing is an empty canvas awaiting my soul
Singing is like vocalizing my calm waters
Dancing as a sexy being
Writing shows beauty
Perfect in its truth
Like a lie vanished

Life Uncommon

This hand writes as a hand that has just plucked
My heart and stuck it onto the paper

315. "Mi Corazon"
(dedicated to Alex)
I feel like throwing away everything I own and everything I am
Because I can't stand the pain of loving you
You got into my mind and my heart
You melted me as though I could dissolve myself in you
I felt a wholeness, a completeness a reality with you…and its gone
I'd love to ask you why…I'd love to know why you chose jail over me
Why you now choose the streets over me
Why you hurt because you're away from me and stay away anyhow
Why you chose to leave me
Why you choose not to come back
Do you hate me?...or just Vegas?...or is it both?
Did you fear me not accepting you drinking?
Did you dislike the fact that I didn't like seeing you being hurt?
Don't you know I love you? Can't you feel that yet?
I've loved you a year and then some and my heart seems wrapped up in dreams of you
I'm not a disillusioned youth, Al
I'm a grown-up woman who just so happened to find the man she could spend the rest of
her life with
The things I've most needed to be real exist in you
You are the honesty, integrity, and compassion the world seems bankrupt of
You certainly are family oriented and self-seeking…you'll change time and again
Even if no one notices, you'll change all the same
You're creative and genuine and honest…you have honor
Though not in the way you've treated me
How do I love you while I know you've abandoned me?
If I could let you go I would but every moment I feel like I need you
I've never needed anything or anyone the way I need you
I don't need your money or any object or material…I need just simply you
And instead I have teardrops and heart aches
I have sleepless nights spent alone and pain that with time only grows
I don't want to go it alone but I fear I will…How does life do this to us?
I know you
I know your heart
You know me and you certainly know mine
And yet we are two foreign travelers wandering the streets of life alone
Both hurting, both crying, both trying to cling to something safe… and finding nothing
but space
If only you'd call or write or let me know…I could let you go or hold you close
It's been nearly a year…I still don't know
I love you but I hate that you've left me

Life Uncommon

I hate that you know how I feel and still stay away
I hate that you keep your reasons hidden from me
I hate that I can't seem to get you out of my mind or my heart
I hate that I found you and lost you
I hate that I hate
Why must there be unanswered questions?
Why do people always leave me or hurt me and then just fucking not let me know why?
I hate the unanswered whys
I hate the twirling fucking questions
If only I had the nerve not to ask but I'm not that girl
That isn't my way and my way sits with settled pain
I'm like a raft on a river trying to find my way
I found it once…maybe once should be enough
Maybe I should learn how to accept that we had love it was nice and its gone
Sounds simple and I'm just not that simple especially not in the way I feel about you
When I can remember someone's words and the way their hands held mine
The way they kissed me, the way we made love
How could I even dream….of just letting you go?
I could throw most anything in the trash but not you
You I hold to as though you are the very life force I need to breathe and yet I feel
choked…as though there's some hold on my very throat
I'm so dried up, a worn out martini at best
I miss your voice…I miss your knowing…I miss not feeling alone
Were you just an illusion? Was the love we shared just a flicker of my own dreams? Did
I make you up?
Gods, how fucked up things are when the one thing you swear you need
Only leaves you knowing less and less
I don't know how long I'll struggle with this inside myself
Maybe time will teach me to let you go…hearts can heal
It'll take some time for me to heal from you though
You're the one I need…I don't know about soul mates and fairy tales anymore
And its not marriage that counts…Its just something about the heart and you're mine
I listen to the wind and wonder if it rustles you the way it does me
I wonder if you even think of me and I cry because I can't know
I don't know the rights and the wrongs anymore everything I thought I knew is gone
Like a vanishing butterfly…gone
Maybe I'm supposed to be mad at you
Maybe I'm supposed to be madly in love with you
Maybe I should just love you or try and let you go
It all seems wrong…Only you seem right
That's the truth you know…The world feels wrong
The suffering feels wrong…Most of the people I know strike me as wrong but you
You've always been right and you still are…maybe you're my north star
The star that will lead me in some sort of direction
I can't see how that could be though
Since I'm utterly lost

Life Uncommon

Between the shores of knowing and not
I'm not really alive, I'm not dead either
I'm just kind of here floating from moment to moment
Knowing only things… and when quietly alone
Knowing only my love for you and I cry because I need you to know I love you
I need you to know I know you love me…I need you to know I'm still here
I need you to know I understand
I need you to know I've always loved and accepted you for you and yet
You may never know
That's life's irony
When we finally figure out some sort of truth
It never gets told
I think no matter how old I get
This time, this love, this experience will be nestled inside me forever
Because you were the comfort I needed
You were the air I breathed and I'll love you for it always
I don't want to let you go
So I won't
I'll just love you
As my home and my heart.

316. "Misery"

People are ignorant assholes
Insignificant tiny minds
Blabbing about chickens
And fuzz
Wondering about lipsticks
Worrying about high heels
Living machinery lives
Incorrigible
He wants to be a figment
I need to be a figment
Of his imagination
Without love
And hope killed nine times by now
Cheer is a laundry detergent
And happiness always comes with a question mark.

317. "Missed Opportunities"

I am relaxing
Thinking of all my missed opportunities
The no's that should have been yes's

Life Uncommon

The cant's that should have been sure's
The some-other-times that should have been right-thens
The maybe-nots that should have been why-nots
I missed so many opportunities
Yet there is one I'll never miss
And that is the time I have to spend with you!

318. "Momentary Drift"

The pen slips...and my mind momentarily drifts
I find myself in a place I don't know
And wish I never came to
But no matter how much
I run or try to really see...
I seem blinded by who I'm meant to be
And even when I make up my mind
To get the hell outta nowhere
It seems I only end up back here
Cursing the light and the gods that be
And whoever made it their choice anyway
To make this life the way it is?
Don't you ever feel lonely?
Don't you ever want to curl up and cry?
Why is it so -wrong- to really
Need someone
Even if just for a moment?

Saddened souls reach out at night
Across the darkened skies
Shelled up like maddened lullabies...
And the tigers roam at night free
But only in their innermost fantasy
We are all caged, aren't we?
Our wings don't fly
And everything dies
And just as you think
You've stopped this hellish ride
You're right back where you started...
Cursing the sky

319. "Monthly Man"
(dedicated to Jun)
As I grow older
I find it easier to deal with the hurt

Life Uncommon

The pain of a brush-off no longer breaks me
I am still whole
Wounded, but no more than before
The lines didn't affect me the same
I saw the promises were made in vain
I can't spot a hurter for the man he isn't
But I can ride the waves now
I can wield the force of pain
I now can love and let go
Happy to have laughed and touched
Glad we never made love
Thanks for showing me light
Now I take on the task of
Finding my way back there
But on my own this time
Without you or any lover
Just me and the strength of my heart
I count my blessings this day
And bid you, farewell.

320. "Moonchild"
(dedicated to Anthony)
Sometimes at night,
You can tell,
The Goddess is there
Clouds are a bit stiller
It is then,
That you can feel her

A half-lit moon looms overhead
As autumn leaves fall silently,
Breezes blow somewhat differently
Your heart fills with a hope

These are the nights
She watches nearby
Winds sing you their lullaby

And you rest easier
For you know,
She is there to protect you
To keep you
And to bless you

Life Uncommon

321. "Moonspirit"

Simple words brought tears to my eyes
Dare I open up and let you inside
To love is pure, gentle and right
Let go of control and just go with the flow
Your words ring so true, I shake
And I quiver at the very thought- of you
You're the gentle child I hold at night,
The whispers of a pillow in the moonlight
The tears of sorrow, the laughter of love
You're the spirit I seek the one I
Hide inside, the poems you write
Inspire, prophesize, care and adore
And I'm always left yearning for more
I ask nothing of you gentle druid of
The night, just bid my farewells
My welcomes, my adieus, and my
Gentle embraces, if we let go where will
This love go, I try to control
To keep you from harm and to protect
Time heals all, perhaps together
We'll mend but I wish only
The best for you my friend

322. "Morbid"

Do you ever think about dying?
Probably not
But I do
All the time
Ten minutes ago I was going thirty miles over the speed limit
Then a truck pulled in front of me
I wanted to crush
Maybe I even needed to die
I am here though
Dreaming of ropes
And wrists freshly sliced from razor blades
Maybe arsenic will work
Others dying brings the only truth I ever seem to know of them
Every day I try to be true and honest
I fail
And I wonder
Will I be honest only when I die too?

Life Uncommon

323. "Mother's Day"
(dedicated to my Mom)
Mothers deserve their own day
During this bright spring month of May
I love my mother
Knowing we need each other
This day is for you
And that is one thing that will always be true

324. "Mother's Tears"

Young goddess
Touch your hand to the smoothness
Grains of sand
Spread your fingers
Allowing tiny particles to seep through
Hold them up high
Show the moondust
And the man in the sky
Tell your mother through fire
Let her know every burning desire
Then smile as Selene rules
The sea of emotions deep inside
Keep them true, nothing to hide

Look into those eyes
Fathers lullabies
See them twinkle
Oh, bright stars

The healing within the sand
Walking you along your path
Onto a better land

Father blesses the sky
And the tears of rain
Are your mother's own

325. "Movie Theater"
(dedicated to Rivertree Court)
People come and go
Together, Alone
Sad, Happy

Life Uncommon

A night of fun
Or one of relaxation
Sometimes an escape
Friends are made
Perfect place
For a first date

326. "Ms Vixen"

Okay Ms. Vixen
What you been mixing
I know its something crude
You been fixing
You want to make things right
But not with that mix tonight
You are naughty, I know you
A bit of a sheepish grin is shining through
Time ticks on
Feel a con
Mistress of twirls
Spinster of whirls
You know you are bad
How many men your heart must have had
Tilt your head
And smile sweetly as you fall back into bed

327. "Murrieta, California"
(dedicated to M.M.)
Home of the guilty and forlorn
Today I visited the Valley of the Witches,
Laughing so loud I'm left in stitches
Homes of the great bitches
California attitude resides within the valley
Spirit work of the dead
Where is Osiris?
I miss the way he led
Burial grounds no good
Going back to Vegas
Where I should
Listening owls tell my tale
The poet and her will to prevail!

328. "My Brother Wind"

Life Uncommon

As a child I ran around in the wind who I called my brother
My reasons for calling the wind my brother were endless
But I knew nothing less than the peace I found as a child with the wind
The wind never left my side
I wouldn't even dare to hide, because I loved my brother wind

329. "My Comforting Blanket"
(dedicated to Shannon & Dennis)
My comforting blanket
Constantly keeping me warm
Torn but still my shield
Colors so bright
That I drown myself
In them
Strands that hold together
Part of my life
When I cry
Here, during the day
And whenever I need to be heard at night
We laugh
We cry
Understand
You, my comforting blanket.

330. "My Generation"

We are the good
Willing to offer a helping hand
We are the bad
Turning our backs on a friend
Always talk of amplifying our best points
Of showing the world the beauty inside
But what if we just gave up that fight?
What if we indulge in our bad points
The dreamer chasing every rainbow
The inner child creating chaos among the sane
The sex maniac fucking all your twin flames
The druggee stealing your spare change
The kittens roaring in your hay
The rock a rollers drumming you out of your haze
The strangers even stranger on stormy days
The rapists taking no time off from work
Wouldn't that just be a lovely quirk?

Life Uncommon

The alcoholics whipping more than ever
If you could be anything bad
What would you be?
And is it being that bad part
That would set you free?
What fills up your empty days?
Dreams of chaos
Echoing through my brain…

331. "My Guitar"

Up on stage with a guitar in hand
Or just sitting on a nice piece of land
The strokes fill the air
While the wind blows at my hair
I feel the music through my fingertips
The sounds coming out of my lips
I strum and strum
I let out my emotions
Always coming out with different notions
My fingers move to the song's beat
And the beat moves through my feet
Showing feeling
Always dreaming
Of a time with harmonized song
It shouldn't take long
At least not if I am playing the guitar
Because happiness never seems far
Whether up on stage with my guitar in hand
Or just sitting on a nice piece of land
If the wind is blowing at my hair
Happiness shall fill the air

332. "My Heartache This Morning"

Last night bitter words were spoken
Between Jake and I
I call him…to apologize?
To wait for an apology?
Who knows?
I feel empty
Almost free from him
But the kind of love we've shared does not ever fade
Not like this

Life Uncommon

Opposites maybe
But lovers
Can this be taken away from me?
Was it ever mine?

333. "My Home"
(dedicated to Alex)
You were the rock that I beat my heart against
You gave me the right to let my tides flow
In your sighs I felt life for the first time
It was like I never lived until there was you
Your drunkenness was the relaxation I needed
Empathically I felt your lack of worry and pain
It was you that made me feel okay
How can I ever repay you for the gifts you gave me?
Love, compassion, understanding, friendship
You were my savior
It was you that breathed me back to life
You questioned me and brought this great passion into my soul
A passion that riveted in every moment I spent with you
Making love to you has been unparalleled
No person has ever gotten to me the way that you did
When you held me it was as though you held my very soul
I've never sat alone in the dark with anyone before you
You knew my thoughts even when I couldn't speak them
You felt my fears and comforted them time and again
How is it that you knew me like the back of your hand
And still left?
Could you not understand that you are the only home I've ever known
I remember your ears and the way your hair fell
I have memories of sitting next to you and knowing you
I love you and I miss you too

334. "My Incident With An Angel"
(dedicated to Dmitry)
Have you ever touched an angel?
Or looked into their eyes (so bright and beautiful)?
To touch one would be like catching a shooting star
The distance is so vast and far
Innocence and love strum through their fingers
And even a glimpse of one's smile always lingers
A near impossibility to even see one

I had the honor of touching an angel

Life Uncommon

I glanced in the eyes of something so wonderful and fragile
My heart pumped because it walked
Then my soul flew as it talked
My luck had surely changed
And my chaotic life was all easily rearranged
When the winds blew from need for change
He left my sight and my mind became deranged

335. "My Love"

A love that branched over the divide of centuries
Swept into my dreams to bring me romance
Nights of peaceful dancing amongst the stars
We walked along shorelines together, making love
Forming a bond we knew straight inside
Something we knew when we met eye-to-eye
Others around us, but none quite within
We knew together that it was me and him
My twin mate with whom I found so much
He made me believe in myself again
Helped me to believe I could go anywhere
That I could fly, or leap, or love and then like an instant
He vanished to death's dismay overcome by a cancer that I couldn't fight
We made love, held each other on those last fate-filled nights
Oh, how we loved…how we laughed
How we knew even in the depths of our own hell
That we had a love that would last forever
His friends helped me clean up his place
Made a video of the sessions weeks long of fun and friendship
Times to remember with laughter and grins…God, how I loved him
By myself on the last days I tidied up the place
Grabbed some old notebooks and pens of mine
Gathered up my clothes and other belongings
And finally with his grace knew his secret
He kept something precious to him, to us
Locked up in a place I had never discovered
But in an instant I knew and went to that very cupboard
I found a hidden supply of paintbrushes, pens, and pencils
Knowing this was his way of saying he'd be with me
Every time I write, every time I dream, every time I love
And with faith in my heart and love by my side
I walked forth onto a new day…called up an old long lost friend
Walked down the street on to tomorrow, hand-in-hand
The old oak tree leaves fell so magically
Today I grieve,

Life Uncommon

Today I smile,
Today I love,
Tomorrow I sing
End Chapter I, Scene III.

336. "My Wall"

I stand behind a wall
It protects me from cruelty
From madmen
From secrecy
From unhappiness
People cannot break down my wall
Its too high
They can kick it
Scratch it
Pull it
Push it
Smash it
Thrash it
Yell at it
Cover it
But my wall won't go down
No, no
I made sure of that
I built my wall out of fear
Unhappiness
Loneliness
Depressed thoughts
Fright of living
No, no
Nobody can break down my wall
My wall
That protects me
I won't drink
Take drugs
Smoke
Trust
Live
Not in this world
Not in a world that has so much trouble accepting what's behind my wall!

337. "Mysterious Woman"

Life Uncommon

Something in her eyes
That glistens like gold
Something inside
She everything holds
It's like she knows where I've been
And knows where I'm going
I see her eyes and I want to delve within them
She knows my soul
And she moves it all
With a smile or a laugh
That's all it takes for me to know
That its her that everything holds
She could whisk me away on a giggle
And comfort me in a whistle
The world fades except in her eyes
Its her that gives me life
Something in her
That tells tales from afar
And lights the fires of passion
Like the brightest star
Something in her
Holds a life I never knew
A mystery I'll spend my life uncovering

338. "Mysty Eve"

For in that time that houses the dead
And the sleep of night
When nighttime yawns
And the world spawns
Demons and devils
And sprites
And fawns
We sprinkle merry dust along the path
Of old and new together at last
We smile so sully and dance so gaily
The moon shines on
Diana there
Encouraging her children
To laugh and dance on the merriest of nights
When cloaks are worn and wands waved mysteriously
When the animal inside us roams
And when the woods become our home
Mystique
Mystery

Life Uncommon

Unknown forces blend
And its on this night... our hearts and souls
Do mend

339. "Nate"
(dedicated to Nate)
Nate, nate what seals our fate?
Bushes of yogel tomato and tomorrow
Thorns of time twice and thrice and
Once is mine
Your knowledge of dragon wars
Memories of thyme
Every thrice and thrice is mine
When the hour strikes solid 10
Wants you to be mine
Through heaven through hell
Through desert through lake
Only she knows what seals our fate

340. "New Day"

I'm going to gallivant around
And then come home
And say hello
What's funny is that-
I have

341. "New Feelings"

This morning I woke up to the sun's rays and music
I jumped out of bed and felt alive
I knew I would strive for sunshine in my heart
Of course on a day like this I could never fall apart
A ray of sunshine just fills my heart with hopes and dreams
The day is happy and exciting
Any old routine takes on a new appearance today
Time to tune in and play
I feel happy and safe- protected even
A world of sunshine- free from cloud
When the sun goes down we see hues
Nature's colors end the day perfectly
And let night take over
The stars and gray moondust clouds are as lucky-

Life Uncommon

As a four leaf clover
But luck was not intended- just the warmth
The warmth that I knew I'd feel
The moment I woke up this morning!

342. "Nguyen Chi"

I am in this room
Wondering and waiting
Maybe a trial will never come
This space may be my doom
Poetry is part of me
Oh! Help me!
Keep my spirit reverberating
Alone I am
Nguyen Chi

343. "Nickel-Dime-Back"

There is this unsatisfaction that comes
When the life you live numbs, Your dreams
And your hopes and your fantasies too
It's been a long time since you were a starry-eyed youth
Wanting to kick everything in sight
Ready at any moment to jump into another fight
You'd bang down the walls of every American city
If you thought it would help this life worth only pity

344. "Night"

Night
Late
Dark
Moon
Stars
Moon dust
Spread
Beautiful
Inspiring
Interesting
Cold
Chilly
Cruel

Life Uncommon

Scary
Dull
Slow
Long
Different
Comets
High
Far
Outside
Pretty
Night

345. "Night Vs. Day"

Dark
Cruel
Chilly
Dull
Slow
Long
Spread
Late
Night
Day
Light
Early
Fun
Beautiful
Sunshine
Colorful
Interesting
Changing
Clouds
Outside
Early
Late
Light
Dark

346. "Nightless Night"

What does tomorrow hold for the fool of life?
Hierophant searches for eyes
Priestess forgetting her height

Life Uncommon

Temperance strums a guitar
Cat plays
The artist draws it
The poet writes it
And the moon cries

347. "Nighttime Dreamz"
(dedicated to Robert)
Alone in the darkness
The hours tick
Sun goes down
World asleep
Kittens dreaming
Bittersweet fantasies
And I imagine myself happy
Just you and me
Years separate us
but what is time?
Time is money they say
But not for me
Alone I dream
Alone I weep
Alone I pray
Alone I sleep

We walked to get ice cream
You bought me lunch
You favored me
I loved you so much
Will you ever know
The way I yearned...

348. "Nighttime Hopes"
(dedicated to John)
You would call me up at night
And I thought you could take away the fright
But I was wrong as I always am
See I thought you could help me, take me out of this jam
But it's a hole I live in
Day out, day in
And I'd tell you of all my troubles and woes
But how could you help, what do you know?
You're just some guy alike in tastes
Telling you anything now seems like a waste

Life Uncommon

But your laughter felt like raindrops to my ears
Felt like you could tenderize the lonely years
But now I know you could not
So I feel like here in my hole... I'm left to rot
I don't know that I told you much about me at all
Perhaps about one or two clumsily made falls
But in truth it just wasn't much at all
We spoke of mustangs and palominos
And several things that no one else knows
But all in all it still feels like we didn't tell anything much
Not even in the cold could I feel your touch
Phone calls and e-mails don't make a relationship
Couldn't we tell, we just didn't fit?
I guess I tried once to escape
But then that didn't seem the real fate
So I went back to you
And told you I'd be true
And I was, that was the truth I told
But I don't think in my heart that you did hold
Maybe as a friend or an ally
But to tell you it was love would only be a lie
And now we have parted for the last time
No longer am I yours, No longer are you mine
You called me princess
I can only hope one day you will find the perfect fit
You are a good man with a strong heart
And may you find a beautiful union of which to be one part
I pray for you a friend that was there for me in need
May you always find your place within the steed.
Merry you part and blessed you be.

349. "No Cheers"

Why are men such scum?
Why do they lack compassion?
Are they heartless-
Or just stupid?
Us girls we give our hearts not just our pussies
But they don't get that
Its just lust
Confident
Another 6 pack
And a joint
Life holds no beauty
Just lust

Life Uncommon

Loneliness
And another beer
Its so disgusting
Welcome to hell
You're bound to be alone
Or with one of these scumbags
I lost my pom pons

350. "No More Outside"

I don't like outside
I liked work
Even loved it
That is until I got involved with someone
Who thought he'd prey on me
Then tainted my boss's view of me
And got asked repetitively to have an affair
With another co-worker
Life sucks
I'd like to pretty it up
And say sometimes life can be not perfect
But the truth is
Life sucks
I hate going outside
And inside
I'm shit

351. "No Words Leave My Mouth"

In this hollow night of November I sit by myself
Loving and laughing
All inside me building up more and more
Fiery eyes of misfortune daunting my brain
Mocking my presence
Intimidating the fire that is me
As it builds and builds, piece by piece
The jigsaw puzzle is being put together
Making an image so clear so beautiful
So mysterious
Reading the poetry of the great ones
Under a simple Pine
This passion inside me intensifies so divine
And I look up
To my destiny

Life Uncommon

352. "Nobody"

Nobody likes me
They don't listen
I just want my soul to be free
And to watch stars glisten
But cruel beings don't care
I dislike their pessimism towards everyone
They just don't know how to share
Or relax and have some fun
Is there no
Help?

353. "Nonexistent in Invisible Territory"
(dedicated to Ryan & Marie)
To trust someone
Such a simple task
Until the one you trust
Becomes the lying lass

You are invisible
To her selfish wants

Knowing you exist
In nonexistent territory
Knowing with every breath
Who you are
As you live
But only sometimes

As she walks by
Forget that others know
Pray
Pray, pray
While she preys
On your trust

The friend who turns
The lying lass
Try not to cry
As her ways are crass

Feeding on your hurt

Life Uncommon

Thirsting for your life
Lethargy comes...

I become what I despise

354. "Not Remembering"

I don't remember what it was like to be happy
Images surround me
But I can never quite feel the intensity
He is so much of what I want
His image interrupts my sad existence
I don't remember how to laugh
And live and love
I may be dead
But somehow I still feel
And what I feel in my mind is him

"Not sure if this is a poem..."

Basically I need to work full time
Nine dollars or more
No sick days allowed
I think I hate the images
That society implants in my brain
Curse the falsities
Fed to my youth
A child who only hopes
Wishes and loves
When robbed of my truth
The feeling is of death
And it rains today
Again, thunder, in my head.

355. "Note To Self"

Challenge the underlying beliefs that drive me to get things "just right"
If you want a reward, find a quicker and more direct way to get it
Employ a different strategy if I believe in existential things
Ex: Self-acceptance
Fulfillment
Or inner peace
What things would I like to change about myself?

Life Uncommon

What could I do differently that would make me feel better about being…Me?
I need to give myself credit for what I do well, even if it isn't perfect
Take inventory of my accomplishments

356. "Nothing in life is stable"

Nothing in life is stable
Everything I perceive can be so wrong
Friends are just enemies waiting to happen
Concern finds itself a rumor so quickly
Embellished and cruel
Love is just fictional
Honesty exists nowhere
These walls of mine were glass
The hammer of life has knocked
And so the pieces shatter
Scattered on my kitchen floor
I try to avoid them
Ignore and repress the memory of them
But I can't
These glass walls were all I had
Defenseless now
And more afraid than ever
Of the one thing I know nothing about
Life

357. "Nothing Left"

Does anyone know how it feels to have nothing left?
I love to read about things like petty theft
But this is not about what I love—it is about what is
There are so many things I miss
I miss feeling safe
Secure
Unharmed
Free
Does anyone know how it feels to have nothing left?
I have no home
Nor even a phone
My money is gone
Evil has been done
It isn't fair to have to be this afraid
Always in the shade
There is no light

Life Uncommon

Just lots of fright
I am broken down
Now I know what it is to drown
To be sucked below the waters
And only flounder
I am alone in a world of terror
Does anyone know how it feels to have nothing left?
I saved a few people a few years back
Now I know what I lack
Curled up once again
I thank you my friends
They try to help
But—Does anyone know how it feels to have nothing left?

358. "Now"

Alone in our homes we weep
So many roses lay in the streets
Oh, so oft we mean to laugh, yet we cry
Thousands innocent have died
In the heart of man lies peace
In the walls of our own prisons
God gives us justice
Fear now upon us
Swiftly we listen with ears so soft
Like feltdrops, Tears of our fellow man
Rain falls hard tonight
The world about us all
Soft we speak, that inner call
We may run for years in fear
But none can numb the inner chill
May we not fall without grace
But rise with mercy
And without injustice

359. "NY Suit"

Doesn't get easier
Not in this world
Travel the trains
And get a little faster
A little crazier
Work on wall street
Up our chances with the stocks

Life Uncommon

Get a little busier
Be a grown up man
Step off of Disneyland
This is the real world now
Where you just walk away
Walk forward onto the new day
Sleeping is a luxury not for us
We're grown ups now in a city
Where everyone walks fast
Everyone has their perfect Starbucks coffee cup
A cinnamon, sugar-filled, creamy, tall cappuccino
We know how to order better than any other generation
And yet no matter how much we work to break down time
We never have enough
The train's about to leave
And I've surrendered my youth...

Oh, the sweet surrenders of the New York suit.

360. "October Dreams"

Love lingers
Sadness dies
My eyes cry
I love you and I

Forever pain
Alone and drowned
I wear your heart
Like a crown

361. "Ode to a Leaf"

Small drops of leaves
Flying through the wind
Telling stories of Italy and France
Bringing to my heart a subtle romance
And telling me of that one time down in Mexico
When the heat had dimmed, sweet and low
Oh, if only I could go!
Hawaii he sailed straight through
Stopping only to bring beauties of every hue
Wisping through Tahiti smiling down on the sand
Watching the tourists form a nice suntan

Life Uncommon

Yes, it sounds like so much fun
Sifting by the Florida sun
Oh, to be a leaf
To travel the world
On the rooftops of the wind
Then come back home
Landing in my lap, loyal friend.

Inspired by the book "Dibs: In Search of Self" by Virginia Axline

362. "Often Crying and Often Curled"

I am a loner in the world
Oftentimes I find myself in a fetal position lying down
Waiting for my doom
Tears easily drip from my eyes
When I look out from the bed I see walls
They surround me and even seem to bind
Me to a place I do not want to be a part of
Outside of my walls are proverbial walls and chains
Bearing down on me
Sometimes when I walk into a room I see all of the
Folkways and mores of our society
My passion chokes inside my throat
I always want to run back
Back
Into the fetal position,
Where I delude myself
Thinking I am safe
Laying down once more
Often crying and often curled
A ball of me, wishing the pain would subside
Awakening, walking outside
I venture into cobwebs of destruction
People force me to work
To give myself up
That is why
I often cry alone on my bed
Because there I am myself

363. "One Fall's Changes"

It is now the time for leaves to fall
Outside kids play their last games of ball

Life Uncommon

Colors are changing, metamorphasizing
It is a time of learning, of choice
To be this, To be that
To sleep, To run
To creep, To have fun
What will our lives become?
We are locked within
Growing on the inside
Striving for the outside
Trying to notice all
We can't understand
Slowly we learn from flowers
And thunder-storm showers
No identicals…
Just nature being itself
Beautiful in its individuality

364. "One Man's Heart"

Can one love another's heart?
He loves her
She's a small town girl who loves art
She's a mother by nature

He helps so many
One could think he's a disguised nanny
A mirage, a fantasy, a dream
So perfect

She sits and dreams of a new life
She wants to grow up and be a wife
Happy dreams are always on her mind
She tries not to stay behind

Maybe they'll never meet
Some friendships never start
Maybe they are meant to be that way
Wow what to believe- destiny or fate?

365. "One True Night"
(dedicated to my gentlemen friends in college)

Gathered round the table of Arthur I dined with some of my oldest of friends

Life Uncommon

Without tuxedos and bowties or the dreadfully woeful black suits of death being our gathering cause
No bouquets needed to be thrown, simply a birthday for which this blessing was bestowed
One whom once was so young and obnoxious turned into a husband before my eyes
The heart's brother grown into a sophisticated gentleman
My newest friend, though four years hardly counts as new, smiled radiantly while,
His subtle humble way showed through
The shy articulate soul whom I've always felt moved by leaned over me all night,
Making sure that everything was, for me, just right
Andy, once I thought he was lost and while watching his elegance I could not help but comprehend
That it is I who am lost within myself and he who simply- is not
Gentleman of olde, the lover, the friend, the fellow co-conspirator of so many youthful fights, the memory of my naïve self, the keeper of the strange beauty of my college years, sat as a cultured individual awaiting, Life
I simply felt as though I was enjoying an evening with six husbands of time
Each aged beautifully, as though some perfect French wine
My heart overflows in happiness to see such friends
Time, in its own strange ways, always mends.

366. "Otherworld"

In mute psychosis
My mind pulls me into the past
Before yesterday
And before the birth of my father
Into a time without civilization
When man and beast were just creatures of the earth
Survival was only threatened for need
Hunted only for food
Without rules
And without law
Prejudice had not yet been created
And silence brought peace
Emotions understood
Innately felt and communicated
A time when instinct existed
A time I wish to be a part of

367. "Our Future"

"Time keeps on ticking into the future"
Tick…tock…tick…tock…tick…tock

Life Uncommon

We keep on seeing shadows of memories
And bright waves of the future
Our lives never stand still
Motion is our future
Yet standing is the mind's maze of thought
Moving…thinking…constant motion…
When will things stop…start…or just stay still
We will never know-
Because we depend only on what we have already learned
From our shadows of memories…our past
Our maze will be solved and our future will at
Some point be known—
Because the "time keeps on ticking into the future"
Tick…tock…tick…tock…tick…tock

Inspired by the song "Fly Like an Eagle" by the Steve Miller Band

368. "Out of Place"

I think the reason I often feel unaccepted
Is because I made up my mind that I am
So I think telling the truth,
Always,
Under all circumstances
Is the key
Wish me luck!

369. "Out There"

Out there lies a drunk
A kid sleeping on the top bunk
In space is a man
Down here a sad baby lamb
Someplace else there is a drug dealer hard at work
In my room is a strange man with a strange smirk
Downtown are innocent animals in zoos
Right now I'm reading some bad news
California just had another earthquake
Across the street is one more destroyed lake
In Washington D.C. the newest president has been shot
The homeless center is striving for an extra cot
Florida is becoming too hot
And my thoughts are being tangled in a knot
Out there people are starving

Life Uncommon

In bars men are trying to be charming
In my heart I am dreaming
And my mind is screaming
Some mother is broke
Some brother addicted to smoke
Life is changing
And pans are banging in an alcoholic's room
Out there someone is for the first time hearing their doom
Gangs are killing more children
Leaving my heart in ruin
Out there lies our government
Finding out how much they've been lent
And realizing how much of our lives they've spent!

370. "Pandemonium"

Tossing the coins of fate
Shitting the bull over
Tequila and cards
Cleared sight streaming forth
Love spoken in subtleties
Listen with ease
Over coffee and bull
This is the ease
Of the star and the fool

371. "Paradise"

Is there really anything as beautiful as the moon at night?
Full and bright
Hanging above you
Freely moving about the heavens
She has this glory that emanates in everything she does
I imagine an ocean beneath her
Glowing with the beauty of sea creatures
Blue and beautiful
All is glorious

372. "Parting"

Kissing her goodbye one day I stood with my back to the doors of the courtyard,
Not letting her leave
I leaned my head down

Life Uncommon

And forward
And kissed her passionately

The beauty in this moment, is, I guess, how masculine I felt
Dominant,
Loving,
And taller- for once

373. "Pathways"

Pathways laid out glittered in silver and gold
One I know, the other I am told
Simple are not the ways of fate
Seemingly on patience I am always late
Tying "cord to cord, knot to knot"
One is right, the other one not

Time solves the things we can't
Sometimes waiting misunderstands
If choices were easier lessons wouldn't be
Like a fly caught in my own web, I am
Straight, then turned
The answers elude me

As I try to figure out the solutions that be
I'm not aware of the bigger picture
But I love, I laugh, and I believe in
A light-filled future
The highest good, the truth I seek
Questions rumble of the strong and meek.

374. "Paying"

Give me hell
I want heaven
Give me hurt
I want happiness
Nothing good comes without a price
Nothing worthwhile comes without sacrifice.

375. "Pegasus"
(dedicated to my sister)

Life Uncommon

They walk with a sense of innocence
And run through the wildest of places
These animals are known as the Pegasus
They have so many great characteristics
Such as white fur which is as pure as an angel
People always tell of how gracefully they fly
I even smile as they walk, run, or fly by

376. "Pendulum"

In the desertion of my youth
I have gained insight
Understanding now what's wrong,
What's right
Missing the maybes
Fathoming the unfathomable
And hating the indescribable
I miss your touch…
Lips so sweet
Missing you much

377. "People and Tigers"

(dedicated to my sister)

People are like tigers
People work and get what they want
By writing, building, cleaning
Tigers hunt their prey night & day
Work for both want and need
Children, Cubs both young, both innocent, both looking for nourishment
To heed one simple bit of advice:
Trying your hardest is the easiest way to succeed

378. "Petals"

Petal by petal
I pluck them in search of my destiny
Maybe this tiny pink miracle will bring me,
The love of my life
I see him
Tall and handsome
Smiling- in my direction

Life Uncommon

Love extends
My tired, trembling body
I will get hurt
But I inch forward anyway
Sweet angel
I come for you

379. "Pets"
(dedicated to my sister)

There were two little kittens
With the whitest fur
They were a cure for little children's pain
No one could ever gain friends like these
They were always together like the Siamese
These two little kittens with fur like snow
Now I truly know what two little friends can bring!

380. "Phantom"

Somber and cold
On a hot day in Vegas
Sweet bitterness
Hate rising in my throat
Thick as a melon
But hatred is enough
More painful than blood
Afraid to swallow
Difficult to breathe
My whole body shakes
As I recall
Not the event
Or the aftermath
Just the feelings
Just the feelings

381. "Phone Home"

If you called God on the phone
Would he answer?
What would you ask?
How insignificant would your questions seem to you,
When you know he's busy as fuck on a minute-to-minute basis?

Life Uncommon

Would you really feel like whining?
Or crying?
Or feeling bad for yourself,
In a self-absorbed pity?
Would God tell you to cheer up,
Or pipe down?
Would he tell you to follow your dreams,
Or chase your own destiny?
What would you want him to say?
If you know the answers, why don't you believe yourself?
Who can you trust, if you can't trust you first?
God doesn't answer the phone-- you do
So ask the question
Hear your answer
Act on it
Act I, Scene I.

382. "Poet"
(dedicated to Matt S.)

Why am I so drawn to him?
Maybe it is his precious words written down on paper
Or how he smiles at me
Could be how he is afraid, but not too afraid
I know I appreciate how he isn't afraid to admit his feelings
At least not on paper
He seems to be all man
But sometimes feminine charms seem to come through
Friendly
Intelligent
Mysterious
I guess that is how I like 'em
My question is answered
But I still don't know
Don't know
Fear why I am so drawn to him

383. "Poor Ducky"

Childhood rhymes
Race through my mind
I recall the monkeys
And the man who bumped his head
I think of twinkling stars

Life Uncommon

And mother goose chimes
I row my boat
And run up some clock
But as it turns out
I forgot the flock!

384. "Prevailing Honesty"

Why is it that when you want to talk to God, he's not there?
I want peace and find none
I find worry
About money, about family, about my home
I find anxiety about the almost always explicitly,
Always rude and hurtful opinions of those around me
We all have troubles
We all have fuckups
Am I your perfect?
No
And why should I be?
I'm fat
Not just a little overweight
Or a little chubby
Or having a few extra pounds
Hell no
I am fat
F-A-T
That means that I don't fit into your clothes
That I'm not welcome in your magazines
Or your movies
I'm not visually exciting
I don't have people around me who love my love handles or big ass
I'd like a slimmer body
For myself
But I don't get one
Because of you
Because your insensitive, deluded, artificial self only sees weight
What's behind it means so much more
But that
"I cannot tell you my truth until you stop telling me yours"
If I find a truth in myself about myself or God and it is completely clear
Is it true?
It is for me
And one's own truth is important

Life Uncommon

Footnote: Excerpt from the book "Conversations With God" written by Neale Donald Walsch

385. "Prince"
(dedicated to Matt S.)

He is in my mind so many minutes of my week
Matt
A character in a book
A movie star
A prince from Europe
Anyone but who I want
But I never really know that
To me he is perfection
Utter beauty
No existence leaves me crying
For his eyes have never really seen me
Or have they?
I think he knows me
Without words we have shared so many heart breaks with one another
So, in the misshapen hours of spring
I dream

386. "Protector"
(dedicated to Brian)

He sings a song of sometimes
And I find myself in tears
Could it be this is true
He loves me
Is that what he said
I know he talks
And even when needed
Will listen
To all the muddled hell inside my head
A friend he is
And a mighty young fella
For he is the simple umbrella

387. "Puppies"

Small enough to fit in your hand
Cute, cuddly, and sweet they are

Life Uncommon

Ready to give you unconditional love
So playful, so happy

388. "Quantum Leap"

Sam's favorite song is "Imagine" by John Lennon
The man who goes around putting right what once went wrong
He's sweet and caring
I look up to his ways
He loves his brother Tom
His parents
And his sister
At sixteen he played basketball
Not all too well
Although he never really fell,
But his mind was stronger
His best friend Al helps him
But all the time a cool man
Sam Beckett

Footnote: TV Name Quantum Leap & character names from the show
Inspired by the television show "Quantum Leap"

389. "Quarantined No More"

Smoke another cigarette
Sip in the toxin with one more breath
Inhale the ugliness the grossness the anger
It won't make things any less unfettered
Sheltered young lady
Don't you know already?
Things that break
Aren't easily fixed
But its those gemstones beneath the hurt
Beneath the gross
Beneath the ugly
Beneath the pain
That shine more glorious every weathered day.

390. "Questions of Honor, Answers of Loyalty"

So I'm walking the desolate valley
A place I know so well

Life Uncommon

At times a distant memory, but now a present path
Time to take arms against the self
Break down those feelings telling me I must help
Is that a conscience buzzing in my ear?
And why is it I should feel guilty?
Guilty for the traps they set themselves?
Guilty for mistakes I was bound to make?
Yeah, okay, so I'm human…its true…I admit it
Perhaps you thought more but I'm just me
This is my life…Take me as I am
She's shipwrecked ladies and gentleman
With nothing to save her from rough waters
So you make it harder, kick some dust in her face
Yell out a couple of names
Use that nasty tongue of yours
So she'll see what you want her to…but she, she is me
So that's dust you're kicking in my face and its me you are yelling at
Maybe I am going to stumble a few more times
This is my life…Take me as I am…or row your boat away
Help or get out…I don't need the lousy lies
The helpless victims…The screaming prophets
I need a line to show me the island or to stumble upon it on my own
What I don't need is words of fate
Shout them at me you fools
But they are words lost on deaf ears
I hear no words just feel your anger and perhaps you were too busy shouting
To notice I had the line to the shores in my hand
All along
Sail on oh oracle of hell
And keep your destiny words for yourself
This is my life
Take me as I am

391. "Quietus"

Infinite sleep I worship you
The utter peace you bring
When my echoing thoughts no longer
Glare so bright
Scorching burns to my palms
Walk me up the ladder
Whistle me a tune
I follow you
Not as mourner
Nor as child

Life Uncommon

As I am now
Knowing you as I do
Understanding twirling nonsense
My ambivalent self sees clearly
The pawns of a chess game
One without start
Questionable end
Prancing and dancing around this universe
Following instructions
Attempting to survive the human threshold
By work
By work
Living on and on
By work
By work
Now that we know
We must find a solution

392. "Quotes"

"When you look beyond illusion and journey into disillusion, when you travel to the bottom of the depths of disillusion, that's where you'll find love." – Jules

"Cruelty and pain are sometimes one in the same" – Jules

"Life is and will be, whether you like it or not" - Jules

"Holyfuckingcrapmyass!" – Jules

"The epitome of fuck" – Jules

"Time lasts forever- inside" –Jules

"Wonders never cease, neither do disasters." –Jules

"Even on a mild-mannered day the sun beats happily." –Jules

393. "Rain"

Why can't I stop the rain?
Its falling down so fast, without change
Another lonely night is filled without him
The light in what has been darkness
Now just a dark shadow on my heart

Life Uncommon

He crawled through the cave I call my heart
Silent
Slippery
Slithering until he found his way
He crawled for months
Observed the switch
The light was on, of course
Dim as it may have been
Then he pulled the chain
There no longer was light

A thunderstorm came about
Lonely and scared
He dashed out of my cave

Thunder crashed my dreams
Shattered the serenity
Pulled the switch

Now I wonder why
Why was there an entrance to my cave?

394. "Rainy Day"

Bleeding heart
Drops of honey
Melted
Pitted prunes
Dried up seeds
What's in it for me?
Yeah okay
So I should have been working and slaving away
I kept saying I'd save up for a rainy day
Five months now
Rain must stay long around the depressed
Went to the doctor
Jury went out
Verdict is in
Nothings wrong with me
Discharged
…What if its all just a dream?

395. "Rainy Vegas"

Life Uncommon

Tired of the rain, I'm sick of the pain
Every day another dime down the drain
I live in a cold-footed city
Even the downpour won't cleanse
Negativity feeding into the hearts of us
Greed settles in like dust
Money never coming in
Not in the city of sin
Tears like clouded thunder
Watching my life go under
Still no relief living on city streets

396. "Random"

Monkey in can
Can in jeans
Jeans have nail polish on them
To fix a tear
The nail polish is in the cup holder
The cup holder is being held by
The bunny
The bunny is lying next to the lotion
The lotion is in my mom's purse
The purse also holds a phone
The phone is next to a pack of Marlboro cigs
The cigarettes have scotch tape around the box
The pen has tape around to keep away blisters
The pen is in my English book
The book is on the windowsill
I look out the window at night

397. "Rats"

Jump onto hot coals
Run across
Leap through the circle of fire
Dodge beneath the ax
Make your way through the maze
Keeping safe from death's hand

Why?
What does one live for?
Love is an ideal
But simplicity is for the real

Life Uncommon

Living without happiness
As hours become years
And memories become an unbearable weighing force
The future, an unknown abyss

398. "Raw Truth"

You want me to be something I can't
I can't give anymore
I gave for fucking years
I won't give again…not anytime soon
Maybe not ever again
I may go unmarried and be single for life
Shit happens, what can I say?
You want me to be all in love and care for you
Well fuck you because I just can't…and I won't
I damn near died in love for a man
I wanted him so bad I would have given everything
And I don't mean this all in just theory
I mean I sent my energy to him
In a jail where he was rotting
He needed it, so I gave…It is all I knew how to do
I cried and I cried…Until that little girl in me died
Can't you see that this is just a used up me?
I'm trying to let go of the past I knew
I've thrown away the love letters
Tore up the journals…destroyed the stories
I keep getting rid of so much and yet it sticks like glue to my ever-failing heart
I can't get rid of the things that kill me
The things that make me know I'm nothing
I loved and loved and loved and was I ever loved back?
Fuck if I'll ever know
So I just want to go and let go
And be really fucking far away from all the shit of my life
So can't you understand you fucking cunt that I can't give
Not to you…not to them…not to anyone
I need me and I will only give me to me for now
So you can wait your turn
Take a fucking number
Stand in line or walk away
It makes no difference to me but you've got to understand
This is my time for me
Get on board or jump the fuck off
Bitch~!

Life Uncommon

399. "Reality"

Sleek and slender
I move
All hundred and sixty pounds
Weightless in high heels
And tripping over my skirt
Beautiful am I
Oh god I forgot to brush my teeth again?
So I smile and wave shyly so as to leave some mystery
Can't walk away though
I'll stand and beam
Otherwise they'll see the tear in my seam

400. "Reality of the Night"

Well, today wasn't all that bad
I actually had fun
Earlier Tim and I were alone
Passionate, and loving were we
His heart is in my hands
And I've placed my heart in his
Love, that's what you call this
After I got home
My parents spoke once more
Not happy or cheerful
Put down and tested
That's my life—right?
Still I sit here not speaking to anyone
Grounded from my phone for a week
I miss, wait I never had,
A happy life
Where is love?

401. "Relation Games"

I don't understand love's games
It sure as hell has brought me no fame
Such fools we make of ourselves
Even when it makes no sense at all
The lies we tell
Can never really help
Something good steps in my door

Life Uncommon

And out again in no time at all
Friends explain that its all about me
But how could that be?
What really says this one is right,
And not that one?
The color of hair?
The job?
The past?
Who ever really knows?
Not even I can make sense of myself right now
I can't understand why something starts off
So great and ends like a slap from fate
How complicated relations turn out to be
But I suppose that's part of life's mystery
How I can meet and like a guy so much
And then feel like fates wheel
Left me on my ass
I don't know
Perhaps this is another time to move on and grow
God help me because right now
I just don't know.

402. "Release Me"

Release me
From the prison of my heart
Release me
From the endless boundaries of pain
Release me
Let me not be beyond the shelter of light
Release me
Let me walk away with some pride
Release me
Allow me some air to breathe
Release me
Just let me be
Release me
I need to move beyond
Release me
Break the bond
Release me
I need to move on…

403. "Reminder of Angels"

Life Uncommon

(dedicated to Shannon)

Dream with faith
Sing with heart
Listen with soul
And write with light

Within your showers of darkness find the light within
Lift up that torch and light up the world
With the love you know inside

Chorus:
*Dream to fly with angels
Embraced by the light
Dream to fly with angels
Through darkened tunnels at night

Know their gentle hearts call you
You'd know them even in death
They'd awaken your soul just so you'd remember again*

Sharing your dreams of a nation meant to be
Falling towers shall stand upright again and the truth shall set us free

Darkened skies fall like rain,
Curses disappear in vain
Terrorism shall rot in the home of the insane and once more freedom shall lift

We'll become a nation again
Standing erect with unity
Lifting our hearts and heads
Remembering who it is we are inside

<chorus>

Close your eyes and whisper to god…the guardian of men
Pray that he'll hear you and give us the gifts again

<chorus>

They'll awaken our souls
Till we remember again.

404. "Repetition"

Life Uncommon

A path for good
A path for fortune
A path for something new
A path to pick up something old
A path to walk bold
A path to walk alone
A path to walk side-by-side
A path to flow with
A path to cling to
A path to let go

Most of these paths I walk alone
Rarely it is that a stranger helps me
To find my way
At times I reach out for a lover
A time or two I've succeeded
This time I look to you
Not as you lay in my arms
But as you walk next to me, friend

405. "Resistancy"

Somehow, I failed you
I thought I could do better than I've done
But I was simply wrong
I tried so very hard
I thought I did
Yet, somehow I know that I failed you
I know that I could have done better
Tried harder
Stayed longer
Given just that much more
I thought
I had it all figured out
I knew, I knew
And yet...

And still...

I don't

I simply failed you
By resisting the temptation
To give you my heart.

406. "Revealed"

Marriage to Self
Is a truth that not even God can conquer
Marriage to one truth, your truth
Bond of eternity, strong with strength
Of life, of self
Any marriage that needs a contract- isn't a marriage
A bond by spirit
Appears as truth
No other bond will last
For time will come
And contract will fall
Marry your spirits
As one
And that truth cannot be undone

407. "Riddles"

In front of me sits a wall
Solid and sturdy- it may never fall
Taller than my little existence
It holds the key to my happiness
I feel the need to run at this wall
Break it down
Tear out the middle
Solve this forbidden riddle
The wall is so plain
White without a single stain
Bricks built up so high
Into it I just want to fly
How little we know ourselves
Sometimes

408. "Rings"
(dedicated to Shawn & Jess)

Like two finely interwoven rings
Shawn and Jessica's love bonds an eternity
From teenage lovers in high school
To adults sharing a romance
You've grown into the adults we now know
Simple love we watched grow

Life Uncommon

The unconditional affection always so evident
We wish for you both only the best
Time's already shown us you'll pass any test
Let the waves guide you safely along
Remember in times of hardship that together
Is where you are strong
Every storm has an eye, a calm, a peace
May you always find it together with ease

409. "Risen Heart"
(dedicated to several of my exes)

I remember what it was like when
The first of you left
Blue shrouded youth on a bus to Indiana
I knew I loved you and fell like bricks
When you never returned
I sunk like quicksand into hurt
I rose though
And the next to leave
Was my heart itself
Went to a prison and locked away
The love we had made
Recovery was slow
I rose though
The last before you left in illusion
Meaning he never really left at all
But was gone all the same
Of course it hurt, like arrow from bow
I rose though
Now once more another leaves
I'll listen to the strength within
I'll live happier than I've been
And time will show
The words I'll breathe once more
I rose though

410. "Robotic Discourse"

Two people may run fast and be allowed
To come together as a fast team
But they can never be lovers
For it was not love of anything
But a hobby that brought these two people together

Life Uncommon

It was just a team of machines- not hearts!

411. "Rocky Horror Picture Show"
(dedicated to Sarah, Gretchen & Renee)

Virgins who haven't seen the movie are tortured
Normal people act like alien transvestites
The audience makes fun of every line
Water guns are shot when it rains
Chains, weird makeup, and costumes
Freaky night

412. "Routines"

The daily routines of every human are futile
We lead machinery lifestyles
Although we think and analyze our movements
We are all robots
Procreating for no reason
Creating ways to keep human life going
Extended our years through science
But why?
My life will be, and is already, meaningless
I may help a child
My entire generation does nothing
They entertain and prolong life
But why?
For some reason I am alive
Expected to work every day
To make money so as to survive
Maybe even to have a family one day
Which is all futile
Conformity does not breathe
Happiness and love are fantasies
I get up in the morning
But why?
My life is an empty box processed
And stamped and shelved and stored
In a corner of a bedroom in a house in
A city in a state in a country
Somewhere, somewhere
Left for the wind – like all the other useless
Pieces of conformist junk!

Life Uncommon

413. "Rubber band"

The phone line stays dead
No ring
Not a sound
Silent tonight
Not even a breeze
My thoughts are inaudible
Crying inside
No one ever calls this late
Just darkness
Birds sleep now, smart
I think now
Remembering too much
Like how we first made love
Funny that was
We had to use a rubber band
Hilarious
Contemplating what to do tomorrow
Knowing I can't talk to him
See him
Love him
Plead with him
And definitely can't change him
Perfection is just a state of mind anyway
And that passes too
So on to tomorrow…

414. "Ruler of the Universe"
(dedicated to Michael)

To rule the universe
Tuck it in and hold it like a purse
Toss it around what a curse
To be the ruler
Of the entire universe
To smile at the sun as you dance around the moon
To wave to Pluto
As you swing on a star
To leap from sandy beach to dusty deserts
Its all yours
AND STUFF

Life Uncommon

415. "S (Simplicity)"

Yellow sunrises
Blue daffodils
Green trees
Bluebirds
Children giggling
The wind softly howling
Rain drops on my roof
A bonfire in the woods
Fairies dancing
Angels flying
Such beautiful treasures
That magic bring
The essential part
Of happiness

Lifting like maybe, loving like you, walking like ice, snuggling in truth.

416. "Sacrificial Rites"

what would you sacrifice to know yourself?
how many books would you read?
how many tales would you tell?
how many stories would you listen to?
how many hardships would you endure?
how many friendships would you survive even after they end?

what would you think of god?
what would you challenge in yourself?
what would you do if you had to go through one more heart ache?
what would you do if you had to fail every subject in school?
what would you do if you had to go through the toughest thing in your life?

no sea is easily sailed
no mountain easily crumbled
no hardship easily endured
no heart break easily healed

so what would you sacrifice to know yourself?

417. "Sadness"

Sadness lurks in my heart today

Life Uncommon

I feel desperate
Why can people be so cruel?
Who gave them the right to always rule?
I haven't done anything wrong
Unfortunately my heart isn't strong
Yes, I'm very emotional sometimes
But I haven't committed any crimes
All I want is good and pure
Is there no cure?
It isn't right
We shouldn't fight
Why?

418. "Sailboat Romance"
(dedicated to Stan)

I miss the moon
Like the sun misses the stars
As the water of the earth
Misses the sky up above
Like a fleeting smile
We're a thousand miles away
Dawn breaks
The river floats away
Wishing to the trees
For love centuries in the making
Simmering stories my heart tells me in rhyme
The lullaby that puts me to sleep
Kissing my dream-filled eyes
You are the sailboat
The lighthouse that brings me to
In the days of tomorrow
I'll still be loving you

419. "Sailor"
(dedicated to Stan)

So sailor, I love you
In my dreams
I love you during the day
I love you always
Have loved you always
Race with me to the stars
Sail my golden waves

Life Uncommon

The mirror is ours
We are one
I love you
I love your soul
I love your mind
I am in love with you
You will never lose me
I am bound to you sailor
And I love you dearly

420. "Saint Who?"

If we're meant to help people
Why are we picking up the scraps of the dead?
Isn't it possible to live with your head above water?
Without worry about every single paycheck?
Willing to be diviners for gods
Able to listen to the almost whispered hum
We understand what lays beyond
And hear what needs to be stopped
Our visions guide us
And yet we fail to be provided for
On any larger scale
Than barely scraping by
Us emotional cowards going into suicidal fits
The mentally drained get exhausted
The spiritually fearful go too far and know not when to hold back
The sexual beasts get so caught up they need that lust
And the physical ones get lost in the lines of feel
You lose us
When you need us most
Don't we deserve more?
Constant terror and fear and need is our sacrifice
Or punishment
For the reward of helping
And healing
So is the story of the saints
Not of Bethlehem
But of the modern day.

421. "School"

Pen in hand, notebook open, classroom filled with ready students
And in the teacher walks with a lesson in mind

Life Uncommon

And a semester of glory facing ahead
The time ticks down and it begins .....
School has started

422. "Sea of Happiness"

The sea of happiness is ahead of me
Lying there peaceful
Flexible to the command of the moon
Each wave holds a happiness all its own
When I swam in the sea I was like a wave
Happiness surrounded me
The tide rolled back onto the beach
Leaving me to lay still
And just glare
Unmoving I remember
The idealistic times
I once had
Will the tide ever pick me up again?

423. "Sea Reflections"

I feel like I'm on the edge of a cliff in Maine
Staring at the darkened sea
Seeing a reflecting moon
Half lit, if you will
Illusions all
A lighthouse spins a light for the boats
I stare out at my own reflections
Memories of happier you, happier me
And here I am
Setting free the ties that bind
For one year you have inhabited my mind
I'll always know how I felt
I'm sure I'll remember wanting to marry you
You'll fade
You've faded much already
I don't remember you clearly
Not even the small details I focused so intensely on
Things once so important-
Now like waves… they wash away
Away out onto some other sea
No longer meant to be with me
Goodbye, little things

Life Uncommon

424. "Seaman"
(dedicated to Stan)

Soul mate in the making
No memories to recapture
You comfort my soul
The challenger, the teacher, the mentor
And the lover
Hello beautiful, hello sailor,
It is true all that is true
For I am for you as you
Are for you
The never overbearing
Friend tried and true
Lyrical poems are all that is you
The most precious stone in the garden
Sail the heavens, dance on the
Moon, touches of an angel,
All in knowing you, you the
Friend who is tried and true

425. "Seasonal Beauty"

With the beauty of spring and the warmth of summer
With the colors of autumn and the passion of winter
Seasonal colors stream about me
Red, orange, yellow, and green
White for winter, yellow for spring

In the beauty of transition…of change…of season
I have been taught how to love
Growing each year with the cycles of nature as they turn once more

New beginnings leading way unto new passions
In color a sparkle is born and in the winter there is beauty

Our love is like this cycle
At times we are summer passionate and romantic
Sometimes we are autumn simply colorful

The cycles of nature
Swirls around us
Leaves of all hues

Life Uncommon

Like a flickering candle
We burn high and low

In you I have found a love and a partner
Someone to stick by me when the nights are cold and the days are long
Someone to understand me
Even when everything feels wrong
You stand like a guardian
Watching over and protecting me
Sometimes I feel like you are an angel sent down to me
To watch me drift simply as the sea

When times were tough, you were there
Holding my hand, holding me dear
Thank you for each kiss, for each touch
Each promise

Thank you for being you,
Thank you for being us.

426. "Seductress"

Look into my eyes
I'm not hiding any lies
Secrets of passionate tales
Firmness that never fails
I'm intrigued by seduction
And sometimes playful corruption
My body is smooth and gentle
These fingers of mine are instrumental
Do you like my teasing?
Is my touch pleasing?
Hair blowing in the wind
Wouldn't you like to get pinned
My eyes will seduce any man
Every boy is a fan
Picture your fantasy on a lake
I'll make it no longer fake
Intriguing I am to you
And to you a little kiss I blew
My red dress is flowing
Our dreams seem to be growing
Want me
Feel me

Life Uncommon

Let me seduce your soul
Feel your emotions flow
Come to my side
Watch the oceans tide
Its strong and powerful
Am I beginning to be a handful?
Throw those strong arms around my body
Just look into my eyes
See any secretive lies
Keep your dreams lasting
And those emotions blasting
Be seduced

427. "Seeds"

Seeds of change grow up all around me,
And the world is no longer the world I knew.

428. "Self-Acceptance"

Can I accept other people's inadequacies?
The lying and stealing?
All of it?
There is so much wrong
I don't know if I can even say I love or
Care about the people who love me
I don't know much anymore

Its like I have cancer of my beliefs and my life
Like this disease is eating my body
And I can't breathe
And I'd move but I don't know which way to turn
The thorns or the piercing needles
It is a terrible existence like this
I need to move, so badly

429. "Self-Hatred"

What do you do when you hate yourself and hate your life,
When your bogged down in so much pain and strife
When the evil world has turned black,
And the clock always ticks,
But you can never go back,

Life Uncommon

Dark forests of the night…
And you hate where you were,
Where you are,
And where you'll be,
Yesterday,
Today,
Tomorrow shall be,
Lacking in comfort,
Eternally?

430. "Senses of Yesterdays"

Listening to the sound of love
I dream of you, an innocent dove
My hair blows in the gentle word of dreams
Envisioning a fantasy surrounded by fantastical streams
Looking around I see nature
And I see everything that's pure
Shadows of yesterday remind me that I am strong
And that I'm not always wrong
Yet, I long for a man to understand
Maybe even one to carry me away to my fantastical land
Memories flow through my mind
Memories how all my friends were all so sweet and kind
I miss their silliness and weird habits
And my siblings, "stop- its"
On the campus I find my piece in a garden patch
A place of beauty that doesn't have a latch
My friends please know I am happy
Never sappy
But I miss you all
Don't worry—I know you'll be there if I ever do fall
And I will be there at all times
You can hear my heart through wind chimes
So know we'll always be side-by-side

431. "Sensitivity Kills From the Inside"

Remember that time when I told you I get hurt easily?
Would it have been so hard to listen just that once?
I know fragility's a joke
To you fine bloke
But let me tell you this sensitive girl
She's been on enough tilt-a-whirls

Life Uncommon

For a lifetime of dizziness and confusion
I just want a way out now, a way off this horrid ride
But I'm guessing its too late, I'm already dead inside.

432. "Seven"

7 deadly sins
High in times of crime, killing, murder, rape, pain, drug deals,
Gluttony,
Greed,
Sloth,
Wrath,
Pride,
Lust,
Envy,
Beaten children, molested innocents,
Incest so casually indiscreet you could trip on the agony of its sinful way,
Physical, sexual, verbal, even emotion abuse makes its way to us all,
Whether we're pimps, prostitutes, whores, sluts, nymphs, playboys, playgirls,
Or even if we're just normal every day people,
You find it everywhere
In your homes, your schools, your churches,
The downtown pick-up bars, the naughty late-night strip clubs, your family get togethers even reek of it
It can be find in simple places like rumors
The actions we take can be to any horrid extent
This is our world…
Now, look at it…do your eyes hurt?
Smell it…does your nose itch?
Listen to it…are your ears twitching?
Touch it…are your hands trembling?
How do you feel now?
Want to take a shower?
Rid yourselves of the grossness
Cleanse yourselves
Then when you're done…look up
Look into the mirror…Is everything all better?
Do you accept yourself?
What do you stand for?
Are you able to accept yourself as you are?
Do you?

Inspired by the movie "Seven"

Life Uncommon

433. "Seven Months Later"

After seven months my life ahead is becoming clearer and clearer
I will be happy
I am content with the way things are now
I'm single and free
At night I remember and love
Sometimes tears fall in remembrance
But I have to love me and my dignity more
My writings might all suck, but I love them
I am ink on paper and the blackness reflects me so perfectly

434. "Shadow of my heart"

One Love
One truth
I gave all I had
Now swimming through a pool of nothingness
My heart was in his hands
For only one man did I allow through my wall
He knocked it down
Walked through
Saw all that was me
One love
One truth
I gave all I had
He took a nap in my cave of warmth
And as his eyes opened
My dream ended
He is a shadow on both sides of my wall
My invisible ghost
Forever he holds in his hands all of me
For he was my…
One love
One truth
He was all I had
I swim on…

435. "Shadows"

Shadows of others lurk in my mind
Night crawlers creep onto my road
Darkness stands hovering over
Shall I go insane

Life Uncommon

No! I shouldn't move
Dammit all my tears are drained
Dark thoughts
Hard memories
All these good things they tried to do
Do it its ok
Hey life will get better
And you should put a smile on that face
Bullshit-
I don't listen to all of it
Hell-
All I am listening to is a knell
Fuck no-
Life isn't moving up its running low
Too many shadows are in my way
Is there anything left to look at?

436. "She"

She's everything to me
She's the birds and the rain
She's June and she's May
And I love her every single day
She's everything to me
Showing me everything I want to be
Oh, baby, you've got to believe me
Everything I am is all for you
This is exactly what I want to do
And forever I'll be true
Because darling, I only love you.

437. "She Tries"

She tries to drink away her problems
But she can't
'cuz when all the drinks are done
And all the bars are closed
The image comes undone
She's still just a girl
Who can feel
She's anything but numb
Afraid to take each step
Afraid of the damage done
So where has this gotten her

Life Uncommon

Another numb and coked down day
Wallowing in self-pity
She's got her life ahead of her
And each night the bar is there
She sits on her stool
And her soul is bare

Walk by her if you must
But its in her you can trust
Tell her a story
Share a memory
She'll see the glory
A dove by day
A wolf by night
She'll help you
Shed some light
Say a prayer
Buckle that belt
And enter the realm

438. "She, The Beauty In The Mirror"

Lost in a sea of troubles
Swimming to her destination
Pondering the wonders of the underworld
Roses of every hue
Fall at her feet
She is the princess of waters
Yet unseen
The keeper of tales
Enchanted in their own realm
She is the keeper
Of dreams
Sailors of beauty
Caverns to forsake the lonely
She's a mystifying experience
All her own
Whenever she wishes
Her dreams you shall own

439. "She'll Move On"

Misty rivers flow around me
Reflections of a younger you, a younger me

Life Uncommon

Hand in hand along cobblestone sidewalks of Paris
We'd fly across land and sea
No doubt you were meant for me
San Francisco rolled fog around our feet
We sipped iced coffee on the banks of Florida
And sang 'til all hours on the streets of New Orleans
Where are those kids? The younger you, the younger me
Drizzling rain surrounds and I remember the love I once found
Last night you told me you needed time
You need to find who you are
We grew up you and me
We stopped being the kids we used to be
Someday I'll know where we went wrong
But by then, you'll be gone.

440. "She's Looking For Herself"

I started to believe again
Something gave me hope
Gave me faith
Tumbling-truths roll by
I trip up my own steps
Losing my way
Finding a path
To a universe gone astray
Always searching for some eternal answer out there
Universal doors swirling empty words
Its hard to know how it all works
She's gone to find herself
Out there in the universe
Candles flicker
I stare endlessly
The moon shares no secrets
Alone I hop back on the never-ending train
Not knowing how to subdue the pain
Mist floats in and I'm back on the road
To finding me again.

441. "Shoes"

These black old pieces of leather stick and stick
Holes are everywhere
The once handsome young shoes are now old and ready
I meander through the woods

Life Uncommon

Savoring sweet memories with these shoes
Rock climbing on Mt. Charleston years ago
Running after Elizabeth while frolicking in the fields
Elizabeth and I danced the night away once
These shoes
Old now
The leather fades
And I am old too

442. "Shoreside Blues"

Oceans apart from the love I hold inside
Alone I sat, Alone I cried
He left on a mission he said
I don't know why times change as they do
I've never quite comprehended the sad but true
Ten years ago we loved so strongly
Mountains moved in our honor

Slowly the guitar strums...

Lilting melodies so blue
Somehow this is the melody that reminds me of you
I remember the times we ran along the beach
Kissing under the stars
Nothing out of our reach
We made love to the sound of the shores
Back then you were mine, I was yours

Every secret shared
Every dream together we dared
I loved every minute then
I lived so happily...so free
Back when I had you, you had me

Then one day the winds changed
You went, you were gone
Silent tears, hearts so strong
Why these things happen I suppose
I'll never know
But I'll love you forever and all of time
Remembering how once
I was yours, and you were mine.

Life Uncommon

443. "Should I Press Charges?

…Sure we can go out tonight
…Sure you can come over a while
…Sure we can go out again
…Sure I'll go steady with you
…Sure you can kiss me softly
Oh, how naïve I was to have said "sure" so many times
Such bad memories just like noisy, annoying chimes
Why did I lead him on?
I keep hearing his name
It won't ever leave my head
I almost wish I were dead
Yes, its true he…
He…
I'll never forget trying to become free
He took my happiness away
But I won't press charges
I can't
I don't know
What should I do?…
He should be put behind bars
After all he's made my life feel crashed
I may press charges
My life is already ruined
No, I can't do it
But if I don't another disaster will be lit
Help…
Why did I say sure?

444. "Shutting Out the Light"

Thunder, Thunder, Thunder Rumbling in your ears as you try to sleep such little dears
and you run from the noise into some type of paranoia and you never get anywhere
because it crashes again and your entire body shakes and you look into the eyes into
someone scared frightened by the crashing thunderous booms that wake up everyone and
all are sent fleeing from room to room and then the poisonous noise stops and things
smooth out and you just hear the drip drop of the drizzling pour outside your home and
you wonder why you're surrounded yet feel all alone and the darkness falls and candles
are lit but you move out of the room to go and sit somewhere in a corner away from the
fight wishing to be anywhere but near the light for you'd rather put up a fight with
someone than sit in that illuminating light that only scares you into a deeper fright and
you fall asleep.....drip, drop, drip, drip, drip, drop and it falls and you sleep in a
meditational type of thought enters your dreams and the screams of the few are lost on

Life Uncommon

your ears which have been deafened by the peace you've found away from the fears, away from the screams, away ..away....

445. "Sigh of Relief"
(dedicated to Jimmy Snuka aka "Superfly")

Old man sitting across from me
Sharing stories of times, of mystery
He sits in front of me with the heart of a lion,
The eye of a tiger
A man
He's lived his life, and I've barely begun mine
I felt so old two hours ago, and feel like a newborn baby coming home now
He, the ever elusive man with a heart so open
He sits in a truth and speaks in a rhythm only he knows
He knows himself as a missionary and me as a student
Telling me how, "Nobody can make you number one, but you"
Did I listen?
Or did the words roll away,
Like thunder from rain?
I'm not sure...
Seems like the wisest come along the very second I lose my way
I wonder where I've been when I'm gone
A voice rings clear
"Where are you?"
"Here."
"What time is it?"
"Now"
Simplicity so simple
Polaroid snapshots to capture the moment for eternity
My hands like the map of a grandmothers toil
The skin I shed each year, as does a snake
Something in me is ready to wake
"Take care of number one" they say
So hard to remember what is with us every day
Mirror strikes back a truth, I am a candle,
And you, the light that guides me through
Love, like rain, drops into eternity
Like blood to vein
I called heaven on the phone last week
And today my friend has wings
Spoke with a master tonight
Processing all the new truths
Like a rolodex trying to organize myself back
Back to normal

Life Uncommon

Back to what works
Back, back, back
He also told me that I have an angel inside me
Asked me, "Do you understand that?"
I replied, "Yes."
He asked, "Do you?"
And then told me that it is for me to figure out
Half-heartedly I agreed
I'm sure I'll understand in time
I am reminded that if you are going to do something, do it all the way
No short stops, No cuts and curves and simple ways around it, "Just do it",
And do it all the way
No left turns when you need to go right
No downs when you need to go up
Just go
And don't look back
He saw a truth in me when I said of how I only trust me and god
He told me I know, and told me how we each have our gifts
I suppose right now I only hope that I know how to use mine
And that I become the person I am meant to become
Tonight I shall sleep like an angel in the flesh
And tomorrow...Here, Now
So much to learn, so much to process, so much, and I'm so human
Which means I've got time
The gate to the kingdom of god is inside us
And the only way to get there
Is through faith, trust, truth, and by being you
I must know me to be me
He told me never to let anything hurt me, ever
If only I could follow that advice
Its so hard to feel so much in such a little amount of time
Such a pressure when you fear the unknown
Fear the days of tomorrow and the truths of the right now
"Where there's a will, there's a way"
So much I forget, so easily too
But I'm here right now, and I get it
Right here, Right now, I get it
And that says a world, an eternity, in an instant.

Special thanks to Dan Millman and his book "The Way of the Peaceful Warrior" from
which excerpts of this poem came from.
Inspired by the book "Way of the Peaceful Warrior" by Dan Millman

Life Uncommon

446. "Silent Peaceful Death"

Who else can I talk to about being raped?
My family history?
Who else cares about my deep thoughts and feelings?
He might not have ever cared but he listened
Not all the time but enough
I wanted sweet kisses goodnight
To be held around the waist
To be treated as someone loved and needed
To actually be needed
To actually be loved
Maybe I want too much but now I can never have it
No one else will probably even be slightly right for me
He was it but even with all that he was
I was never happy
Always upset
No "I love you's"
No feelings
No long term commitment but full trust
But now I know how untrue that is
He never trusted me
He knew me…he studied
He stalked and he learned
I tripped and he remembered every second
He learned from my downfall
His uprising talent
Will I always suck like this?
Being nothing
Living without love
Without hope

Destined to go nowhere
But maybe to sleep and maybe sleep will bring a silent peaceful death
Yes…that should be my goodnight

447. "Silent Speaking"

Friends
Sit over there
Burning from the warmth of the
Fire
Calm, but empty
And just One sits here
With me

Life Uncommon

We are small
Together
Tiny
Easily invisible
Light turned
Blanketing us
Without shadow
We are free
And it is only
Her and I
On this
Silent
S
I
  L
   E
   N
    T
     Papery
      D
       A
        Y.

448. "Simple"
(dedicated to Alex)

Simple tears shed on a truth
Even cosmic attraction is no match
For human rejection
Love can bind you up and twist you
Get you believing in knots
And still you feel alone
When the man next door
Doesn't see your heart as home
Simple tragedies happen here and now
A beautiful man with a smile to kill
Compassion of a king
And love of the world
Simple little me
Trying to find footing on soggy sand
If only you could see my love
Even then, would you even reach out your hand?

449. "Singer"

Life Uncommon

Now is the time before I sleep
Where I feel most alive
For in that forgetful time
That houses the dead
And the sleep of night
I may drift away
To sleeplessness
And try as I might
I cannot forget the truths I find
The darkness that brings
Inner peace, comfort
Off in the daze I see
A sea of trouble
A sea of woe
But, alas
I must travel tell
Not in tales
But in honesty bestow
The intricacy of a cloudless sight
The place inside
A swan takes flight
Upon a sea in the sky
Where dolphins rise
And fish swim high
Its the holder of the castle
Of which youth brings
And its during this time
That the moon sings

450. "Skeletons"

The wretched beasts
Unearthlike creatures
Beings that taunt you
Dreams that maim you
You wake up hoping for something new
Ready to grasp on to any parcel
And they trample on your every fantasy
Take your wishes and put them in the ground
Stand six feet over and dance on the grave they made
They laugh at your smiles and hate all that you do
No respect for that which is you
And what joy do they get from this?
Do they sleep better at night knowing they've tormented your very soul?

Life Uncommon

Do they get richer?
Do they all of a sudden become beauty pageant queens?
What? What is it? What is it that they get?
Your home, your clothes, your bed and your faith?
Well I say this is still my home and this is still My life
So trample as you will, but it is life I choose
And you may NOT take it from me
These are my hopes and mine they will remain
So just kiss your stardrops goodbye, dear friend
For you are sailing to a place with no end

451. "Sleep"

Last night I had a yearning for sleep
My alarm clock couldn't have been set more times
Over and over
Each time getting my lazy ass up
But it wasn't until the last moment
I got up. Procrastination
Lack of sleep does that to me
Tired. Exhausted.
Yep, that's how today begins

452. "Sleeping"

Tonight I will sleep alone
Without light
No arm around me
Just a kitten nearby
One stuffed animal
To comfort me
Once again
I am always so lonely
But in my dreams
Oh- there I love
And I live
He kisses me
And silently knows me
But truthfully I am
Simply
And
Sadly
Alone

Life Uncommon

453. "Sleeping Stars"

In a bubble the water falls
Coming down in waves
Leaving no room for flowers to bloom
But feeding the roots all the same
"Oh, I kept the first for another day," Frost proclaimed
Knowing that fall gives beauty its very own name
Somehow in this illustrious fame
Where singers dance in the dazzling rain
I've died and been reborn again
Among the stars and moons that orbit the earth
I find myself alive in this rebirth
Sheltered no more and never before
Feeling so free
Finding the only road that really led to me
So tonight when the stars come out to shine
Tonight it'll be me to sing them to sleep
With my very own lullaby

454. "SMAERD"

My dreams consist of one bad image after another
And the good images are lies
Like the cute Mexican entering my dreams
Has anything to do with reality
He is not attracted to me
No one is attracted to me
I've given up on men entirely
I've spent the last nine years giving them a chance
I could just be alone and probably will be
But I'd like to see if women work
If anything could work...with me

455. "Smiling Star"

Twinkle, twinkle
Light and serenity
Beautiful
I shine in your sky
Brightness
And you smile

Life Uncommon

456. "Smoke Me"

He twists his bony fingers around me
I am compelled to yell in agony
He has the power to break me into nothingness
And I am just a weakling
There is so much to me
But he is this overbearing evil
And I will probably be crushed
Done with
And shut away from all happiness.

457. "Snake"

Snake
Bite
Fierce
Teeth
Cold
Eyes
Cruel
Killer
Mean
Fierce
Big
Tongue
Hiss
Scary
Snake
Ouch
Eyes
Cold
Scary
Eyes
Kill
Eyes
Flashing
No
Kill
Snake
No
Thrill
Scary
Snake

458. "Snow"

Snow
Winter
Cold
Chilly
Frozen
Ice
Slippery
White
Pretty
Innocent
Smooth
Smooth
Innocent
Pretty
White
Slippery
Ice
Frozen
Chilly
Cold
Winter
Snow

459. "So this is Life"

All my ideals are gone
Crushed, smashed, burned, dead
Love is a fallacy
Trust is inevitably betrayed
Care gets twisted
Friendship is a weakness
Loneliness-the easy way-
Fucking sucks
So this is life
A bottle of shit
And nothing to clean up the vomit of it all
I am not impressed
If this is what I've been waiting for
I should have chosen death over liberty
Fuck-up
Next time,
Next time I'll get it right

Life Uncommon

460. "Soaring Souls"

Two different worlds
Be them houses or neighborhoods
Be them countries or entities
Holders of lovers
Sparrows and doves
Eagles and falcons
Dressed in golden garbs
Eyes of romance
Lips tasting of sundance
Drip sweet memories
And drown me with your fantasies
Pick me up
Bring me forth
Fly me away to that place I know from my mind
Where the fairys swarm
Laughter surrounds
Mountains sailing through blue skies
Fly me there dear lover
So that we can forsake it all
Let the worlds die away
Houses turn to dust
Neighborhoods vanish from my sight
Countries dwell in lands unknown
Our identities shall no longer tear us apart
Love be felt
Tears be cried
Together we'll fly
You and I

461. "Sold You Out"

I had this dream once
But I forgot it
I had this house once
But I got up and left it
I had this dog once
But she died
I had this family once
But I moved away
I had this talent once
But I didn't want to play

Life Uncommon

I had me once
But I think I sold me yesterday

462. "Soldier Off to War"

"I must leave you now, sweet Adrianna. Go off into territories of thine own enemy.
Please wait here for it will be until I shed my last tear that I shall be only yours…hush
now."

Crying alone now I remember these words with such sorrow poor soldier always tender
in his affection his voice echoes my name again and again Oh, how I remember that
night

He ran across those acres when the sun had already gone to sleep those legs just ran and
ran arms came to wrap around me but my dear old father had trapped me inside that
wretched tower I was trapped like an animal father held the key and my poor soldier
just cried not defeated he rushed to the castle wall and climbed like a cat he was by
my side so quickly fingers bleeding from the climb but his only pain was in leaving me
he loved me so and I he I remember his hair straight and brown eyes of endearment
and he whispered such sweet things before he left time must have gone by quickly for
my soldier went back down into the territory of beasts he left me with those words

463. "Solemnly"

I don't know why I feel for him like I do
I've heard his list of things going on in his head
And yet somehow I can't get myself to grasp it
Sure, alcoholism is a road to ruin
Pot keeps you high and out-of-tune
Suicidal thoughts on a one way train to hell
Well, sure I can see his point and all
But I also see a light
A crescent-shimmering
He may not know my love
Nor how deep my care goes
But I know it in the gentle whispers
Of Autumn's evening
I feel the striking blow of that rejecting 'no'
Strength carrying me through
Tunes my only solace when all else leaves
Why he has to be so beautiful...
Completely eludes me
Compassion, love, kindness for all
None of it saved for himself

Life Uncommon

None at all
The gentle creature of beauty
I'd be with if I had half the chance
But, alas, he in his words has rejected me
Time to stand tall and strong
And I suppose in this October sun, move on
God willing life's wheel will spin
And I'll be set free again

464. "Some Days"

Some days you wish you were someone else
Anyone but you
Some days you wish you could escape
To some other planet, some other place
Some days you wish you knew which direction to go
"As above, so below"
And still you are lost without a friend in sight
Directionless map
Compass-less night
And you wonder which path will be right for you
Dark and twisty
Or straight and lonely
And you reach out to tomorrow
But yesterday grabs you by the waist
And as you close your eyes
My, what a waste

465. "Something Beautiful"

Loves lost on blue tides
Purple dawns
Can never embrace
The hero he was
Valiant and charming
A true lover
Chained to a cell
Only in his mind
To love sometimes
Is better than to write
He closed himself in so tight
Nothing could free him
Of the agony
Of love

Life Uncommon

Lost on blue tides

466. "Sometimes at Night"

Sometimes at night,
You can tell,
The Goddess is there,
The air is different
The clouds…a bit stiller
It is then,
That you can feel her
When the moon is half lit
Leaves fall silently
The breeze blows differently
Your heart is filled with hope
And a spark inside is lit
These are the nights
She watches nearby
Breezes sing their lullaby
And you rest easier
For you know,
She is there to protect you,
To keep you,
And to bless you.

467. "Son to Mother"

Well, Mother, I'll tell you
Life for you ain't been no crystal stair
I've seen the tacks
And splinters
Even the torn up boards
Its been bare
But all the time
You've been climbin' on

Its my turn
I won't fall
Even when I come across tacks
And splinters
Even the torn up boards
I won't let it be bare
Even if it ends up
As life without even one crystal stair

Life Uncommon

468. "Soul Mates"

The perfect reciprocal
The mirror image of my own
That which is either so like me that we can barely see the difference
Or that which is so opposite that it fits me perfectly
They all fit in a way
They are all loved by me
And I admire each and every one

469. "Sparrows"
(dedicated to Alex)

Like two sparrows without a home
We found each other, found some hope
Lifting up our wings
For the first time in ages
Let go of some old fears
We found solace in each other
Time hurts the already wounded soul
What happened to the childlike love we shared?
How did we get so far from
Where we once were?
Are you the one who got away?
Or the one who'll come back to stay?
I know not your truths or past
But I'll never forget the warmth
Of your hands
If the moon should set on our love…
I'll strengthen up
You'll go your own way

Once so surely in love
Just look at us now
The hope that sparked each other to life
One night asked me to be your wife
Sometimes dreams come true
And believe it or not,
I'm still in love with you
Once so surely in love
Just look at us now…
Will I go it alone
Without the soaring sparrow?

Life Uncommon

470. "Special"

Smile at the weak
And laugh at the lonely
Yell at the poor
Cackle at the rich
Giggle at the victims
Chuckle at the battered
This is the way
Of all that is shattered
Demented and uncouth
Wretched but true
Be the one in a million
Who does not do these things
The one in a million
Who happiness brings
You need no followers
You need no leaders
Just be yourself
'cuz you're already special

471. "Spirals"

Poetry flows
Pulling the reader
Into its in depth, Descriptions
Sometimes making you...
Look further into...
The black and white words

472. "Spirit's Embrace"

Have you ever loved somebody so much that you feel them in your blood, in your veins?
That's how much I love him
But I don't even know who he is, just the pain
It riles and winds inside me like a snake without a name
Its the wind pulled into an abyss of unknowns, water risen all around
Tides that bring me to a place with no name
The earth should ground me, hold me, embrace me
If it does I am unaware
The passion that comes from fire feels faint, weak, near death
If anything it is spirit alone that is holding me now
Firmly, gently

Life Uncommon

Embracing me.

473. "Spirituality"

What is spirituality?
Is it believing in God?
Believing in death and its aftermath?
Does hell exist?
Or heaven?
Is there eternal life?
Have we lived before?
If you never sin- are you still spiritual, or just good-natured?
Is going to church all it takes?
Does wearing a cross make you a spiritual seeker?
I think for me, spirituality, cannot be found in a book,
Or a building, or a belief
It is the vibration in every word you speak
Every breath you take
It is the energy you emanate
When I feel alive and whole
When the parts of me connect
I am then spiritual

474. "Sponge"

Go where the wind takes you
Follow the sunsets, let them lead you
Listen to the rhythm of the crickets
And the silence of the ground
You'll find new things at each turn
While you hurt at leaving the past,
Know the future awaits you,
With only greatness in store
The key already joined with lock
Is knowledge that this choice, no doubt-
Is right
So follow the yellow brick stones
And allow yourself to be home.

475. "Standing Stone"

I am stone
Steel in magnificence

Life Uncommon

Hit me
You'll never hurt me
Slam me
And I will still stand
Not water nor rain
Can move me
Erect with confidence
Incinerate me
And my image is anchored
In the streets
Your home
And even in your bedroom
Your mind can't shut me out
For I am the perfect wall

476. "Star Truths"

Have you ever loved someone the way you love the rain?
The way you feel when all that pain washes away?
Like the cleansed feeling of a sea salt bath
Fresh and new like daises growing straight to you
Swimming guppies singing you a tune
Likened berries bringing you red
Wishes come true that you long ago said
Thinking the moon didn't hear you
And the stars must not have heard you that night
They listen though those twinkling vixens
Tricking you into thinking they weren't fixen
One morning when the sun has just come up
The dawn will rise
Singing your dreams lullabies
When your eyes flutter awake
That is when the wish will take
Unfolding throughout the day
You'll remember the wish, remember the way
And when the moontime comes about
With joy in your heart you'll want to shout
Praises to the lord and lady that be
Goddess bless the hearts of all we see!

477. "Stepping to Love"

Walking along the glistening sands
Tide rolling in from the West

Life Uncommon

Hearts gently uplifted
In loves embrace
First encounters
Sweeping us away
Into a world oh, so magical
So stunningly real
With possibilities- endless
And the truth, wrapped, in us
The first unsure steps of love...

478. "Stiff"

I am stiff and dead trying to hold on to the one happiness I have
Him

479. "Story for A Willow"

Everyone has a story
What's yours?
Isn't it funny how in the movies people just know
When the love of their life is around the corner?
Isn't it funny how everything seems picture perfect
And time efficient in the movies?
And in the books there is always that 'one true love'
Circumstances are all that keeps them apart
But how does one know their own love?
How does one know that the other 100 lovers,
Weren't the real one?
How does one know shit about their love life?
Movies, TV, music, books,
They all have us fucked into thinking love is simple
Love is about as simple as eating only with a toothpick,
And no knife
But we ramble on
Rock rolls us
And we dream

As eternal dreamers always do.

480. "Stranded Insanities"

Love bubbles like butterflies
And truth circulates like numb

Life Uncommon

Try me mister
Just try to inflict that thumb
Carry your own weight young man
Time to grow a beard
Kiss me sinister
Color me mad.

481. "Strange Land Greetings"

In the tests of time
Swirls of rhyme
Thoughts of kindness
Going a long way
Helping a stranger
Find their troublesome way
A hand across the street
A pat on the back
A simple hail to call them a cab
Its so easy to be the helping hand
In a time, In a land
Where peace just takes
Simple utterances
"How are You's"
And "Can I help You's"
Said to a stranger brightens the darkest cloud
Lifts a shroud holding them from the light
Finds a way, finds a might
A will inside strumming up
Like the snake of laughter letting us know
Who we are, how to grow
Simple gestures at hand
Smile to a stranger
You see?
Its not such a strange land.

482. "Streamlined Thoughts"

My heart is torn between two shores
That of yesterday and of tomorrow
Sometimes I don't even understand
I know I have to heal within
The time has come for me to go home
To the inner child, the inner truth
I believe you may find yourself

Life Uncommon

Somewhere similar, sometime soon
Thank you for your words
Thank you for the question
My answer not meant to hurt
Is simply the honest truth
That friendship is all I'm prepared for
Loose ends I'm tangled between
So I must do what is right for you
And for me

483. "Strike"

A movie struck into my heart tonight
And brought into my sadness a little light
The earth has not currently experienced a deep impact
And all our skyscrapers are still in tact
The statue of liberty stands tall and free
And so do the powers that be
Tonight I cried wondering about you and me
Lonely nights like these will let me miss you
Human nature is different for so many
Some have sacrificed their lives for others
Some will never again see their brothers
Some were once mothers
Humanity struck me deeply tonight
My life may be meaningless inside
Yet, my love for others I will never hide
I will remember all those that have passed away
And those who have gone astray
Thank you all for being so dear
I love my siblings dearly
And in my dreams see their smiles clearly
Thank you for leaving the world as is!

484. "Striving to Be the Gum on the Bottom of Someone Else's Shoe"

I can watch a movie or some television show
And point at the screen and say, "I want that"
I know I want more
I'm sick of the guy with endless problems…I want someone to take care of me
Someone who can deal with the baggage
Someone who will find out I'm broken and understand
Someone who will hear I've got mental problems now and not run out the door
I can't remember what it was like before depression

Life Uncommon

I've forgotten what it was like not to have anxiety
I guess it feels like I've just always been this way
I want more passion…more romance…more love
And not the sappy oh we're in love shit…The real kind
The kind that you wake up for in the morning and that you go to bed dreaming about
I used to think wanting someone who could hack it wasn't asking for much
Turns out I was wrong – it's like asking for a gold mine in your own backyard
I didn't know that then and some parts of me don't even know it now
I don't always want to be the strong one…I don't want to fucking smile
I don't want to act like it's all okay because the truth is-- its not and god only knows if it ever will be again
I don't want the best looking guy or the most well-dressed one either
I want the guy who can be sensitive to me as well as himself
I'm sick of the arrogant fuckers who know everything in the world
Is it really so hard for two people to encourage each other?
All these movies…all these wonderful stories and I never had that
I had the casual relationships but nothing that made me feel so alive
Nothing ever that strong and you know what? I still gave my all
Because I believed it was this great romance at the time but it wasn't
It never was…So what's a girl to do?
Have friends to hang out with-- right? Maybe I'm sick of their chatter
Maybe I'm sick of hearing how their lives are wonderful
Maybe I don't give a fuck about their dozen plus boyfriends
I'm sick of everyone thinking they've got something great
I don't want to be there when they realize its not even half of what they expected
I don't want to see their faces when he finally cheats on her or lies to her continuously or makes her feel like a queen and then like a slave
I don't want to see them go through that and I don't know if I can go through it again
I try to look for all the signs…I try to figure out what I want but I never quite do
I never quite get what I want

485. "Stubborn Scorpio"
(dedicated to Nick)

From pool fights to romance
From friendship to love
From pain to joy
We've seen it all
You've been there to catch me
When I took the fall
You've been there to sturdy me
When I seem to lose it all
I've been here,
And I will continue to be
Some friends

Life Uncommon

They do not leave
We've seen it, seen so much
Trust in what you know.

486. "Sturdy Strange"

The unwavering rock
May waver beneath the skin
He might smile yet hold that light within
And while he knows I am there for him
Sometimes he wonders
Sometimes love wins
The answer's always elusive
And the power never abusive
And still he sits and ponders
Still he strains and wonders
He believes in the truth
Yet wanders around claiming to be so uncouth
Strong and tender
Bold and glorious
Ask me dear if you can trust me
And my answer is
You already know this.

487. "Suicidal Thoughts Runaway"

I do not have any real friends
Meaning there is no one that I can,
Speak freely and openly to every day
I do not trust any one
A reason to live- I'm without
Forced to give up
My last joy- gone
I hate superficial people
Conformist jobs with no purpose
Survival is not supposed to be selling useless-
Gadgets to wealthy fucks who don't need them!
I have no purpose
And so I should and maybe even shall commit suicide
Die! Die! Die!

488. "Suicide"

Life Uncommon

Cry for it
Because its crude
Scream because its terrifying
Help the lonely
Be an angel
Because without you their heart fades
Their soul goes up to heaven
And their body just lays there in blood
Yeah, look at it
Its disgraceful
So are you if you don't stop it
Stop it
Stop the horror
The horror of
Suicide

489. "Suicide Note"

I think if my attempt to commit suicide goes well
There will be some questions asked
Why did I do it? Life is pointless
I have no reason or purpose to live
I escape pain and that is a purpose for death
Were you loved? Of course
Did you love? I love each person I know
Extremely love them
For watching out for me
For supporting me
I wish them success and love
They've all been role models in my life
Showing me where to go
I have always wished for us to be closer
I doubt we know each other enough to know what to say
If only we took the time
I wish I could have stayed forever
In some happy place
I would have
I wanted…
I miss those times…

Grow up
Care about you first…care about others later

The friends I never had…I guess you're busy
That is too bad…I really did like you

Life Uncommon

The lover, but only in dreams

Fantasies are a crying sign

Well I'm finding some stuff out
I don't want to see tomorrow

Find your hope and live life, not just live, but Live

I love a man
I will never get and never had

I love writing and want more than I can afford

490. "Summer"

The summer has come back to bring happiness for all
This bright season is as colorful as fall
All of us teens think we know it all
We can't be broken or heaven forbid, fall
We are strong, hopeful, and the future for all
While standing we will be strong and tall
This is our summer to be young and free
Even a tree will be inspirational to our young hearts
Our strength will hit the weak like darts
But over all- it will go right
From now on our future nights will be
Hopeful
Experiences
That
Will
Make
This
A
World
Of
Nature and hope
The true future is us!

491. "Sun Rising"

Oh my,
The sun is rising once more

Life Uncommon

I can feel the daylight throbbing for more
The house of night
And the days of yore
It is there that I live
And I'd love to live once more
If I could just for a moment
Stop all time
Think about it all
With the toss of a dime
Heads I move forward
Tails time stands as it is
I don't know which I'd rather have
But, perhaps, both wins.

492. "Sunset Rain"

When the rain falls
I hear you crying
Its your tears I see
as the ocean daunts my feet
You see I think of you
and shall for eternity.

493. "Sunshine"

At nine on a fine Sunday a young child sees bright sunshine
The young child calls out a rhyme of the times
He says, "The sunshine is mine"
Yet we have to tell the child
Time is short for the sun
When night comes and day goes
That sunshine is too high for us to climb, reach, or try for
Hard to define, explain, reveal
Which is why this young child will never call out, "The sunshine is mine"
For now he knows no matter how high he climbs, how much strength he reaches with,
Or how much he tries he will never have this undefinable thing

494. "Surreal Twists"

In a place that's not a place
In a riddle that's not a rhyme
In a cavern that holds nothing
In an abyss filled with time

Life Uncommon

In a secret that holds nothing unknown
In a work of art without any strokes
Its a painting without picture
Its the illusion that is truth

A disbelief without certainty
She is the one for you, my dear
She is the dove
And you the eagle
It is her whispers you hear
And her calls you should answer
Her gowns flow through your dreams
You should see her
Clearer with each thought
Just reach out your hand
So she can hold you all life

495. "Sweet Twenties"

It's a curious thing what happens to a woman
Twenty-two years of age
Alone in house
For it is not home without family
Working her way
Mindlessly weaving herself into the web
She's modern enough
To have technology at her hands
And she is no illiterate either
Boy she has many a novel
While the videos and novels
And other technological advancements
Lie at her feet
She sits and ponders
What it is that life means
Quiet shack
She rocks in her chair
In a symphony of silence
Rekindling old flames
But only in mind
Thinking of the treasures
That truth and honesty bring
She's a vixen by any mans means

496. "Sweetheart"

Life Uncommon

(dedicated to Dmitry)

When you're hurt I cry
When you rage my hand forms a fist
When you're tender I tingle
Inspiration lost
Bring it back
Love can exist
In my mind
Or maybe even in ours
One heart
One love
Stronger than hate
Fierce enough
To defeat
All
Show me
Arm in arm and hand in hand
Love in us
A need in me
I didn't know existed
A need in us
In love.

497. "Swinger"

In the tattered forests of my heart
Swinging are the branches of my youth
Lying on the lilies of tomorrow's hope
Faith, being, perhaps, the strongest word of all
Settling down to memories
Of yesterday's youth
Swinging today on the branch of my own truth.

End Act I, Scene 11

498. "Swirling Petal"

Out above the lake
Is a single petal
Some flower shed it just a moment before
Now it wanders
The blue waves unaware of the presence
A beauty just drifting

Life Uncommon

The waves flow soothingly
Calm like the stars
She just goes on and on
Fearful of falling into the water
But as gravity is her enemy
She tumbles down
Lying helplessly for a moment
Then she is gone

499. "Symbolism"

My poems symbolize my feelings
I try to write the truth
But not everyone will always see the meanings

Right now I feel many things
I feel torn between two gifts
Love is a word almost tossed around
The truth is not easily found
I only love one
Yet have strong feelings towards another
Hurt, loved, understood, and hidden
My life is tangled up
Can you understand me?
My feelings are symbolized
To an exact point
Can you see them?

500. "Teardrops of An Angel"

The angel cries
as she feels that hope inside of her die
and try as you might to show her its alive
her ears don't hear the words spoken by you and I
and so I reach to you my son holding you close
trying to let you know I was wrong
and let you know you're not alone
I wish I could reach the angel as well
my heart loves you both
as a mother does her angel and son

501. "Tears"

Life Uncommon

Often I just burst into tears
Lonely in my surroundings
I hate it
Even deny it
Pretend I am liked
Should be loved
That my secret admirer is really just around the corner
Sometimes I'll act cute just in case
Somehow his head never pops out though
So I think
Analyze
I concoct a great solution
As I execute
I think again
Without response, as always, I shift back into the loneliness

502. "Teen Orphan"
(dedicated to Nate)

He sits on his porch smoking away
Waiting for the leaving of the day
Watching pitifully down the street
For some lass that he'll never greet
His cigarette pack rolled up nice and neat
Sitting in cotton 'til he needs that treat
Hours wasting away day after day
And inside he's nothing but a stray
Waiting for a home to open up
Tell him "come inside lost pup"
But that won't happen tonight
And nothing stops the fright
That inside he feels so strong
Dusk will set and before long
Stars will rise and he'll close his eyes
And he'll hope someone will sing him lullabies
But he'll sleep alone as he always does
Wrapped in blankets that never warm his feet
Lonesome as always is his endless feat
And when he rises again in the morn
He'll be the boy still torn
That street will lay empty as it did before
And still he'll wait for something more

503. "Temperance"

Life Uncommon

(dedicated to Will M.)

Sitting in empire
Building in truth
Earnestly seeking
As the youth
To find the reasons
The answers and
The core
To find who he is
And search for more
The ears of a listener
Silently attuned
Finding his strength
Under the full moon
Time holds no energy
For a man wrapped in timelessness
Shrouded in cleverness
Gifted with talent
Learning the chords
From the source within
He strums the truth
As it comes to him
Balancing our unity
As only Temperance can
He's the front line
Singing Guitar Man.

504. "Terrorism"

Tragedy strikes not far from home
A few thousand miles, that's all
I slept in my bed calmly
While planes crashed into twin towers
The pentagon stands
Yet, it stands in ruins
Victims of the crashes calculate to 266
I slept in my bed
And knew nothing of all of this
Woken up by a phone call
"It's fucking Armageddon" he said
I knew not what it meant
And to tell you the truth,
I still may not grasp the horror
Yesterday America was a strong home

Life Uncommon

Today America is a scared land
What will we be tomorrow?
I pray in silence
And I hope for better hours
But I expect worse
I expect a doomsday for days to come
So while I wait, alongside my fellow Americans
I wish to tell them
That they are loved
And to look to the next few days with rays of hope
But also to proceed cautiously
For in the face of tragedy
One must be aware
Arguments will erupt
Fights will occur
And more importantly
human kindness will prevail.

505. "Test"

Yes, another test
They never seem to stop coming
Multiple choice confuses the fuck out of me
What challenge is left?
Open note
I'm unprepared
But I pass the test I'll betcha
Simple as that
No brain power
God made it this way
I can't change it
Its just the way it goes

506. "Thank You"
(dedicated to Alex)

I wonder if when you left you took a piece of me
Or, I, of you
I guess it doesn't matter
It was experience
Do you know what its like to be left?
Do you assholes ever care?
In that self pity place inside your oh-so-tormented soul, do you know?
Do you get that it goes beyond "I'll only hurt you"?

Life Uncommon

Your lies so good for you, you hide behind them
You forget the hurts that you stained others with
You suck for it, ya know?
I needed you I thought
I was wrong
Somehow I've lived, I've managed, I've moved on
Thanks for your support and letting me know you were really gone
Thanks for saving me the hope and the pain
Thanks for having the ability to care

507. "That is Love"

I know what love is
Its that feeling that chokes in your throat
So that you can hardly breathe
You might turn to walk away
But you'll never leave
You have a home now
Burning passions stream through you
He brings to you heaven, the stars, and goddess
Even the moon
Outside both so different
Inside so identical nothing could tell you apart
It's the feeling that shakes you
Moves you
And finally becomes you

508. "The Balcony"
(dedicated to M.M.)

Time to talk
In a deadened silence
Try to speak
But the words won't come
Fear of loneliness
And unfinished thoughts
Need to tell all
Or none at all
Compassion they give
Freely and at will
But nothing comforts
The inner ill
Confused and lacking stability
Mourning tears of years long gone

Life Uncommon

Letting go of the girl I know
Coming to terms with the woman I am
Smiling thoughts of loves and lovers
Wondering how it came to be like this
A blue feather lands to remind me
That all exists
As one

509. "The Beauty"

Sparkling rivers rivulet your auburn hair in the sunny days we were young and in love
you're beautiful lady with the flowers in your hair and I think of all I would do for you
dance through the moonlight point out every star in the night and bask in the glow of all
inside of you that's bright and the river flows gently into a moving trance and together
under that moonlight oh so bright we dance moving not stopping just going together 'til
we flow intermittently as one and I wave my hand up to the sun letting the world know
that in this dance we never fall for we balance each other like earth sun sky and moon we
are together an elemental trance into this sundance and we shake and we move and we
love in this dancing groove and I feel you baby right under the moonlight where you
make everything feel oh so right and in your arms I feel so alive that I could just take that
dive into eternity and forget my feet and just feel that fleeting glimpse of the night and
take that flight everlastingly into the oblivious truth of it all and in you I find my soul so I
dance and I dance in our spiraling romance and I think of you and all we could do and
then I dance and I dance and I twirl and I spin and its never quite fast... enough and we
keep just spinning and you're a beauty quite the beauty to behold if only you knew how
much life those eyes of yours hold and I think of it and I look into your eyes and I drown
in the sadness and the colorblindness I bask in the gentleness and as we twirl a few last
times I realize that baby you are my world and I will get down on my knees and propose
eternity to you please please be my wife for you baby are my life and I'll twirl you
around a fantastical world where diamonds and pearls are always within the grasp of such
a beautiful lass my what a sight to behold you are and forever I will love you our lives
will twirl us together in a oneness so few know and that's how we'll grow like two
intertwining vines, thank you my valentine.

510. "The Beauty of Tomorrow"

In the grace of gods kiss
We feel something we've long missed
Jaeles are high
The world is nigh
Defeat is anything but near
The kings are coming here
In the travelling halls of time
Linger words of thoughts and rhyme

Life Uncommon

Singing tunes, drumming beats
Hear the call of tomorrow's feats

As autumn leaves fall along our sidewalks
The caw of ravens will fill our skies
Yesterday's song is sung
Today our hearts beat so strong
The future holds us in a warm embrace
Ready to help us in our place
The juvenile hall will fill with blessings
The strangled man will lead his own
The man with maybe confused will be
The child with knowledge shall be seen
The grey knight will come forth
By a fortnight the truth be told

In truth and rhyme you'll know the story
Darkened skies clear for strong clarity
As the clock strikes two you'll know who
Will lead you through
Clouds will part
The stormrider will appear
You'll know his foot stomps, you'll hear them near
Today we smile upon the lady
Raise our glasses in toast, in cheer to
The maiden, the mother, the crone

511. "The Belief That Makes the World Go Round"

If you believe in love
It'll believe in you
Just take the chance
And sing out its tune
Shout it out all night long
Its the breath in your lungs
The blood in your veins
Its the magic you feel
In everything
When you smile,
When you laugh,
When you feel,
That's it
And you know it
Yes, you know it
So shake off those doubts

Life Uncommon

Scream 'em on out
And never forget
What loves all about.

512. "The Boy at the Popcorn Machine"
Oh, how sweet those lyrics sound on your
Tongue, you steal my heart, we dance
An eternity on a flame of a line so say
You'll be mine, red bears red leaves not
Brown, taller not even at eyesight
What is it about you that enchants me so?
You wrote me lyrics, lyrics, lyrics emotions
I'm shaking my head and smiling
Something about you just gets me
Your honesty, loyalty, arrogance
Your smile over the phone, your teasing manner,
Maybe its all just imagination… you have that
Everything-will-be-okay way about you
I'd love to cuddle in your arms, taste
Your tender lips—you are gentle yet strong,
Fast yet slow I love you I do
For this I wish you to know its true

513. "The Burnt Wick"

Although I believed the wick had been cut off
I was wrong
She's still there
Black and burnt
But there
Slowly the flame has inched upon her
Tempting, teasing
Burn, burn
Flicker with desire
I feel hot and hurried
Dizzy, Lustful,
Waiting…
Sweat drips from my forehead
The flickering wick
Her and I
We
We burn again!

Life Uncommon

514. "The Car Accident"

Driving was slow and relaxed
The music was at a slow tempo
The road was wet
The leaves rustled softly
I was on my way to school
Following the same old routine
One road changed
But not too much
Traffic was not horrible
It was not fun either
Everything seemed so slow and relaxed
Raaar…raaar…raaar…
I wondered
Cops…fire engine…ambulance…
I thought, "Great. What happened now?"
So selfish moments before recognition

515. "The Cat"
(dedicated to Cat)

Sitting quietly she stares out at the world
Watching its every move
Learning its every aggression
Keenly observing the common and uncommon
Our behaviors become her knowledge
Her own movements minimal
Eyes aware
Entirety on watch
Knowing only as those eyes can
Strength strums through her
Ready to defend her territory
Claiming where she's at
Sternly the creature
The beauty,
The laughter,
The joy,
And the lacquer,
That we simply know,
As the Cat.

516. "The Celestial Dance"

Life Uncommon

Celestial bodies of steel
Hanging on the edge of something ethereal
Twisted about, ringing to shout
Silent whispers of angels
Heavenly cherubim
In the dance of the fae
The moonlight gives way
Glittering eyes of gold
Spiritual bodies so bold
Sun giving us warmth and light
Helping us grow until the night
When the moon comes about the sky
Singing its sweet lonesome lullaby
Slowly the dazzling stars appear
Tides settling down our earthly fears
The celestial dance streams forth
As we are caught up in the trance
Of birth, death, and rebirth.

517. "The Cellar"
(dedicated to Alex)

I think you are the love that I needed to hate
You are the master who opened my cage
And then stuck me back inside
Reasons never given
Lies never unfolded
Truths never handed
So I sit and not know
I'm meant to be the soaring bird
Surely I'm an ostrich instead
Smaller though, maybe an unflying kiwi at best
I know I'm strong
But I flap my wings as if they still work
And I guess as soon as my heart gave way to woe
The ability to do anything
Stopped knowing how
How do you ring your heart back into a beat?
Or yell your misery out of itself?
Can you write so much that it'll all get out?
Even my tears don't let the pain go
You are nestled inside me like bad wine
And the fuck of it all
Is you still get better with time
Out of my sight, but of my mind? No way

Life Uncommon

I still love you every stupid waking day

518. "The Coffee Cup"
(dedicated to Erin)

There are some days
Not any days in particular
Just some days
When I feel like picking up my pen
And just writing
Old afternoon sweeping me up,
Into the sun, and the warmth thereof
The feel of remembrance
And warm youth
Its like holding a silent cup of coffee
Still...
Just long enough to wonder
Finding ourselves in the far reaches
Of mind
Whisked away to that alluring land
Where smiles and lilies are all about
And coffee is always at hand.

519. "The Color Blue"

Like an elusive arrow
Finding its way straight through my heart
Tearing walls and dreams
Deadening the silence
Heightening the screams
Color of ocean fonts
And lakes I'll never see
Color of sadness
For you and for me
I'd like to get away
Visit some lake
Catch a smile
Find a star worth hanging onto
Find my way
To sanity
Leaving my hurts in the sand
Before I drift onto another...empty sea.

Life Uncommon

520. "The Crash"

So I took a fall
Fell straight into your wall
Walked straight in they say
How I'll never know
But I loved you from the start
I knew it in my heart
I cried to the heavens "thank you"
And that was just where it began
After that we talked
Humbly at first
We knew each others secrets
And we knew each others thirst
We desired to know more
And with each passing day came allure
We fell into the arms of love
We flew high
My pain you knew
And together we grew
Strength we gave each other
We both talked of love for our mother
Souls so alike
Yes, that's right
So one day I took a fall
And crashed through your wall
Forever that day will remain a loving memory
To bind to my heart, to bind to my soul
To keep within me, so that forever I'll know.

521. "The Dark Period"

I wonder who I first knew love from
I may have been loved and just didn't know it
But it probably wasn't until I was 15 or 16
That I finally knew someone cared
Though, I still didn't know
I was loved
Maybe my high school sweetheart…
Either way the last 9 years of loving people has taught me
Exactly one thing:
Love sucks.

522. "The Drifter"

Life Uncommon

Floating in a sea of angst
I drift away
And remember your face
When you were young
And you were free
You were you
And I was me
No masks or lies
Just truth realized
So we grew up I suppose
Oh, how we despised pantyhose
We could have been anything
We used to say
Remember what you used to play?
All the games of pretend
Who did you want to be?
I can't remember
I just see your face

523. "The Drifter's Dream"

Swimming like a fish in the sea of your heart
I whisper sweet prayers hoping you'll hear
I know you feel we've drifted apart
I know you feel we were never really meant to be
Like we fooled time and fate just to be together
But I never told you how I feel
I felt like I was waiting for the shoe that would fit me
Cinderella style
The princess that always was, but never knew
And then came the day when I met you
Sweet and charming you romanced me all the way
I pledged my life to you on that day
So now when I hear you feel we've drifted apart
I wonder what sea we landed in that could allow this
For I only belong in the ship where you are
Voyaging off to destinations near or far
It matters not to me
It only matters that you are there
And that I…am with you.

524. "The Empath's Song"

Life Uncommon

They log on to an invisible friend
And hope to connect to the world
But they stand behind a wall
Its impossible to know that which does not know itself
They can stand there and whine their way begging for help
But my advice is useless
And my love is just there
I can sit here and wipe invisible tears
But none of it will help
None of it will right all their wronged years
I know they feel pain
And their emotions are all bottled up inside
They must have memories swimming over them like tides
I can reach out my hand but to no avail
There they stand, alone and pale
Trying to convince one that they are loved
Man, what a task
I was never in their rooms late at night
Awaiting the sexual fright
I never took a razor to my skin
I never bled outside, no, I bled within
I don't know the pain of starvation
And I certainly don't have a clue of the hurt of molestation
But I care
And I suppose in truth that's why I am here
I have never been inside their shell
But I have existed in my own constructed hell
So maybe I think because I have felt pain and fear
Maybe I think their screams I can hear
I don't know what I expect
No one is perfect
I wish I could get through to them
Or at least succeed at not hurting them anymore
But I suppose only time will tell
Of that I can be sure.

525. "The End"

Drop drop drop
Drop
The lenses rise
The world begins
The world spins and expands
Something new
Dropping the false

Life Uncommon

Gaining gaining the new
Slowly drifting learning anew
The world begins and I
Begin with it
Step step
And the world is mine
I grasp ahold
And feel the want to fly
To be one with the drops of rain
And the whispers of pain
And it starts again
So suddenly starting over
And I lapse into dream
Where I've never been
Before floating about wanting to soar
And then there is something new
I know not what it is
But I am drawn to it
Pulled
Brought to the truth
Like blood
Through my ever flowing veins
I must follow this truth
Drops of rain upon my hair
I feel covered and I close
World ends.

526. "The Everybody"

Just for a minute let me breathe
Let me catch my breath
Before you make me bleed
I know your words will sting
Before you've got me wishing to die
I'm preparing for your judgement
I'm not perfect
I'm flawed you fool
So easy it was to sit me,
On a pedestal
Angelic saint-like girl
I always was to you
Drink to me,
Cheers to you

We're shattering belief

Life Uncommon

I'm a liar and a thief
I'm a bitch and a seductress
I'm a child molester and a rapist
I'm a rebel and a manipulator
I'm a terrorist and a drunk
I'm a victim and a perpetrator

I've used knowledge for bad
I have sinned time and again
You've known my illusions
Alone

I've hurt and been hurt
I've wept, slowly cried
I've lived on both sides of abuse
Can you handle this as the truth?

I am your everybody
I am human
I am the humility
Of equality

527. "The Feminine Power"

Each of us struggling
Each of us yearning
We strive to be so much more
And yet inside constantly feel torn
We hope tomorrow things better will arise
But at night its so hard to close these eyes
Mommy-dom never as simple as you'd think
But my what joy these miracles do bring
Being a wife not quite the task we thought
But what an excellent love the husbands brought
The mask we hide behind shelters us so well
Especially while we each struggle in our own personal hell
Somehow we smile and continue on through the day
That is the woman's way
So we calculate the exact time we will fall
And somehow the goddess uplifts us all
Work can be a hassle for each of us
But we get there by boat, train, car, or bus
Tomorrow the sun will rise
And tonight I shall rest my eyes
Because I am a woman.

Life Uncommon

528. "The Fix"

A mind moving non-stop through the train wrecked thoughts of a maniac and you walk back to a life you never really knew and before you are through you recognize that cigarette you've been smoking most of your life and you wish you never started the down spiral staircase yet you're on the tripping line of a way never to really get back to a time of peppermints and loving holidays when things were always all right and you parents would never tell you a lie wouldn't it just be nice to slip back into that time and never waste another dime on the escapist routine? forget it babe, I need some nicotine...

529. "The Forbidden Streets"

The forbidden street lie there all day and all night
I'd watch it light or dark,
Day or night
Rumors spread all the time-
Pss...pss...
There was another murder
I'd ask what murder was
I got the typical bad thing people do
After all I was only 4 or 5 at the time
Pss...pss...
Someone got robbed last night
I'd ask what robbed was
My mother said robbery was taking something that doesn't belong to you
I figured that meant the pennies I used to "steal" from my father's huge penny jar
After all I was only a child-
Who knew robbery could be taking someone's happiness away,
Stealing valuable merchandise-
Or a penny to me
Pss...pss...
Another girl got raped last night
I'd ask what raped was
My mother wouldn't talk about it
That was not a nice question to ask
Yet, I kept wondering
After all I was only 4 or 5 why shouldn't I be curious?

When I was 8 I moved
Yet, that street still lurks in my mind
Walking past there was like walking around a graveyard
My friend lived there
Sleeping over was like sleeping at a ghost's castle

Life Uncommon

The street was scary
The murders, robberies, and rapes
Still go on today
The street is unchanged
Only more people are hurt
That street was always forbidden
Why should I have known the reason behind that?
That street was forbidden, but it will always be a wonder in my mind
Its different colors – sad, gloomy, unchanging
Not very different- all sad- untouched
Will it go on?
Will more kids grow up around America's forbidden streets?

530. "The Garden of Saints"

She stands wrapped in a garment of white
Floating on heaven a dove comes to rest,
In the palm of her hand
Yesterday no god for her existed
No heaven above
She was alone
No fluttering dove
Today she found
God
Wrists of Nails
Slashes of pain
Nails in the ankles
God came again
Upon the forehead
A crown of thorns
Today she is stigmatic
In a city of whores
Heaven resides in us they say
Today she joins the angels
And strolls among the saints
In a garden of beauty,
A garden of Saints.

531. The Girl I Left Behind"

Somewhere in my search for self
I finally tripped that line
I fell flat on my ass
Without a dime to spare

Life Uncommon

I went searching for some time
Without a real care
Wandering from East to West
Trying to make the lousy dime
Doing what I do best
So many a challenge came flying
I tried to pass each test
But when the clock ticked stop
I still hadn't caught up
Came in this town a youngen
Spent years living the naïve
Now I'm twenty-four
Just trying to find time to breathe
Tender years gone to me
Toughened up for what's ahead
I may not be at the start of the game
But chess ain't won yet
So I'll buckle down
I'll grind my teeth
Put my balls back in my deck
And when the gambler comes a-knocking
I'll be doing what I do best

532. "The Girl That I Am"

Suddenly standing in a darkness I'm not used to
I curse the heaven and the hell
I slowly walk through
I feel alone
And terrified
Trying to be a woman
Failing to be anything but a girl
Youth seems to swarm around me
Fantasies and dreams
Hopes that will never come true
I try to be stronger
But completely forget how
I reach out my hand
And find my own walls
Burned by the stove of my
Own heart

I retreat
And find only me
I wonder where all

Life Uncommon

Those who claim to be
Here have gone
And again question
But as for answers
I find none

So I search in silence
For a truth that never comes
Trying so hard to move on
Who thought up these
Rules anyway?
School and work
Depression fades your life away
And still I stand
As the girl yearning to be
A woman
That I am

533. "The Glass Figurine"

The glass figurine sits across the room
She has hair as golden as her innocence
A smile to wipe away any rough spots on her cheek
Eyes as curious as her swaying gown
And a touch with the feeling of a new beginning
I spot the innocent glass figurine of a child
My eyes cry
And my heart aches
I walk across the room and pick her up
She is soft and gentle
She hides no secrets for her heart is as clear as glass
Gracefulness is all around her
Yes, she is the perfect figurine
As I hold her in the palm of my hand
I wonder why I am not the same
Although I do truly wonder who is better
She holds no spots of a dark nature
But since I do… I have the gift of experience
My reasoning is useless
But my heart shines bright
We all have our glass figurines in sight
Maybe one day we'll have nothing to hide
And we can be innocent
And free
And graceful

Life Uncommon

534. "The Joker"

We're all fools in the deck of life
None quite wrong
None quite turned right
Circling balls thrown overhead
Juggle the load, or you're dead
Think quick, but act a fool
Never give away the game of pool
Quick witted embraces
Of the truth
Watch the mannerisms
Societal or uncouth?
Laughter resonates in my ears
Mysterious
Mysterious
Myst.

535. "The Justice"

Is he right or is he wrong?
Is he weak or is he strong?
The balancer of truth is never quite wrong
He seeks to be just in all he does
He seeks to be fair to every cause
When death appears he sheds two simple tears
One for life, one for love
The two that never come
Are the peace and the dove
Held in the balance of time
He seeks...
He seeks...
But will he ever find?

536. "The Kiss"

Across the room he stands
His hand fidgeting
My stomach contracting
Nervous flames shoot through me
Desire overcoming
His eyes are turned this way now

Life Uncommon

He sees me
Walking my way
<sigh>
Feet move forward
Stare into me
Sweet prince
Eyes of such passionate wants
His hand hits the wall
My back pressed against
The wall
Lips move in
Close my eyes
Sweat in anticipation
My lips unlock
For a second I stop breathing
The warmest touch
A lock
Lips close
Push forward
Arms wrap around
Blissful embrace

537. "The Knight Who Just Isn't"

How to be happy when your knight in shining armor is neither a knight nor does he wear
armor When the criticism piles up at the end of the night you look down and you've
become a shadow of what you used to be. The headstrong girl now just sits quietly and
hears all she does wrong. And where did the good things I do go? I suppose they sit
somewhere up on the moon because I don't see them often anymore. Her- she was
striking and people stopped to listen to her. She talked of real things to real people.
When her friends walked by they looked at her admiringly. Maybe she wasn't gorgeous.
And perhaps she wasn't the smartest girl of all. But she sprouted an aura of confidence
and truth. Even when she failed she succeeded. She would stumble and fall and brush
off the rubbish from her jeans and then turn and smile danger in the face. Yeah she was
beautiful for just being her. And now I am just a shadow of her. To reclaim her could be
dangerous. To lose her completely may be a disaster. What's a girl to do with the knight
who just isn't?

538. "The Leaders"

The birds of prey swoop close to the village of settlers
Silent abetting in hope of truth
Finding none in the clouds nor along the shores
Finding no truth in our hearts nor in our words

Life Uncommon

Our actions ring across land and sea
Our hopes and prayers whispered too silently
Even god has trouble hearing us in our time of need
Even god doesn't know the truths we heed
In a time of sadness we went to work
In a time of loss we showed no remorse
Now with the chance to move the world
Now with the opportunity to lift and be heard
We sit and we walk and we watch it all
We listen and we hear but we do nothing at all
This is the time to stop listening
This is the time to start talking
Pray, shout, scream, and dance
Let the world know that you are
Partaking in this chance
The mountains will stand
The birds they will fly
But who will be the leaders
If not you and I?

539. "The Lies We Build"

Drifting off to a place where the windows may gleam
But just a sparkle will shine through
Timing is so perfect, but doesn't even exist
We build up these mysterious cloaks to hide ourselves
Only we find ourselves in denial, instead of in truth
Black, White, Red
Red, White, Yellow,
Red, White, and of course, Blue
Colors we surround ourselves with
The color wheels of time
Spinning the wheel that only fortune can spin
And still, we still, can't really find the 'me'
Though we search and we try
We end up never really knowing why
Isolated to ourselves
Holding on to some unsubsiding pain
Truth inside, held too close
Choosing so haphazardly ways to destroy ourselves
Ways to dwindle what is left of our youth

When we are 12 we want to be 14
When we are 14 we want to be 16
(Driving we think the key to freedom)

Life Uncommon

When we are 16 we want to be 18
(So we can have smoke-filled lungs)
When we are 18 we want to be 21
(So we can fill ourselves with liquor)

The older we get the younger we want to become
And still we're isolated inside
We have rights and responsibilities
Is that the age where we stop wanting?
And we still build these lies for ourselves....

540. "The Lingerer"

Lingering kisses
Serene truth
Smiling twists of youth
Daffodils and tulips grow in truth
While flowers of gold bloom
She smiles a distant smile
In love she sings to her own heart
Wondering about the love she let go
As all men leave
She has grown in strength
And her love
Lingers on.

541. "The Little Boy in Blue"
(dedicated to Nate)

I love you more than I can tell you Nate
But somehow us being together doesn't seem to be our fate
I'll love you anyway as I have from day one
Praying you'll make amends in yourself
And as you found your parents, may you one day find your son
I know we aren't going to be together
But I guess sometimes I'll wish we could have been better
You understood me in ways almost no one does
And even when it hurts to admit it
I know that doesn't make us one
It just makes us alike, perhaps kindred
Our souls are alike and the flame within burns
So close in nature that its hard to tell
But I know it can't be for us to be together
If it was it wouldn't be so hard

Life Uncommon

Circumstances wouldn't keep tearing us apart
Things would be easier for us
And we'd feel more right
As we tried to sleep through the night
Your dreams and mine will have to live on
And someday in the future we'll hopefully come upon
The one who is actually meant for us
We'll meet our soul mates
And have a date with our true fate
I wish you the best
But know this
I'll love you now as I loved you then
And I'll love you forever
Because you found a place in my soul
A place where no one else ever goes
And now that place is yours and forever will be
Regardless of where you or I are meant to be
I love you, Nate and wish you the best
Bless your heart, your soul, and your love
May you soar like the eagle and love like the dove
Merry part and blessed be, my friend
But somehow I don't think this is our friendships end.

542. "The Loner"

I don't know that I'm completely a loner
I mean, I have friends
Some, not many,
Not any whom I confide to
Still, they are friends
Go to work,
People there
When I get home from work
Neighbors
I have cats
Yeah, I grasp weakly,
I know
I'm a loner
Its just hard to admit it
I guess some part
Likes denying
Alone it really is

543. "The Love"

Life Uncommon

Yes you make the stars shine
And I'll gladly call you mine
It might be a while
Before either of us smiles
But I'll stand my ground
Watching the world tumble round
The scenes may fade
But my love never will
Strolling the streets
Penniless I may be
But I'll always love you
And you can show the world
That you've got a man true
The one who'll always love you
I'll write any poem
Sing any song
I'll dance any room
'cuz I'm where I belong
Enchanted by your eyes
Tranced by your kiss
And this is where we
Both can live.

544. "The Love That Never Was"

So peaceful and serene as beginning of romance could be
Time only ages us…as the heart knows
Even when rain falls…it hurts
Even when love comes…it kills
Time tells me of a story of a man and a woman
Meant to be, bounded by time
Connected by a string of love and tonight I face it
Lonesome and dulled
Wondering what its all for
Why we try so hard,
Fight with such will,
Then give up so easily…

Is trust really what its all about?
Was this love that I feared to shout?
Will I in time realize I messed up?
How does one face this?
What will give me the strength to move on?
How will I ever know if he was the one?

Life Uncommon

It used to be I thought I'd know
Now I sit here unsure of it all

How can love break two in half so easily?
Or is it just humanity?

I don't know what to think or where to go
I know my purpose and know it well
I will continue to help and to heal
To love and to feel
To live and to care and perhaps somewhere in time
I'll find the truth

Maybe in time I'll grow and realize this was just a hoax
A false promise of my own heart
A false belief from the start

Maybe he was sent to throw me off my path
Maybe, but I'll never go back
I'll go forward and on
Finding time for all I am
God help me, I need you now.

545. "The Lovely Dove"

A lovely dove
Sweet and seemingly harmless
The dove walks over to me looking for food
So I throw some down for the sweet thing
I imagine the dove took a liking to me
For the dove came back to me every day for more food
Each time giving me a feeling of being needed
Now the dove shows up at various times
Seeming to be careless that I am the giver
Sweet and seemingly harmless is what I saw
Maybe the dove has found another giver
Should I keep bringing the food?
All I saw was one lovely dove

546. "The Luna In Us All"

Feminine energy
Rising and falling like the tides

Life Uncommon

Whispering through the wind as she hides
Slowly, gently peeking through the clouds of time
Smiling as she taunts in rhyme
She is a trickster of the night
And has the ability to put all things right
From raven to dove
From the depths of the sea, to the sky above
She holds the keys to all you know and love
She's the wife, the mother, the sister, the bride
Grandmother of wisdom
Mother of love
Maiden of magic
And woman of tenderness
She is the feminine aspect
In each of us
Embrace her for her truth
Trust her with your inner most self
And soar with her in dreams
For she knows you.

547. "The Mage"
(dedicated to James)

A young man, not yet aged
Lives his youth as a learning mage
Reading and listening to all there is
Reaching only for truth in the worlds mysteries
Cloaked up in his room
He learns his trade
Wand set about, ready to float
Sparking the illumination within himself
And while he is ready for much
His focus is clear, to the touch
Learning alone is his trade
A trade with which all of his time
And energy flow into
Theories flow throughout the years
And while he will grow in age
For now he is simply...
The seeking mage.

548. "The Mirror That Hides No Dream"

Standing alone

Life Uncommon

In a reflecting mirror
I see the truth and the lie
The twisted fallacy that once believed
Turns into a truth far too real to comprehend
I stand in front of the mirror
Dream of my youth and my old age
Remember that I am only here
At the age of twenty-three
Trying to figure out where it is
And who it is
That I'm meant to be
Wondering why each decision makes such a large effect
When decisions in truth are all lived out
And one is no more real than another
One is no more disastrous than another
And yet, each one makes a huge impact
And why is it that no manual comes for these decisions?
Nothing tells us how to deal with our fears
Or how to avoid them
Nothing tells us how to live with the disorder of money
Or the haphazard way our parents raised us
So we struggle in front of mirrors
And ask questions that regardless of answer, matter not
And we write poetry to a void that shall never answer
Because that is what we do
"We are, we are, the youth of a nation."

549. "The Night the Wind Snuck Up On Me"

The wind snuck up on me
Sighing at my every movement
I could tell it was there when I didn't move
The wind only coughed--
After flashing his bright white light down the sky
I tossed and turned in my bed
My muscles were weak
My eyes kept tearing
Crying was not the answer
Why was I crying?

I wanted to free myself of the wind
But it kept on grabbing at my every thought
Pulling at each emotion
Toying with my fright
I was scared

Life Uncommon

I guess any six year-old would be
I was lonely
In a space with only a few friends
My Charlie Brown friends stuck to cloth
I could tuck myself under the warm cloth
While having my friends watch over me

I held onto my Cabbage Path doll
Hoping her bright little face with pigtails
Could help me
Yet my eyes kept tearing
Crying was not the answer
Why was I crying?

I cried what seemed like forever
The ground kept shaking
Making that horrible noise
I could have sworn people were taking pictures of me
Left and right
Flashes
Noises
Tears
Why couldn't I stop it?

I closed my eyes
Tossed and turned
Once in a while I even screamed
I even was able to stop the tap, tap, tapping

But the wind kept grabbing at me
Creating noises
Shaking my room
Pulling at my emotions
Twisting my every thought
Swelling up my throat-
And then letting me shriek
Tapping at my window
Whistling like a ghost
Wearing white--taking pictures
Why wouldn't it stop?

I kept tossing and turning
Crying until my eyes were dry
Closing my eyes--
Hoping my friends could help
Then slowly drifted away into a deep sleep

Life Uncommon

Dreaming about nothing in particular
Just peaceful
The tapping
Shaking
And photograph taking finally stopped
I was at peace

550. "The Nothing that is Me"

.

I'm not normal
I don't cook
There are no friends in person
And mostly only people I haven't met online
I cling to a girl I haven't been with in three years
I fear stepping outside to go to work
Agoraphobia you call it
I feel dead
Dead and alone
And I'm hating the man who put me here
I blame him
For I gave him my heart
Stupidity never learns
I am a destined failure
A loser
This is all I'll ever amount to
And-I-am-nothing

551. "The Pink Rose"

A flower of hope hangs
Pink and beautiful she sits there
Still and silent
Symbol of a new beginning
Live forever my rose
Be my love and destroy my hate
Be me and none of my enemies

So beautiful

My rose of hope fades
She is my destiny
And she fades.

Life Uncommon

552. "The Ring"

Don't you know I love you?
Can't you read it in my eyes?
How can I show you my fears I've been gathering all my life?
Do you want to know the real, inner me?
The beauty that cries even as she sings?
How can I tell you all of me when I'm still lost at sea?
How can I share my secrets when the lies have yet to be revealed?
I don't know who or how I am
I only know that I'm lost and in love with you
I only know that I care and that with each unmade phone call
I trust that much less
If you love me at all, if you care for me one bit,
I ask that you reach out your hand and dial
So that I may receive
The sound I wait for
That melodic, simple, sometimes fair, sometimes not…
Ring.

553. "The Sigh"
(dedicated to Shawn)

Travel each moment like its heaven
And you'll never look back and wonder again
If you were in the right place, at the right time
If the moment you followed was your destiny
Or the road you took all by yourself
Time takes a chunk out of your dreams
Yet, it miraculously gives you, you
The times when we stand still
And the overhead look from God
Winks
These are the times
When we live
A breath of nothingness easing out of our tired lungs
The sigh, the breath, the ease with which we know...
"This too shall pass."

554. "The Silent Stare"

He sits across from me
His eyes share a beauty
In him

Life Uncommon

With me
They give me comfort

Untainted by verbal communication
We feel each other
In this
Ongoing stare

He looks
Into
Me
Knowing
Me.

555. "The Song"

Sounds formulate echoes
Gaze upon images of trust
Scrutinize
Anticipated a downfall
Each uttered sound tells me
I was betrayed
<stupid>
Musical notes linger
Ears hurt now
My head throbs
Because the tension
Yanks at my scars
<worthless>
Bum, dum, da, da, dum, bum
Pound
By
Pound
I recall
Trepidation transmits
Through my veins
<ignorant>
Unravel
The past
Like a bandage
Unrolling
Across the carpet
Pain
Now visible

Life Uncommon

Stopped
Lyrics ended
Yet, my suffering advances.

556. "The Sparkling Ocean"

Tides roll in every night
The waves move to the moons command
Beauty is one of nature's demands
Every wave flows freely-individually
The destiny is the same,
But the adventure is always different

When the sun sets the ocean sparkles
The ocean lit up by her
The sun beneath
Sun leaves, moon rules once more

As the waves move to the moon's command
The color gets darker and darker
For a while its pitch black

Then suddenly stars seem to spontaneously appear
Every minute more stars become visible
And when every star you could ever possibly imagine seeing-
Is actually there
The moon dust appears

The sky sparkles so fully with pride
That the ocean looks up to it
The sky leaves a piece of itself on the ocean
And once again the ocean sparkles

Sun arising
Reflection fades
Water becomes warm- homely

557. "The Trusted Warrior"
(Dedicated to Nick)

In the silent whispers
Of the moonlight
Even when the dawn breaks
And I cannot see the light
Even when the clouds arise

Life Uncommon

And even when the sunset dies
I know you are there
Lurking beneath the sorrow
Hiding beneath the fear
And fight it as I might
There you are
Shining your light.

558. "The Typical Teenager"

The typical teenager wants freedom
They want to succeed, and to be lazy
To go for the glory, But only by way of a small staircase
The 90's teenager usually has a cigarette in hand
They want to be themselves, and kill their brain cells
To reach for fame, Then only wisp it away
The alcoholic teenager sips away their days
They want happiness
But drink
To expect problems to disappear
But actually drag themselves through them
The druggee teenager starts with pot
They want a cool buzz
But find the result devastating
To ask to have life as a party
But kill their own tormented, explosive minds
The typical teenager wants freedom
So do I
So do you
But what is freedom in this world?

559. "The Undeniable Truth"

When lonely and vulnerable life can be empty
Emptiness going into an abyss of lifelessness
Life without love is sad and lonely
But always pure, innocent, merely vulnerable
Like a flat patch of snow
Still, unmoving, afraid of hard rain or sleet
Hoping not to melt away
Or maybe wishing to melt away into nature
Becoming one with something... anything,
Snow- a cycle of nature
Where's love?

Life Uncommon

Who knows- are you afraid?
Or just empty?
Waiting for water to fill the pitcher,
Flowers to fill the vase,
Trees to brighten up the forest,
Or just plain waiting for love to take you out of the abyss,
Out of loneliness,
Vulnerability,
And sadness…
That's where you belong…
Where you were…

560. "The Unenlightened"

I still love him
Amazing isn't it?
He can do anything
Hit me
Hurt me
Yell at me
Tell me I'm nothing
Tell me I'm stupid
Ignore me
Threaten me
Use cynical criticism against me
Destroy my friendships
Fuck with my goals
Trash my morals
Set aside my beliefs
And I still love him
I picture flowers
Remember candlelight
Taste the champagne
Smile at his beauty
And still I am nothing
Just a lovesick girl
Getting used to
Her dream going black

561. "The Waiter"

Time erodes my bittersweet thoughts
I wish for such beauty and grace
But it feels for naught

Life Uncommon

And in the stillness of my own breath
I wait
Glittering stars and buzzing bands
Hold your love close, clasped hands
Angels wings surround me
While fairies cheerily play on
I've changed in such little time
I've grown into the woman I am
And still...
I wait
I feel that darkness will come
Before I am free of what I am
Bound unto
The Moon shall rise
Above my beautiful tides
My eyes shall joyfully sing as I cry
And even then...
I shall wait.

562. "The Walls of My Youth"

Drinking in the bitter tastes of life
I sit and wonder what I've done with these years of mine
Uncertain of the childhood lullabies I was lulled to sleep with
Wondering why it is that I have kept this truth from myself for so long
The truth is that inside of me I know who I am
Even though I hide it even from myself so often
I am a girl haunted by the walls of my past
For they know secrets I've tried to hide from all
The secret that I've known all along
That I am a strength behind myself
That I am the only one I must answer to
That even in hardships
I still remain true

563. "The Wanderer"

He seeks sights not possibly known to him
He searches for gratitude and finds truth
He moves from rock to stone with steady hands
He travels near and far
Searching for hidden lands
In the wisdom of hidden truths he finds
Himself, then moves

Life Uncommon

Searching to answer all his answers
Constantly questioning all his questions
As soon as the answer looms close
It moves and is out of his grasp
Once more
Because forevermore he will be
...the wanderer.

564. "The Wandering Feather"

A wandering feather can be twisted and turned
It will follow the wind's lead to the heavens
The soft white piece of home isn't distraught

Instead, it is peaceful as it floats with the rhythm of rustling leaves
The soft noise and playful nature
Encourages our own hearts to be that light and free
Happiness could be felt in each of us, moon and sea

And then the feather will land on the tree
It will settle in perfect harmony
Without being bent out of shape at all

And when it finally falls it will combine with the grass
Shining as beautiful as silver, gold, or brass
But alas! It will be picked up by a new breeze
Floating high above the trees, and just be
A wandering feather that can be twisted and turned
As it follows the wind's lead to the heavens.

(Inspired by the movie "Forrest Gump")

565. "The Way I Want It"

It would be nice if my night wasn't so boring
but as it is, boredom overcomes
I am overflowing with unintelligent stigmas
I want to battle the idiocy
break down the walls of falsehood
I want it real
I want it cold
I even want it harsh and blunt
I'd rather have it real
than fake

any day of the week
everyone talks about sex
and alcohol
like its cool
I'm just sick of it
I'm not like them
I'm so different its scary
and yet we are all
the same
such is life
on this idle Sunday morning
before dawns first light.

566. "There's Something About You"

There's something about you
I don't know what it is but in my heart I know its true
There's just something about you

Its in the way you smile and cheer me when I'm blue
Its in the way I can say anything to you
I'm telling you its true…There's just something about you

I feel it in the grace of my heart…and the way you touch me
I'd be lying if I didn't say it wakes me
When I'm with you I feel alive and I know without you I'd die inside
Because, baby, there's just something about you

When it rains the clouds part…they let you into my lonely heart
Lightning strikes an eternal glare and I just look at you there
Watching you laugh with that endless flair and I'm smiling inside
Because, baby, there's just something about you

Listening to the raindrops falling from heaven
Dreaming of places I've never been
Wrapped in your arms…under the stars…lying awake, watching you sleep

Chorus:
You see it's in the way you smile and cheer me when I'm blue
Its in the way I can say anything to you
I'm telling you its true…There's just something about you

All through the night I'm loving you in the lonely place inside
Watching the emptiness fade from your eyes…Loneliness ends in your smile
Loving you makes it all worthwhile

Life Uncommon

Under the moon…Staring at you…Loving the man in you…And I'm bound, baby, to be
with you…Because, baby, there's just something about you

There's something about you
I don't know what it is but in my heart I know its true
There's just something about you

<chorus>
There's just something about you…there's just something about you...
Something about you.

567. "Thought"

Being at home sucks,
Facing the future is hard,
Stagnating leads me nowhere,
And denial never helps

568. "Three Dimensional Me"

She is the source of my calm
She is the solitude that frees
She's the compassion I should seek
I left her somewhere months ago
Leaving behind magic
I almost left behind myself
She is the woman I truly am
But I am this me too
Two sides of a coin
But a coin is three dimensional
Top, Bottom, and Side
Where do these lines connect?
I know there is a place
I must find it
And unlock the mystery
Set the true me, free

569. "Through A Windowpane"

Ah! The life of a poet
Living a love of words
Filled with such intensity

Life Uncommon

In fiery stormed words
Filtering through pages of novels
Scattered at my feet
Surrounded by brilliance
Lifting me up, letting me sleep
The calm of an ocean drifts near
Loons sounding their call
To our sleeping souls
Eagles fly overhead
White wolves roam the woods
Protectors of the children
Bringers of emotion
Slivering notions in my veins
Loving you
Each time it rains
Neon lights shine your name
May none of it be in vain
I found you
Looking through my windowpane

570. "Thugs Galore"

Life is full of motherfuckers
Why?
They don't own me
They don't own you
Confidence stacked like
Hundred dollar bills
Goddamn!
They treat you like cattle
Can't the world move them out?
Can't we evict them from the universe?
Assholes the lot of them
I'm sick of the school teacher rap I get
They drink, they smoke, they fuck
And they hurt others so deeply you'd barely believe it
Its horrid
What happened to kindness?
Was it all lies I grew up on?
I fucking thought love was real
I fucking believed in genuine people
What bullshit
Assholes are a dime a dozen
Dozens and dozens
I'm sick of it

Life Uncommon

I hate it
And yet my world is full of it
I complain
But thugs remain all the same

571. "Time"

Leaves of grain
Fly through the summertime rain
Stains on glass windows
Creaks in the hallway
Days of yore
Hours of remembrance
There he stood
Eloquent and handsome in his own way
We dances for hours on hard marbled floors
A rose in his pocket and a smile on his lips
For hours in his embrace
A scholar on his way to change the world
I proudly placed my hand in his
As he spoke his enchanted words to the other folk
As I sipped some wine I saw him watching me
We returned to the dance floor for one last spin
He twirled me into eternity
The night stars above us throughout our ride home
Before my coach turned into a pumpkin
He leaned down for one last kiss goodnight

572. "Time Alone"

A divine mess I had become
Twirled and hurled until I lost my way
Didn't know left from right
Nor right from wrong
I found myself woven into a reality
That I wish I had never known
I was alone without a friend.

573. "Time and Again"
(dedicated to Alex)
There's a new man in my life
Or was
I'm not exactly sure at this moment

Life Uncommon

He seemed nice
They always seem nice
Can a doctor be a thug?
Does every man need to be an asshole as a prerequisite?
He took me to dinner
Smiled and laughed with me
Where did the gentleman in him go?
Where did the happiness I had run to?
Does it matter, now, that I love you?

574. "Time Told"

Loneliness kills in a way nothing else does
I've forgotten love
I don't remember how it feels
Ever long for a mystery?
I hate the unsteadiness of my life
I want a stable job
Not a new one
I want to work my ass off
But not to the point of illness
I want to care
But not to an overwhelming degree
Why does this always happen to me?!

575. "Times"

Times get hard and sometimes they get harder than you first imagined
You figure that you know how you'll do and where you'll go
But as the days go by you realize just how little you've prepared for
So you decide that you need to take that step and start taking matters into your own hands
And you begin with the first steps that lead you uphill
The hills I am climbing are leading me towards me
Two months ago I began my voyage, searching
I'm not sure where the path will lead me
I only know that I walk with my head upright
My heart ready
And with my future, my own

576. "To Be a Kid"

To appreciate beauty in all things seen
To believe in make-believe

And make a whole days activity out of pretend
To sky rocket to places never before seen
To win at hopscotch before you're a teen
To chase a dog at lightning speed
And have no better friend than your teddy
To be certain you will own the most
Magnificent horse
And be happy to sit down and play
Tic-tac-toe for hours
To be a kid
With a busy schedule every day
And when at night in bed you lay
You kiss mommy and daddy goodnight
And have dreams of the sweetest delight

577. "To Dream"

Sleepless storyteller
Young hazy-eyed woman
Slender she's not
But gentle she is
She sits up at night
When in the city
There shines no light
She rushes herself along
In a process of nothingness
She feels lost in an abyss of darkness
She runs frantically in her mind
Looking for something, something she must find
But her heart is still
Her vibrations calm
Her inner working
Serene
She smiles at the moon
And kisses her fingers to the sky!

578. "Toil"

Days and nights
Working
For what?
A car?
College?
A family?

Life Uncommon

Money- does it keep me going?
Does it keep me surviving?
No, but it's the most important necessity
Love…that's what keeps me going
But I like

579. "Tomorrow Comes"

All those backs were turned on you time and again
Door after door shut in your face
You asked for a friend
And fell from grace
You told yourself you were strong
Lie after lie fed to your soul
How could you know you were wrong?
No heart is really made of coal
Those streaming endless tears
Falling like raindrops
Through the years
Of all you could have gotten
Why did it have to be this way?
Sometimes you just wish you could be forgotten
Instead of the star of this eternal play
But you get up
And you open the doors
And you wish for the next day
And you believe once more
That tomorrow will come

580. "Tomorrow's Affair"

I can't believe that I'll see you in just a few hours
My heart is running
I sweat in anxiety
Excitement ripples through my eyes
Feet are numb
Hands are stiff
My back tenses
You are so
And I am just
Wow!
Air is so hard to reach
I grow dizzy
You will be

Life Uncommon

And I will see

581. "Tomorrow's Paper"

Love is in the heart
But it lives in the mind and soul
Simple knowledge
A kind touch, a knowing glance
These, they last
Its not the clothing or the words
Its the way we are touched
When we know we're understood
Like a fellow sufferer of our very own pain
A common strain of DNA rising up our veins
Like blood flowing from heart to brain
We come together like truth to rain
Simmering in sadness, loving in paradise
Swimming in happy, ready for sappy
Stop the dew, yesterdays news
Romance is a comin' to you
Slip past the maybes
And open tomorrows news.

582. "Topaz Colored Walls"
(dedicated to Danielle)

Sparrows on the bed
Doves in the window
And eagles over my head
I try to sleep
But all I can do
Is think of you
How many times you've said we're through
But I can't let go
So I go ahead and hang on
I guess the hopeless romantic in me just can't see
Blinded by love
Clutched in the stronghold of time
You say you're gone
Yet my mind holds on
People tell us we were never meant to be
Why can't they see?
You mean the world to me
Blue teardrops

Life Uncommon

A feather landing
The guard keeps me distant
But I'm never far
Just open your window
I'll be sitting outside waiting in my car

583. "Tom"

Taller than me
A smile of glory
More violent than other men
Sweet
Charming
Flirtatious
A back rub from him
Made all my worries disappear
I like him
Yes, I do
But I love Jake
That's where my heart stays

584. "Tornado"

In the distant past of the mind
where oblivion never shined
Spirals of gas flailed about
never pinpointed a place or whereabouts
Stars sparked a new wave of the universe
the sky was allowed to be diverse
All interconnected in this radiant beauty
and we sit here dazzled by lack of ingenuity
Lets stand tall, in conformity
not even being ourselves what a pity
Stand in line for the heavenly gates of hell
we're all going to die anyway, can't you tell?
Silent speakers live in a world of truth
those of us who talk must look so uncouth
But that's the way of the unintelligent
we believe if its there we know it
So we're fucked by what we think
better than those that just waste away in drink, eh?
Fuck that's a thought for another day
I'd better go dive back into some thoughtless routine
Since that's all anyone thinks it to be.

Life Uncommon

585. "Tragedy Strikes"

In this time of silent unutterable prayers
In this time when each of us face our own worst fears
In this time when our own freedom is being attacked
We stand tall
We stand United
We stand as one Nation, under God.

Two planes crashed into twin towers of what was
The World Trade Center
The Manhattan skyline has never looked so empty
Sirens still blare
Remaining in homes, utter despair

Another plane crashed into the Pentagon
A symbol of who we are,
what we fight for,
and a sign that says this is OUR land
Crashed into
Lives taken.

And yet one more plane crashed
An hour after the other three landed
in buildings
No direct target hit
Lives lost though
Gone from us forever.

Vigils are being held
Candles being lit
Prayers being sent
And love being said.

What do you tell the children of our nation?
Or the adults still not yet grasping?
How do you calm the terror in your heart?
And why must it be so hard to sleep at night?

Still we stand tall
We stand United
We stand as one Nation, under God.

And we will PREVAIL!

586. "Truth"

Tear stained pillows
And dreams of crimson gold
The warm blood turns something once good
To smoke covered mold
I don't want to be old or young
Fucking societal standards
Labels of shit
Ideas only to be sold
So I'm quiet and shy
Or is that my anxiety disorder
Upsetting your eyes?
And what the hell do you care anyway
You who claims to be so fine
But you're not
You are tainted too
Perfection you claim
What fantasy are you living in?
So I'm not the person you thought I was
So fucking what?

587. "TRUTH CHANGES"

Each day a struggle
Each breath a toxin
I said I'd been hurt
I told you I was broken
You said I could trust you
You said you were my friend
I gently took your hand
I graciously gave you my heart

Each step I take is wobbly
Each night I sleep a mess
I needed a companion
I needed someone to trust
You said you'd always be there for me
You said it would always be you and me
I told you I'd been molested
I told you I didn't know the meaning of family

Each moment another dark secret hidden inside of me
Each memory another striking pain

Life Uncommon

I wanted so bad to move on
I wanted you to be the one
You said you'd guide me along
You said that time will heal
I told you time hasn't healed me yet
I told you it probably never would

Each time I glance in the mirror I see a broken and battered face
Each time I see myself, I turn to walk away
I needed to believe in me
I needed to have some dignity
You said you'd help me gain back all I had lost
You said you had pride in me
I begged god for mercy
I begged god to watch over me

Each morning I wake up I fear the day ahead
Each time I go to sleep there are so many noises in my head
I told you I just wanted to be held
I told you I wasn't so hard to please
You said you'd do all that and more
You said I'd be a breeze
I gained some more confidence
I trusted in the words you spoke

Each morning I wonder is it me
Each night I ask why is it me?
I told you I would try again
I told you that I believed
You said that was good
You even said you were proud
I didn't do much at first
I couldn't handle much at all

Each morning I curse the gods of light
Each night I curse the gods of hell
I told you I was doing better
I told you about how I wasn't cutting as much
You beamed with pride
You told me this was good
I didn't think I was doing much
I didn't think I was doing much at all

Each morning I try to trace where I took the first fall
Each night I try to forget, but the memories will not go
I told you I wasn't drinking as much

Life Uncommon

I told you I shouldn't smoke
You seemed happy at this
You didn't say much though
I should have told you the truth
I never stopped those things

Each morning I remember your face
Each night I remember the screams
I told you that I was cured
I told you things and you believed
You went on with your life
You went on with ease
I should have known you'd hurt me
I should have known it was only a matter of time

Each morning I want to go back to sleep
Each night I wonder if I can ever go back and change all those things
I told you so many lies
I needed you then
You didn't need me
You didn't need anybody
I should have known you didn't care
I should have known you were selfish all along

Each morning I wonder why I didn't see
Each night I curse myself for not seeing
I hung out with your friends
I did things to please you
You fought with me so much
You yelled and you cussed
I asked you to be patient
I told you I needed time

Each morning I ask why I'm alive
Each night I wonder why
I didn't really ask for much
I just wanted a friend, someone with a gentle touch
You were supposed to be kind
You were "fake, a pretend and a phony"
I told you I wanted to be with you
I stayed with you for so long

Each morning I wonder how I could have been so wrong
Each night I think of ways I could die
I could die so many ways
I could take my own life

Life Uncommon

You were supposed to be my all
You were supposed to be my wife
I thought I needed you
I thought together we were right

Each morning I wake up alone
Each night I cry myself to sleep
I was raped again
I was broken to begin with, now what am I?
You weren't supposed to hurt me
You weren't supposed to lie
I thought you were special
I thought you would never make me cry

Each morning I wake up and face the new day
Each night I do everything to push you from my mind
I try to be the strong one
I try to be a fighter
You took that strength from me
You took my integrity
I try to smile happily
I try to fit in

Each morning I know I never will
Each night I think of tomorrow
I try to believe I will live
I try to believe I won't kill myself
You took away my belief in loyalty
You took away the last shred of me
I try to gain myself back
I try to believe things can't always be bad

Each morning I know no one else will ever understand
Each night I know no one ever did
I try to make others understand what I've been through
I try to tell them of my pain and my sorrow
You stole that sparkle in my eye
You raped away that special part of me
I attempt to have hope
I attempt to succeed

Each morning I get up for work
Each night I think I'll succeed
I should have known
I should have seen

Life Uncommon

You see now I blame me
You see I don't even blame you
I try to make it all my fault
I try to place every wrongdoing on my own shoulders

Each morning I wonder if I'll ever forgive myself
Each night I think I never will
I let you walk away free
I never even went to the police
You get to hurt someone
You get to walk away free
I get to wallow in self-pity
I get to be this me

So this is how you left me dear
Broken and battered
Shedding every single tear
This is what you took from me
You took every part that let me know who I was in this world
You took it all
And so here I am now
Writing to a nothingness that will never know
For you will never read my words
No, you'll never know
You'll go on with your life
And this is how I'm destined to live out mine.

Footnote: "fake, pretend, and a phony" from Movie: "Grease"
(Inspired by the movie "Grease"

588. "Truth Speaks"

Its the time to speak out
Forget the past
People rag on Eminem and his raps
Does the truth always shock like that?
Fucking kids shoot up schools
And we're still striving to live by old society's rules?
That's shit,
And you know it
We've got to make the world ours
Its here for the taking
No need to be up in arms
Shallow rivers run nowhere
So why are we still living off of meaningless fear?

Life Uncommon

Hiding is out-
How many youths do we have to lose to suicide,
Before we realize what the rebelling's all about?
Truth matters, that's all.

589. "Trying Desperately to Find My Strength"

Where did my strength wander off to so quickly?

He put a stamp of stupidity on my life
And I was almost his wife
To hold me was a bore
And it was so much of my strength that he tore
I didn't trust him at all
But even that couldn't break my fall
Moving on won't be so easy
But tomorrow he will no longer hold the power to wound me
Without him I may once again live

Oh, where did my strength wander off to in the middle of the night?

590. "Trying To Sleep"

Sometimes at night
While I might look asleep
It may only take me a few minutes
To wake up with a scream
Because I just had the most horrifying dream
About the way
That children can't even play
Without fear of a fight
With another child who's never seen light
I dream about the sadness
Caused by all the color wars and violence
Some people seem so far from something that would make sense
I scream at the tugs of death
And the alcohol on peoples' breath
I scream at the cigarette smoke
Certain people that go broke
And death around the old folk
I dream about the Holocaust
And the people that were just tossed
I dream about the gangs
And those horrible sounding bangs

Life Uncommon

I dream about the Draculas with fangs
And scary lions with manes
I scream at the animals who aren't tame
And too many wrong people with fame
I dream about slavery
And wonder when it will end
Although I realize life will never bend
Especially for those without a friend
Who tend to go the hard way through life
I scream at a life-threatening gun
And the people who shoot them for fun
I dream about a dead president
Wishing for peace
While a young man just shot a little child too weak to tie a knot
I wonder when it will stop
And still a mother's only hope is a mop
Then I fall back asleep
My last thought being
All the people buried so deep
While I'm just trying to sleep

591. "Twangs of Truth"

Tonight a chord was struck in me
About death and about beauty
About emotions and about lovemaking
About the acts we do and the people we become
Opinions seem mountainous when we have them
Decisions seem groundbreaking at first
Time spent undergoing a harsh lesson…Seems life-threatening
Each of us makes so many choices…Not just one
We travel so many roads
The people we become
We only become for a moment
The moment passes and we are new

We define ourselves by so many things
By the way we love, the way we hurt, the way we cry, the way we mourn,
The way our pain affects others so often that we forget to just let ourselves be
We condemn people, sometimes ourselves
We choose religions and places of worship
We judge ourselves more often than not
We forget to see beauty and to seize life
Death shakes us, but only for a moment…when we think we're invincible
The world seems a playground…when we think we're alone

Life Uncommon

The world seems a place from which we need to hide
When we wipe our tears, do we wipe the pain?
When we curl up, do we keep things more locked up inside?
Who is it we wish to become?
Sometimes we try to be invisible, sometimes we succeed
Sometimes this is you, sometimes this is me
We weep and we mourn for people, for time, and even for regrets
We sing an emotion, and dance a feeling
At times we dream, we fantasize, and we hope
At times there are nightmares with which we cope
Times are rough in this world, but only when we let them be
I suppose the truth is we each have a choice
Another choice…to let ourselves feed the deadening of us
Or to help ourselves encourage life in us, around us, within us
These are just words...just thoughts
Struck by a chord.

592. "Twenty-Something"

I'm not happy
In fact I'm so depressed
I either need a pill or a drink to sleep
Physical problems while plentiful
Don't even touch the mental angst
I have come to hate love
I just don't trust it anymore
I think love is a lie
There is no happy ever after
Even if there is it wouldn't be my happy ever after
There is no real love or acceptance
I'm a fucking spiritual pagan-like, not-so-very-Christian, bisexual, intelligent, female
You know what that makes me?
Fucked up
And just like most other 25 year old losers
I have no idea who I am
But I hate me anyway
And I'm lost
Have no idea who to turn to
So turn inward
And hide
I have a game face
Lies
Shields
All the tools necessary for survival
But happiness

Life Uncommon

I have none of
Isn't it great...to be twenty-something?

593. "Two Entities of Royalty"

To kiss
Oh…to touch
Living to live,
And not just to survive
Loving to live,
And living to love
Romance in two entities
So majestic in their beauty
Filled with hot-blooded passion
When books become part of the family
And people are all sovereign
To think a tiny apple can sprout a university of such amour
Grasp on true lovers
Servant and King

(Inspired by the movie "Ever After")

594. "Uncurtained Truth"

Truth musters like wine in my hair
I slither along the valleys with care
Like droplets of wind, the world rises up
I lift and I veil and
I raise and I fail
Like truth we all fall like dominoes
And yet, we have faith
And with that alone we are strength
Put away childish fantasies of becoming
Something great
Something more, something better,
Something not-so-you
And start living life
By recognizing you already are
You see our challenges don't make the 'real us'
For, they are us
The trials and the times we fall
Make us who we are every single day
It is the truth of hardship, stress, hurt, and tested stamina
That makes us who we are

Life Uncommon

It is not the new care, home, boyfriend, or wife
It is just simple in us living our life
So stop the head-spinning trying to be
Something more
And love exactly this: Who you are

595. "Under the Big Ol' Oak Tree"
(dedicated to Old Man Tree)

Phoenix rising in the north
Chicago drivers looking forth
Over coffee and cookies
We found romance so easy
Chess playing 'til the last cookie crumb
Finding new love is so much fun
I wrote you letter after letter
Sharing my heart in words
The stories we tell
The lessons we learn
Never telling you who I am
You found that all on your own
Sending off sweetness
Embracing the world as a whole
Under the oak trees
We call our home
I became your loving poet
You became my star-studded wife
Filling each other with as many emotions
As there are words
Time tells no lie and holds no secret
Which is why
Here in loves domain
We found the angels
In our own two names

596. "Unfulfilled"

I'm going through one of those idle nights
When my hate for life, and for falling in love is no less intense
Than love itself…to fall in love so deeply that rock bottom still has his warmth
To explain this would be a feat I do not want to attempt
Every movie has a scene that reminds me of him
The marriage proposal rings constantly in my ears
Every rose I see reminds me of those romantic dozen

Life Uncommon

On the road I check for his car
My necklace always hangs on my neck even when I don't wear it
Every time my phone rings I jump to answer but it never is
Not the way it used to be
We could talk for hours…about religion…about kids
They say he never loved me and sometimes I agree
The chills down my back still crawl every time I hear his name
Making love has lost all its charms
Where did it all go?
Arms that would secure even me
The insecure coward
Complained too much…hoped for the perfect man
Didn't I know I had him?
Maybe I thought I didn't but then why is this love still strong?
Should let it be…let it go…move past this
But my mind is in the past
Sweet kisses…poems dedicated to one another
Friendship…trust…was there that? I forget
He had all of my love
I said "not again"…but all along…I meant "yes"

597. "Unicorn and Her New Friend"
(dedicated to my sister)

A young girl sat by a tree softly
Reading her book
When on her face she gave the most satisfying look
Then she jumped at the shocking horn
On her favorite animal, the unicorn
The animal turned its back and pranced around
And soon it came upon a unique flower
Then she turned her head and looked at the stream
She thought it was as pretty as the thought of a summer nights dream
The young girl smiled at the unicorn's interest in the stream
Then the unicorn signaled the girl to come and play
They chased each other around with all their might
And later during the night
The two had become best friends

598. "Unmotivational Fear"

My heart is so frail
Like dry skin in the middle of winter
Not dried up, just red and sore
I'm not the girl I was before

Life Uncommon

I don't exactly fit the warrior profile either
Healer?   How can a bruised swan heal any,
When she herself is broken?
I cry at so much
I'm lost between two shores
Once more
How do I end up here so often?
I'd say no more this
No more that
But when life throws you a ball you can't help but catch
As you stumble- there's no avoiding the impact
Our fears cause us to avoid the things we think we know will hurt us
How does one really know?
If a lesson is meant to be learned,
We're bound to hurt
Pain is a part of life
Part of the inevitable balance
We're not gods
Just mortal wounded fawns
I could try to escape life
But fear does not resolve
Wisdom isn't doing what everyone else does,
Wisdom, alone, is being you.

599. "Unreal"

I guess I always wondered where my road ended
But I never realized that it isn't all one road
I turn and then I take a different one
It is disgraceful the way I am
My life has been destroyed
I know that I can't control things
Not even myself
Responsibilities I can never live up to
I can't flee who I am
Although sometimes, many times, I want to
Where is the sensitivity in life?
I have no clue what could make me happy
I just haven't found it yet

Nature is so perfect
Peaceful and calm
Without worries
Why can't I be that?
Skies so smooth

Life Uncommon

Clouds long and free
…Oh well

600. "Unreality"

Unreality sifting through my veins
Like dried up tears falling in vain
Who knows why we cry at all
Or where the tears so endlessly go
Like Alice in a puddle of salty tears
Asking the caterpillar to dry her fears
No rabbit ever has the time
To tell you why you're too tall, or too small
Or how you fell out of rhyme
The unhappiest birthday of all
Is the one when you forget it all
Nursery rhymes that lullaby us to sleep
Fists raised in rage at the lies we keep
Tangled webs of chaos
Live in our own minds
Trying to figure it all out
And answering nothing
Comfort only in the strength
To sleep...

601. "Unrelinquished"

For a long time
My heart was closed
I couldn't truly love
I waited years to open up again
Years to hope again
Time spent dreaming
Poetic nightmares
And I'm a disaster
Trying to understand
How I could hurt myself again
So sorry to myself
I'm sorry you're crying
Sorry you're torn
Some thorns cut deeper
At least I finally loved again
Even the hurt is worth
Knowing that

Life Uncommon

602. "Unsuccessful"

I don't get it
I just do not get it
What am I supposed to do?
I can't pry my way into their souls
I certainly can't be myself in front of them
I cannot show myself and hope they'll do the same
And I certainly can't win any points by listening to their pain
No, they know best
And no one will ever know them
No one can EVER understand
They know, they know
So what the fuck am I?
The empath who is a dumbfuck?
Or are they trying to help me?
Am I their project?
I don't get it
All I know is that trying to help
Gets me nowhere
Another fucking waste of time
Congratulations just ran out

603. "Us"

I am the good girl
Who works
And does well in school
I chit chat with whoever
My smile is radiant
And my heart is big enough for it all

And I am her shadow
With her always
Just upset by the peace she tries
To find
To make
Peace doesn't exist
I know here in the shadow
That life is without reason
Death escapes pain

Life Uncommon

604. "Vacuity"

Slip through reality
Into a time not known
Sail on a star
Swingdance on the moon
Bend the rules
Make them swoon
This is your time
No clock to hold you back
No boundaries to make you lose track
Nothing to restrain you from excellence
So scatter through the mazes of hell
And puzzles of heaven
Flip the coin
And soar on

605. "Vagrant"

The surrealness of reality never ceases to amaze me
Toss a coin
Select a maze
Catch the tail
Of a cat
But tonight
You're just a rat
Run as you must
Time slips
Reality fades
Insanity slips
You forget the tail
Forget you're a mouse
So what's reality in your own house?

606. "Valentine's Day"

Lovers parade
Throughout the day
Candies and teddies given away
Cards to sweeten romance
Lace dreams hung in streams
Heart filled days
And sunshine rays
Tonight the sweethearts will cuddle

Life Uncommon

Loving one another
Worshipping the one they love
Embracing souls shall soar
As their boat docks ashore
Sweetly smiling synergies
Meet on a star
Sparkling happily along the way
Happy Valentine's Day!

607. "Vegas"

Dancing ages sing again
The low rumbling beat
Rhythm and band
Tiny scarlet graceful feet
Living it up on ol' Main Street
Guitar strums all through the night
As we each wish one another "good night"
Beauty seems so simple
The ways of children, so youthful
Each cycle swirling itself
This is Vegas nightlife, baby!

608. "Vengeance!"

Thunderlight Strikes
I'm a man thrown to the wolves
Bitten by the bitter unconsciousness of life
I'm dead to the sea and I scroll for truth
I'm a wanderer without the desert
Quenched thirst like forthright knowledge
Vanished to my being
I'm like a king without a kingdom
A horse without a rider
And I storm into the neverlands of life
Like a warrior unbidden
I am untouched
I am unseen
I am the dream and the dreamer
And I scream with lust
With life
With vengeance for the one
Who stole from me
I vow to live only to take life

Life Uncommon

With blackened heart I avenge!

609. "Venting"

I keep being told to vent
A week ago no one cared what was wrong
Now I'm supposed to spill the glory
I just love that!

Ok so here goes…

I'm in the middle of another lovely depression
I want friends
I'm a hermit
I want money
I work in a low-paying bookstore
I want love
Could it get any more lonely?
I want meaningful conversation
Can it get any more boring than, "so how are you?"
I want a non-smelly, clean house
I have cats- need I say more?
I want to have energy in the mornings the way I have energy at night
Hmmm not gunna happen!
Its like when you hit the lottery right after receiving a huge inheritance!
Ooh gotta love irony
I want a fun online life
But its like talking to a cigarette almost burned out

610. "Vessels"
(dedicated to Alex)

Where is truth these days?
I lie to everyone but my own heart
Its like I live still in the past loving Alex
As though no moments have passed between us,
In the world, where we are not together…I miss him, his lips, his touch
The way he loved me without saying anything at all
The way he knew me, my fears, for fear lived inside him too
He knew my love, for he loved and loves passionately still
His compassion stronger than my own a wise understanding of things
He loved me in the quiet moments in the dark when no light shone on either of us
Both our hearts still, dark, tormented
He felt the terror of his past as I feel the terror of my own

Life Uncommon

He knew how it is inside my mind when everything is ugly and black
He felt all that I do and he drank...filled up his woes and let him silence them
Mine were silenced but only because my strength overcame them
I am not strong anymore for I finally opened the gateways to my heart and let him in
I opened my heart anyway, whether he ever came in or not is another story altogether
Like the raindrops that fall on my pavement I weep for him, for us, for who we were
We had a love like I've never known, like I'd never dreamt of
It was beyond the simple love at first sight stories you hear
And more than just a we-lived-happily-ever-after...he lived as my heart
He held me and I felt safe and whole
Alex is the only home I have ever known
I will love him forever and I fear never knowing whether or not he truly loved me
If I could run into him and hide there seeking only the shelter of his embrace, I would but
I live in a time of circumstances and obstacles
I live in the twenty-first century
I have this over-abundant need to become a financially independent woman
And I hate money...I'm an ironic soul, I admit
Why can't there not be places? Not be times? Not be serious and committed?
Why can't there just be simple? Why can't there just be love?
I close my eyes and see his
I hear a song and I cry for the patience neither of us really had
I want to let him know I love him...I want to scream at him for leaving me
He was my entire heart
Will not the world ever know how much I loved that one estranged soul?
Love... like a sailboat drifts away and I am but a vessel that must accept my fate

611. "Voices"

There are choices to be made
Important ones
If I don't "get better" I may need to go
Back to Chicago
Will they make me see physical doctors?
Or live in a sanitarium?
Insane asylums may just be my style
No work
Bad food
I don't eat much now anyway
Constant attention
I want an easy way out
There are all these statistics on violence
Why can't I just be murdered or killed
I want to die fast
Without pain
Just dead

Life Uncommon

I want my organs to be donated to science
Maybe someone else will find me not so futile
Societal conformists – probably
So I'm sure one would think
Commit suicide already!
I'm sure I should
Why live?
I do not have a boyfriend
The only man I thought I loved
Turned out to be just another fantasy

612. "Walking By"

He just walks by
Ignorant of my presence
Unaware of my desire
Unaccepting of my need
I am nothing to him
Invisible as a ghost
Alone in this want and will
His is so beautiful
And I am just me

613. "Walking The Line"

There is a tether tying us together
Both sides are equal
The middle is strong and loved
Stuck between both sides of the cloth
Each side is special
Shaded with its own happiness
Is the knot supposed to move
Will it come undone
Or will it shine out above all else?

(Inspired by the movie "Walking the Line")

614. "Wandering Thoughts"

When your best friend leaves you
Do you cry?
Do you hide?
Do you inside silently die?

Life Uncommon

I mean what is it one is supposed to do
When the most important person to them- is gone
Whoever she was to me, she can never be that to me again
And that's a sad, very sad thing
I want to blame myself
I want to hate myself
But I can't
I approve of who I am
I approve of my beliefs
I know I'm not perfect
I know there are things I should change
But all in all I don't feel that
I'm a disaster
But she does
And best friends don't think that about each other
I have all the negative thoughts
I guess in the eyes of others and
Currently myself- I entirely suck
This is the kind of view I used to have when I was suicidal
So I mostly try to stay away from it now
I keep thinking how I should just move on

615. "Wanting"

Suddenly I am six years old again
Walking around my grandmother's house saying,
"I want that."
Always wanting something
The pretty silk blouses
The immaculate china
Her house was so beautiful
Now at twenty I ask again for what I want
I long for a love so deep that I would travel anywhere
To find my lover
Darkness or light
Any hue
And any shape
I want that
My body could go through a thousand deaths for him
I would be stabbed or choked
Shot or strangled
Starved
Starvation from food could be no worse than starvation for him
I want that
I would dive into the deepest sea if I could find him

Life Uncommon

And I would give my life to securing us
So that we would never lose one another
These are just dreams
And mythical promises
But if he is out there
And I believe he is
I will do it all

616. "Warrior Child"

Let the warrior within
Rage war on that which is sin
Allow her to protect all which is kin
Let her metaled shield of honor,
Hold you close to all you hold within
Brothers and sisters align alike
And it is on this indigenous night
That I look to you sadly
With a single solitary tear in my eye
Knowing inside,
That one day you will die
Then something picks me up,
Lifting me to newer heights
Letting me know that even on
The most lonesome of nights
That I shall hear your words
Whispered into my own ear
And it is then,
That I shall know,
You are always near

617. "Wasted Whispers"

Cover me in a blanket of stars
Comfort me when my sun stops shining
Hold me with sensitivity
Understand me the way I am
Have compassion towards me
Even when its hard
Know my soul and know its core
Know I act out of love and light
And that so rarely do I feel the comfort
Inside or outside from another human being
I find love and family in temples

Life Uncommon

I find peace with animals
But the love of a human is so rare
I'm sick of fights, headaches, and discomfort
I want to be done with hurting
With being hurt
Help me to get there
Please, I beg
I scratch and hear no reply
Still...I listen...

618. "Wax"

Sweet tasting
Soft and moist on my tongue
Filling my taste buds with perfection
Tantalizing and mesmerizing
My heart is filled with this warmth
Weak in the knees
Knocked into concentration
Strawberries so red my eyes are hurting
Fresh from the barrel
My teeth sink into the fruit
And-
Irony surrounds me

619. "Web of Deceit"

The beating of the drum
Beckons pushes pulls
Pulsating terrors of the height ending
When the killing of calmness may slash me next
Cigarette after cigarette I attempt to escape
Yearning for freedom from myself
The dungeon in my mind
I fail myself on purpose
To spite everyone who puts pressure on me
"Human Sir!"
That is what I am
Not a doll or a robot or a computer
All these people with expectations
Who am I trying to succeed for?
Their spidery legs crawl over me
Tangling me in their webs
I become ghostly, ghastly

Life Uncommon

Awkwardly transparent
Yet they still see errors
I'd kill the mother of them all if I could
But like the internet- there is no headquarters
Trapped in a web of expectations
Gasping for breath
Dying slowly
By heartache and misfortune

620. "Wednesday's Clock"

Wednesday afternoon has come
Sky-blue, sun-warm, wind-mild
Rustling my hair slightly as if the strands were leaves
On a desert tree
Las Vegas is an interesting town to live in
We have hotels and strip clubs
But those are written about enough
We have something more
Something rarely written about
Kind of like we never left the 70's
And every crime we read or hear about
Is really just part of a sci-fi news show
Surely no child would kill classmates
No way planes would crash into buildings
On a day flashing 911...911...911
Impossible that coats worn would
Scare us of our own youth
Instead our clothing is the same dull colored,
Flower-patterned design
And while people, 5,000, move here every month
Nothing changes
We don't move
As if our clocks have stopped
It's a beautiful trance that's taken us over
Kept us from catching up
From moving forward into a time of war and hatred
Endlessly caught in the webs of time
And it's beautiful

Like a sun ray that stays
A butterfly clumsily dancing in time

Maybe someone forgot to patch us
Onto the newer

Life Uncommon

More futuristic
Fabric of time

Or maybe, just maybe...
We like it this way

621. "We'll Never Run Short on Love"

We might run short on water
But we'll never run short on love
Things might be dry for a while
The money might run tight
But the love will abound
Each and every night

622. "Whasup Kid?"

What's going on kid
Is life good?
Is it bad?
Or is it just plain history?
Well for me
Its good
But too bad its not ecstasy

623. "What Lies Do I Tell Myself?"

If I were to lie to myself maybe I could answer, but I find I don't
Sometimes I pretend
But I always know
Others do not hear the truth
Not as I do
At night I am the most honest
Ambivalence is not a sin
To lie is a cruelty I cannot commit towards my own heart
So I advise you
Accept you
Accept me
As I will keep in search of a love
A great one
Tomorrow I will still write because paper will still be my only friend
Yesterday I called myself fat
So what?

Life Uncommon

Some things I don't find derogatory
I don't find my habitual television watching a bad thing
Truth is I do live vicariously to those I read about
So what?
My hair does look as shitty now as it did this morning
And still I have no love
Tonight my phone will be silent again
One month from now I will have the same obsessive compulsive routine
One year from now I will still check my watch every five minutes
Ten days from now I will still be crying about the yucky girl stuff
And forever I will still be me
So what?

624. "What Matters"

What matters comes from the inside
And never from without
No factory, company, or franchise
Can give you the key
You can earn money and build houses
You can raise families and empires
I'll bet you can even be popular
But none of it matters
Not unless it comes from within
A house built on emptiness means naught
A life built on emptiness holds no meaning
But build a life in the house of you
Then perhaps you will succeed
At knowing what matters
It is not just to know you
But to accept you
Good, bad, ugly, and flawed
To accept your sins and failures too
To accept all those things that once left you blue
To give way to love and throw away the hatred
This is when you come closer
Closer to home
Closer to living within the home
Closer to the you, I'd like to know
And this is when you come closer
To finding that what matters
Only matters, Within

625. "What Seeking Finds You"

Life Uncommon

Tommy, I'm sorry for any dishonest words that I have spoken to you
I never meant to be anything but one who spoke true
I don't know that I lied or told you something untrue
But something tells me that somehow I have wronged you
Maybe its possible that my attention-seeking sends out a vibe
Perhaps you felt that somewhere inside
Yet, I know that its not love from you I need
I'm meant for something different and that's a truth I should heed
Friends are all I should have for now
Because I'm not ready to recite any vow
I'm no girlfriend or lover or even someone to bestow love upon
I'm not the type of person who deserves such a great thing
I'm probably not the person who others once thought I could be
And I'm sorry I failed you, Tommy
Because I never meant to and its my fault
Forever friend I hope you stay safe and well
May you escape that inner hell
And live a life of beauty and peace
May the truth be your release
Blessed be and Merry part
And may the goddess watch over your wounded heart

626. "What the fuck?"

What the fuck people?
I mean what in the fuck are you thinking most of the goddamn day?
Can't you look in the mirror and see you're wasting away?
How the fuck can you sit there and hurt yourselves?
What do I care, right? Maybe I shouldn't.
Maybe I oughta learn not to mess with other peoples lives
But inside I see you
I know your pain, I know it well
Can't you see that in my eyes? Can't you tell behind my lies?
If only you could see what really lies there
Then maybe you wouldn't tell me tomorrow of your troubles and fears
Maybe for once you'd listen to my endless tears
They fall silently they do but they fall nonetheless
And maybe its about time I confess
That I'm no healer anyway
I'm just some girl in a grown up play
I couldn't help if my life depended on it
I'm just a joke for you to laugh at
Maybe I'm not worth love
But I sure hoped one day I would be

Life Uncommon

But I guess something that beautiful isn't meant for me
So come on and tell me again that you love me
Just like everyone else does
And I won't forget to wave goodbye as you leave me
And I'll even close the door nice and neatly
It's too bad though how it always has to go
Because it sure would be nice to really be loved
And not for the emotion I bring or the security blanket I pretend to be
But for the crap inside, the real fucking me.

627. "When Can I Sleep?"

Sounds
They are loud…waking me up…wrecking my dreams
Forcing me to think consciously
I want to sleep…thoughts…they keep on coming to me
Waking up the thoughts of night
Wrecking my dreams of innocence
Forcing me to move on through the day
I don't want to go on…movements
They are constant…waking up my body
Wrecking my tired muscles…forcing me to walk
I don't want to go to school…class, work
They keep on handing me assignments
Waking up my memories of yesterday's lessons
Wrecking the easy going mood of this morning
Forcing limits on my thoughts
I don't want to stay hungry…lunch
They keep on talking around me
Waking up my tired thoughts
Wrecking my lazy mood…forcing me to eat
I don't want to work again…class, work
They keep on lecturing me
Waking up my lazy thoughts
Wrecking my happy mood from eating
Forcing me to hear their stupidity
I don't want to stay here…driving
They take too long to move…waking up again
Wrecking my bored thoughts
Forcing me to stay awake
I don't want to stay awake
Sleep…they keep on telling me to stay awake…but I won't
I'm finally going back to peace…sleep…happiness…and…innocence

Life Uncommon

628. "Where Do You Turn, When Everywhere You Would Go, Is Gone?"

Who can I trust?
The answer is no one
Not one person
How can this be?
Why?
It isn't fair!
It just isn't fair
Friends should keep secrets
Friends- something I don't have
Trust is gone
Respect demolished
Will it ever end?
Will it?

629. "Who am I Today and Who Were You Yesterday?"

Who am I?
Am I a beacon in the sky?
Or perhaps a bird who couldn't fly?
Maybe I was the baby who couldn't cry

Well today I am me
Whatever that's supposed to be
Perhaps tomorrow I'll cut the chain and finally be free
All I want to be is me

You can come inside my house
Quietly as you may come you are still no mouse

The noises you create in my head
Leave my happiness next to dead

I want to shout this from the rooftops
Of a New York skyscraper surrounded by cops

I will say with no uncertainty
That you are you, but I will always be ME!

630. "Who am I?"

I am a young woman
Exploring the world around her,

Life Uncommon

Or rather swimming stroke by stroke in a sea of turmoil
My past is the strength to keep me moving
And my heart holds the inspiration
Why am I?
Such simple questions too often seem complex
Mom and Dad are the answer
Sure I've encountered many things and people outside my parents
But the voice always there is them
The discipline has given me strength
The pets have given me a love for animals
The siblings have taught me to be a control freak sometimes and other times I share all I have
The household chores have taught me household manners
The babysitting has given me a motherly instinct
The fights have taught me to live and learn and to compromise
The big disagreeances marked all my transitional movements
The constant devotion through my Mom & Dad's hard working, fights of their own, trips away, housewife consistencies, Mr. Mom on sick days,
And the list could go on
Have all taught me to have a big heart
Not to mention to work a lot
Thanks Mom and Dad

631. "Who Are You?"

I am a priestess and a healer
A warrior and a philosopher
A teacher and a pupil
I am more than just words
Disconnected though I am
There is a center
A place within where all collide
It is not lost
But I must journey if I am to find
How long have I been this way?
Was I once whole?
Will I be again?
The journey begins

632. "Whorl"

Perhaps I always knew he didn't love me
Perhaps I just needed to think he did
Maybe in ten years I'll be ready for love

Life Uncommon

I care, I hurt, and I heal
My nature so cyclical
Thank you God for allowing me pain
The future is unknown
And today I love a man
Who probably doesn't love me for me
And probably doesn't accept me for me
Maybe I'm too screwed up for love
Maybe, but I don't know
I just don't know those answers
Maybe God will find them in
My tear-filled prayers

633. "Why?"

Why did he leave me so destitute and lonely?
I loved him and love him now
I need him so much right now
To hold me
To love me
But he isn't
Oh God
He'll never be again
Car crash or drive-by-shooting
Even though I know he isn't dead
He is
Illusion has blackened
My painting burned
The ashes haunt me at night
I would have done anything
I have lived and died for him
I've lost myself in the terror of love
My strength has dwindled
In my dreams of him I am so hopeless
And I love him
I've loved him so many hours in this lifetime
Dread anymore
Dread him
Dread this love
Dread it all
Terrors in the night
Fall
Fall
Fall
I am so fallen

Life Uncommon

Crushed by his shoe
Flicked like a cigarette into the harsh streets
Shoved away like an annoying insect
And yet I still love him
Always love him
And where is he?

634. "Willow"

Darkness stares down at me
A black cloud clears my vision of light
It hides me from my fears
It protects me,
Holds me inside its shade
Claws are breathing fire
Blazing
Lightning bolts of darkness
It sounds crazy
Almost easier

Because outside of the darkness
Are beautiful branches
Lively,
Friendly,
Caring,
Loving,
And none is better than any other

635. "Wind, Leaves"

On a windy day the breeze is cool and comforting
I feel like a queen when it blows at me
In the car leaves come swiftly towards the front window
On the ground little tornadoes form
Circling endlessly and mysteriously
Exotic and fun the wind with its
Children leaves
I love them
Their beauty
And uniqueness

636. "Wings of a Love"

Life Uncommon

Simple melodies for a simple tune
And there you were, I looked up at you
I've loved and I've lived
But today I found you
In your youth
You made me smile
Breathless I agreed to walk the mile
Tomorrow will come
And a bride I will be
Independence I clung onto
But, baby, its you that set me free
Thank you for the tears of joy you bring
Thank you for fulfilling my every dream

637. "Winter Night"

Leaves crumble to the ground
New tiny miracles are found
The night is cool
But still warm enough to enjoy a swim in the pool
Each branch symbolizes something amazing
And bonfires are always blazing
Excitement is in the heart of all trees
None of us have to fall to our knees
A warm winter light
Is like watching out a window on a cool fall's night
Different shades of blue
Colors in our hearts all so true
Trees are swaying in the breeze
What a beautiful winter's night its turned out to be!

638. "Wish Poem"

Star light
Star bright
Glorious and whole up in the sky
You fill my soul with hope and faith
Fly fly away to the distant regions of the universe
Where angels are born and dragons fly abroad
Where oceans are pure and clear like the hearts of young ones
Dreams coming back and fantasies return
I wish, I wish—
For a glorious
Sense of completion

Life Uncommon

The cup is full no matter how much water is in it
And the water satisfies my thirst no matter how much I drink
I wish, I wish—
For peace and humanity
Serene surrounding
A sense of connection that envelopes the individuality of each of us as human beings
The time when wars and guns becomes futile
When a kind word is a mile
Words spoken with ill intent are only a step
I wish, I wish—
That the artist of truth and honest paints a picture on the world
For all to see
Each of us has a picture in our head
Painted with happiness instead of pain
I wish, I wish—
That pain can be shared without limitation
And that healing can be done together
I wish, I wish—
Again I wish for near impossibilities
Your environment and mine
Your domain inhabits mine
My painting completes yours
Individuality within connection
Oh how I wish

639. "With"

Dance with me
In a forever that I can only dream
Walk with me
In a night, a cloud, a light,
That frees me from the burdens of my soul
Take with you
Only the dramatics to ease my-
my loves, my hates, my fears, and most of all
My desires
Lay with me
In a moon, in a star, in a sun,
In a dream where we can be
In some dream, in some anywhere,
Where we can simply
Just be.

640. "Within"

Life Uncommon

I'm going to set aside the truths of others for a while
And just sing my own song
Wisdom is
And silence is not
In the times of Egypt, when dynasties were around
Gods were noticed and worshipped daily
Today we notice so little
And I talk so much
I seek times of silence
The flowing peace within
Without the words of others
Filling my precious space
Yes, I'll put them aside for a while
And come back to the places
Within
Within
within

641. "Without"

Through my glass eyes I stare
My hands hold Teddy bears
Tight as prayers are said
Wine sipped
Dancing slowly to the sound of love
Pretty smiles
Twinkling of delight
A tear drops
Moved by the cherished memories
The ones I never got to have
My curtain falls
Blackened by my own fear
Shadowed mysteries of pain
And the rest is quiet
I stay in peace
Serenity and bliss
As your world moves about
I stand still
Just here
Alone

642. "Wolf's Moon"

There's no moonlight

Life Uncommon

No light at all
Darkness befalls
And the nighttime flows
Candles illuminate our darkened souls
Your soul calls me from miles away
I'd hear it in my sleep
I'd know that call anywhere
You're like my key
And you give me life
Awakened as only one can be
In the night

643. "Working Again"

Yes, its true I am working again
It seemed so much fun back then
We would laugh and joke
But not these folk
They are bored and boring
Unless of course—they are flirting
Teenagers are they
Always out and ready to play
Some are older
And never colder
These are the ones I talk with
Oh—I'm back to work again

644. "Writer"

I'm a writer
Isn't that great?
I can do something everyone else can do too
But maybe I pour a little more passion into my unspoken words
Or something of the sort
Maybe its because I know how to spell
It certainly isn't from my disastrous attempts at grammar that I came to see myself as a
writer
I doubt it has anything to do with I.Q. or talent
More likely its just my inadequacy mixed with the need to express something, anything
Being a loner is just so amazing
I can do nothing by myself
Or something
And hate it all exactly the same
Boy, life just has some glorious turns!

Life Uncommon

645. "Writing"

I write about how I feel
Sometimes I just can't write at all
Some feelings I want to keep to myself
It is hard to talk about death
It is hard to talk about feeling completely isolated

I feel my best writing comes when I have an extreme emotion
Like when I am melancholy and depressed
Sometimes I get to the point of despising my pen
So when I am in love my poetry beams
Or when I am crying
Tears will drop in the form of letters

646. "You"

Moon drops on willow trees
Tiny remembrances of things that used to be
Passionate kisses,
Glances so sweet
Our souls, meet
I remember
Even through the anger
And tear soaked eyes
I can still see
The real you, the real me
I've hated you a thousand times
I'll hate you a thousand more
But I'll love you
Twice as strong

Funny, the imaginings of my youth
I never dreamed an alcoholic
Never fantasized a thug
Couldn't have imagined a drug user
Nor a father of two
I would have never
Imagined you

Silly girl I must've been
Because I should have
You've been the rhythm

Life Uncommon

For my rhyme
The answer to my prayers
Every time

You're the love I always needed
The touch that soothes
As long as I live
I'll never know another you
Perhaps we're through
But you'll remain
As an affair of my heart

My life will spiral
In directions unseen
You're the anchor
I'll find in dream
Whenever I'm ready to go
Home to my heart

647. "You Remain Perfect"

Why do I think love means you'll stay? Or accept me?
Am I so abhorrent that its better to leave?
Am I not enough? Do you even care?
All those tears I cried, sounds you're never around to hear
I pity myself alone. I comfort my own self.
Without you- I grow younger
Through my own destructions'
Leaving you perfect
It's unfair, isn't it?

648. "You Sir!"

You sir!
Do not turn, move
Not an inch, you know you'll lose

You sir!
Let your anger drain
I've no use for useless pain

You sir!
You'll not take me
I stand far too steady

Life Uncommon

You sir!
Get used to me, For now I stay
I remain

649. "You Surround Me"

During the summer hours you surround me
When your rays dance on my face, I laugh
As you shape clouds I stand in awe
Respectful of such intelligence
When your breeze hits me it is as if to say
I know
When the stars glisten
You understand
But you care
For so many
I may just be a speckle
But you care
And so in you
I-
Find life
My life

650. "Young"

My heart is with Jake
My soul is with God
And what they leave with me is what I own
As a teen I know where I am
I know what I want
But my innocence lies in the fun of flirting
Guys, men doesn't matter
Younger, older – who cares- its fun
Don't get me wrong that's not all I am
But it's a summary

651. "Young Beauty"

I stand between time
And no time at all
I lift up my arms
And pray you'll hear my call

Life Uncommon

I walked down the road
The one you pointed me to
I saw her there
I saw her crying for me
She needs love, the young girl
Battered and torn
She lets out a shrill
I need her still
For I know that I am forever bound
With this young beauty
Who inside I found

652. "Young Thoughts"

Everyday I walk
I walk on to a point in the world
The point where child's play ends and adulthood begins
Adulthood beginning to bring me in to understanding more about life
As I begin to understand life I begin to mature
The more I mature the more I have a chance
To move on to the next point in the world
The point that brings me closer to a realistic dream
The dream will be my first step into my future
This all starts with me just walking to a point
We all walk to a point in our minds and physically
We can't ever stop walking
Otherwise our
Minds will shatter
Our dreams will lose hope
Our legs will break
Our feet won't move
And life won't move on

653. "Young Waterfall"

I see the magic
I see it in your eye
And I for one
Refuse to let it die
You can cast off people
Places, events
But you cannot cast away
This magic
Which to you

Life Uncommon

Was sent
You hold it deep within
Its the hours before dreaming
The minutes after waking
Its the smile you give
For no reason at all
Its in the beauty of you
Young waterfall
So smile on your knees
And raise your hands up high
Gods bless the rain
And heaven bless the sky!

Life Uncommon

Life Uncommon

Life Uncommon

Life Uncommon